Music Copyright

for the
New Millennium

Foreword by Mike Curb
Edited by Patrick Runkle

David J. Moser

236 Georgia Street, Suite 100
Vallejo, CA 94590
(707) 554-1935

Library of Congress Catalog Card Number: 2001088666

Publisher: Mike Lawson
Art Director: Stephen Ramirez; Editor: Patrick Runkle

236 Georgia Street, Suite 100
Vallejo, CA 94590
(707) 554-1935

Also from MixBooks

The AudioPro Home Recording Course, Volumes I, II, and III
Creative Music Production: Joe Meek's Bold Techniques
Professional Sound Reinforcement Techniques
I Hate the Man Who Runs This Bar!
How to Make Money Scoring Soundtracks and Jingles
The Art of Mixing: A Visual Guide to Recording, Engineering, and Production
Music Publishing: The Real Road to Music Business Success, Rev. and Exp. 5th Ed.
How to Run a Recording Session
Mix Reference Disc, Deluxe Ed.
The Songwriter's Guide to Collaboration, Rev. and Exp. 2nd Ed.
Critical Listening and Auditory Perception
Modular Digital Multitracks: The Power User's Guide, Rev. Ed.
The Dictionary of Music Business Terms
Professional Microphone Techniques
Sound for Picture, 2nd Ed.
Music Producers, 2nd Ed.
Live Sound Reinforcement

Also from EMBooks

Studio-in-a-Box
The Independent Working Musician
Making the Ultimate Demo, 2nd Ed.
Making Music with Your Computer, 2nd Ed.
Anatomy of a Home Studio
The EM Guide to the Roland VS-880

ProMusic Press, Mixbooks, and EMBooks are imprints of artistpro.com, LLC

Printed in Auburn Hills, Michigan
ISBN 1-931140-16-2

Contents

Foreword

In my experience as the president and founder of record and music publishing companies, I have found copyright law to be a fundamental component of the music industry. Copyright law creates an environment in which creators can share their music with the public while enjoying the profits from their creations and knowing the integrity of their creations will be preserved. The protections of copyright law are critical in motivating creators to continue to create music and have a willingness to share that music with the public. Those same protections also offer an incentive to record companies and publishing companies to provide the funding and resources necessary to produce, market, and sell music to the public.

Anyone who currently works in or aspires to work in the music industry, including writers, artists, publishers, musicians, and distributors, should have a basic understanding of copyright law and how it applies to the music industry. Understanding copyright law is particularly important today, a time of rapid technological advances including the rise of the Internet and digital technology. Distribution of music now encompasses these new technologies. The changes in distribution methods alone present novel questions of copyright law that, depending on how they are answered, could upset the delicate balance between the interests of the music industry and those of the public. Drafters of copyright law are attempting to answer these questions, and members of the music industry have a great interest in those answers. A basic understanding of copyright law and the protections it affords musical works and those with an interest in those works is essential to success in today's music industry.

Music Copyright for the New Millennium is a valuable guide to copyright law as it applies to the music industry. It is a vital resource for anyone contemplating or pursuing a career in this exciting and ever-changing business.

Mike Curb
President
Curb Records, Inc.

Preface

As we begin the 21st century, we have entered what may be one of the world's greatest periods of growth in creative expression. This growth is primarily the result of advances in technology that have made it easier and much less costly to produce and distribute creative works on a worldwide basis. Civilization experienced an explosion in creativity in the 18th century after the invention of the printing press. The end of the 20th century may have begun a similar explosion in creativity as well as a means of distributing the products of that creativity using digital technology and the Internet.

Technology, however, brings challenges as well as opportunities. New technologies have made it much easier to copy and distribute creative works; it is also much easier to infringe upon the rights of the creators and owners of these works. Part of the early Internet culture revolved around the notion that everything available over the Internet should be free. Many people still mistakenly believe that they can copy and exchange music and other creative works freely over the Internet even though virtually all of the lawsuits involving Internet infringements have held otherwise.

Copyright law has always involved a tension between two important competing interests. On one hand, creative works should be readily accessible to the public so that society can benefit from them. On the other hand, authors and publishers who invest their time and money in the creation and marketing of these works should be compensated for their efforts. The United States was founded upon the principles of liberty and justice. The principle of liberty suggests that people should have free access to creative works. Justice, however, sometimes imposes limitations on liberty. The principle of justice suggests that even though society benefits from having access to creative works, it is not fair that some members of society can appropriate other member's creations without permission or payment. Copyright law attempts to strike a balance between the competing principles of liberty and justice by providing authors with a right to be compensated in order to encourage them to create new works that will be made available to the public.

Whether we realize it or not, copyright law affects us all during virtually every day of our lives. For instance, consider whether a day goes by in your life in which you do not turn on the radio or television, listen to a CD or cassette, read a book, newspaper or magazine, watch a movie, run software on your computer, or surf the web. If you do any of these things, you have had access to copyrighted materials.

While copyright law and the ownership of intellectual property may be a confusing concept to many people, it is the lifeblood of many industries, a crucial part of the American economy, and a necessity to authors and producers of creative works. Many of the businesses that comprise the entertainment industry such as book publishing, motion pictures, computer software, and music are based on the ownership and use of copyrighted works.

Copyright is absolutely crucial to the music industry. While music would certainly still exist without copyright, there could be no industry based on music without copyright. This is due to the fact that the main products of the music industry (songs and sound recordings) are forms of property that are protected by copyright. Without copyright, songwriters and music publishers could not own and derive their income from songs and artists and record companies could not own and derive their income from musical recordings.

However, many participants in the music industry, from songwriters to record company executives, fail to understand and appreciate the importance that copyright law has on their careers and their livelihoods. There are many common inaccurate beliefs about some of the basic principles of copyright law. For example, the belief that copyright allows people to control ideas is a mistaken one. As discussed in chapter 1, copyright only protects certain ways that ideas are expressed rather than the ideas themselves. Although some aspects of copyright law are technical in nature and very complicated, certain basic principles should be understood by everyone who works in the music industry.

The idea for this book originated when I started teaching copyright law classes to college students in a music business program. Other professors teaching the class had been using a law school casebook (a collection of court decisions) as a text. Although that may work well for teaching law school copyright classes using the Socratic method (teaching primarily by asking questions rather than providing answers), I did not feel it was the ideal text for undergraduate music business students (especially since relatively few of the cases dealt with music). After some searching, I realized that, although there are some good books dealing with copyright in general, there were not any specifically geared toward music.

The goal of this book is therefore to provide an overall understanding of copyright law as it applies specifically to music and the music industry. Some of the main issues that this book covers are:

- What is copyright and why is it important?

- How did copyright law originate and how has it evolved?

- What types of creations are protected by copyright and what types of creations are not protected?

- What provisions of copyright law are especially relevant to musical works?

- What is copyright infringement?

- How do you know who owns the rights to a copyrighted work and how can you get permission to use it?

- How has copyright law responded to advances in technology?

- What does the future hold for copyright law?

In writing this book, I have attempted to arrange the material in a logical fashion and to explain provisions of the law as simply as possible. Unfortunately, I have not always been completely successful in doing so since some provisions of copyright law are technical and complex and since certain terms have specific legal definitions that must be followed. I have also incorporated many examples (some based on real-life situations and others of my own concoction) and practical tips to illustrate how specific provisions of the law are applied. I hope that the result is an informative and useful reference.

A few basic things to keep in mind when reading the material presented are: (1) all references to "the Copyright Act" refer to the United States Copyright Act of 1976 unless otherwise specified; (2) the Copyright Act is part of the United States Code, which is a collection of federal statutes; (3) the Copyright Act comprises Chapter 17 of the United States Code; (4) the Copyright Act is organized by chapters and sections within those chapters (for example, the first section of the Copyright Act, section 101, contains several pages of defined terms, and the legal citation to this section is 17 U.S.C. § 101); (5) the symbol "§" means "section" and refers to specific section numbers of the Copyright Act; and (6) the full text of the Copyright Act is available from the Copyright Office (Circular 92—Copyright Law of the United States of America) and can also be found online at **http://www4.law.cornell.edu/uscode/17/.**

I would like to thank all of the people who have assisted in the creation of this book. Although the list is too long to include (and I would be afraid to leave someone out), many individuals including colleagues and students have reviewed chapters and offered suggestions.

Finally, in an effort to keep readers up to date, I have created a web site to supplement this book—**musiccopyright.net.** Some of the information contained on the web site includes:

• A short summary of how United States legal system works—how statutes are passed, the federal court system, etc. If you don't know the difference between a statute and a court ruling or between a plaintiff and a defendant, it might be helpful to take a look at this information before delving too deeply into the chapters that follow.

• A brief overview of copyright law—For those of you who don't have the time or inclination to read the entire book or just need to locate very basic information quickly.

• Updated information—summaries of legislation dealing with copyright which has been proposed and enacted; current court cases dealing with copyright, etc.

• Information and resources on other areas of intellectual property law such as trademarks, trade secrets, publicity rights, etc.

• Useful copyright and music business resources including books, trade publications and web sites

• Miscellaneous information about legal issues affecting the music industry (music publishing, record contracts, artist management, etc.)

Disclaimer

It is my hope that the information provided in this book will be helpful to readers. Every effort has been made to make this book as complete and accurate as possible. To the author's best knowledge, the information presented was accurate at the time of its writing. However, legislative changes to the law and court decisions interpreting and applying the law are made on a continuing basis. At the time of this book's writing, there are several important proposed amendments to the Copyright Act and several important pending court decisions regarding copyright law. Consequently, it is impossible to guarantee absolute up-to-date accuracy. Accordingly, readers should not rely on this book as their sole source of legal advice or as a substitute for qualified legal counsel. This book is sold with the understanding that the publisher and author are not rendering specific legal advice and the publisher and author shall not be liable or responsible to any person or entity with respect to any loss or damage caused or alleged to be caused, directly or indirectly, by the information contained in this book.

CHAPTER 1

What Is Copyright?

▼

"Music is such a tremendous proposition that it probably needs government supervision . . . I also advocate much more rigid laws so thieves may get their just desserts. There are many who enjoy glory plus financial gain's abundance, even in the millions, who should be digging ditches or sweeping the streets. Lack of proper protection causes this."[1]
Jelly Roll Morton

I. What Is Copyright?

Copyright is a form of property ownership for certain types of artistic and creative works such as songs, recordings, movies, and literary works. Copyright can be defined as "an intangible right granted by statute to the author or originator of certain literary or artistic productions, whereby he is invested, for a specified period, with the sole and exclusive privilege of multiplying copies of the same and publishing and selling them."[2] In general, copyright law protects all types of original creative expression. Some, but by no means all, of the types of works that can be protected by copyright are songs, sound recordings, movies, television shows, plays, dance routines, books, poems, photographs, paintings, sculpture, computer programs and web sites.

In general, there are two broad categories of property, real property and personal property. Real property protects land or things that are built on land such as houses and buildings. Personal property basically protects everything that can be owned other than real property. A car, for instance, would be personal property. One subcategory of personal property is intellectual property, which protects products of the mind and covers property that has no physical existence. The main categories of intellectual property that can be protected are copyrights, patents and trademarks *(see section III below for an overview of other types of intellectual property).*

The concept of copyright is difficult for many people to understand, mainly because it protects intangible rather than tangible property. Tangible or physical property is easier to visualize and understand because it can be possessed. People generally do not find it hard to understand that things such as houses, cars, food and compact discs are property. These types of property can be seen, touched, and sometimes tasted, smelled or heard.

Intellectual property, on the other hand, cannot be possessed by anyone, although this does not mean that it cannot be owned. You cannot, for example, possess a song although you can certainly own one. You cannot see, touch, taste or smell a song. In fact, you cannot even hear a song although you can hear a particular performance of a song. In other words, the thing to which the property right applies (the song) is not subject to direct perception by the senses and cannot be possessed in itself. It's a bit easier to understand if you realize that property refers not to the actual possession of a thing, but to the right to use and control its use. A copyright owner's right to prevent the unauthorized use of a work is therefore somewhat analogous to a homeowner's right to prevent trespassing on his or her property.

The idea behind the law of copyright is that products of a person's mind (such as songs) are just as much the creator's property as products of a person's hands. Unfortunately, it is difficult to draw clear boundaries around intellectual property. Over 150 years ago, in a case involving an infringing biography that contained letters written by George Washington, the Supreme Court recognized this difficulty:

Copyrights approach, nearer than any other class of cases belonging to forensic discussions, to what may be called the metaphysics of the law, where the distinctions are, or at the least may be, very subtle and refined, and sometimes almost evanescent.

Many people find it difficult to regard mental creations such as those protected by copyright as a form of property. This may be because the rights granted by copyright law conflict with many expectations people have with respect to their rights to use tangible property. Most people believe that when they purchase something, they have the right to do anything they want with it. However, if that property is a compact disc that contains copyrighted works, the owner of the compact disc cannot do whatever he wants with that piece of property, at least not legally. For example, he cannot legally make copies of the compact disc except for his own personal use. Although the majority of people would probably agree that it is wrong (not to mention illegal) to go to a record store and shoplift a compact disc, a much lesser percentage of people are likely to consider it wrong to make a copy of a compact disc they own and give it to someone else. The harm to the record store due to the stolen compact disc is much more apparent than the harm to the copyright owners of the intangible works infringed upon by the taping of the compact disc.

To make things more confusing, although copyright law protects intangible property, copyrighted works are embodied or contained in physical objects that can be possessed. For example, a song can be embodied in a recording (on tape, compact disc, or other recording medium) or in written notation on paper (such as sheet music). So, although you cannot possess a copyrighted work, you can possess physical objects in which the copyrighted work is embodied. However, it is important to understand that possession of a physical object embodying a copyrighted work does not equate to ownership of the copyrighted work. If you buy a compact disc from a record store, you are the owner of that compact disc. Acquiring ownership of that compact disc, however, does not give you any ownership rights to the copyrighted works embodied on that disc (i.e., songs and recordings). Copyrighted works are separate pieces of property from any tangible property they may be embodied on.

One major disadvantage of intangible property as opposed to tangible property is that it can be easily infringed upon. If you own a car and someone takes it without your permission, that person has stolen your property. Similarly, if someone uses your copyrighted work without your permission, that person has infringed upon your copyright. If someone steals your car, it probably won't take you long to figure out that its been stolen. However, when someone infringes upon your copyright, you may not be aware that the infringement has taken place because a copyright is not a physical object. If someone wants to steal your car, they have to take possession of it. However, if someone wants to infringe the copyright to your song, they can do so without taking possession of any physical object and quite possibly without your awareness of the infringement. Further, someone can infringe upon the copyright to your song from thousands of miles away. Finally, if that weren't bad enough, more than one person can infringe a copyright at the same time.

Initially, copyright only involved the right to copy literary works and applied only to printed material. Over the years, copyright law has evolved and now gives authors of all kinds of creative works certain exclusive rights to their works. These rights include the right to reproduce, adapt, distribute, publicly perform, and publicly display the copyrighted work. By granting these rights exclusively to copyright owners, copyright law also prevents others from using copyrighted works without the copyright owner's permission. It is the exercise of these exclusive rights that allow copyright owners to make money from the use of their works. Permission to use a work is usually granted by a license which is an agreement stating how the work may be used and what compensation the copyright owner will be paid for allowing the use. There are different kinds of licenses for different types of uses and the compensation paid to a copyright owner under a license is usually in the form of royalties.

II. Why Do We Need Copyright?

In order for society to function smoothly, it is necessary to have rules governing who owns and who can exert control over tangible as well as intangible creations. Copyright law provides such a set of rules to govern the ownership and control of certain intangible creative works.

Before discussing the development of copyright, it is important to understand why copyright law exists in the first place. The issue of whether copyright should be recognized in creative works challenges fundamental assumptions about why society has created property rights in the first place. Historically, most property rights arose from the act of possession. However, intellectual property is unlike physical property since, once it is made available to the public, it is not subject to exclusive possession. The Supreme Court has stated that:

The general rule of law is, that the noblest of human productions—knowledge, truths ascertained, conceptions, and ideas—become, after voluntary communication to others, free as the air to common use.[3]

There are several potential justifications for copyright. One involves considerations of privacy. An author may not want a work he or she has created to be made available to the public. Copyright gives the author the right to decide whether or not to make its works available. Another justification involves the belief that an author who creates an artistic work should be able to control how that work is used. Finally, there are strong economic justifications for copyright. It can cost a lot of money to produce and market artistic works. For instance, the average recording released by a major record company involves an investment of over half a million dollars while a major motion picture involves an investment of over $50 million. Consequently, authors and copyright owners rely on the hope that potential revenues from their copyrighted works will repay their investment and allow them to make a profit. An alternative would be to have the government subsidize the creative work it believes the public wants and then distribute free copies. However, the public would ultimately still pay for these works through taxes.

A songwriter transfers her copyright ownership in a song she has created to a music publisher in return for an advance and potential royalties based on commercial uses of the song. The publisher will then attempt to exploit the song by licensing its use in various ways that will generate income (e.g., recordings, movie and television soundtracks, commercials, print, etc.). Both the songwriter's and the publisher's actions are based, at least partly, on economic considerations—they both want to recoup their investment and make a profit.

Although most people will agree that authors should be compensated for their work, it is also important to realize that copyright protection comes at a price. If copyright gives control to one person (the author or owner), it takes away some degree of freedom to use the work from others (the public). This does not mean that the public will be totally denied access to copyrighted works. Rather, it means that the public will be forced to pay for this access. The right to prevent the use of a copyrighted work also implies the power to allow the use of that work for a price. Most physical property, once used, is gone forever. However, since uses of copyrighted works generally involve copies of the work rather than the original work, the price paid is usually a relatively small amount per copy or use.

Additionally, copyright is not an unlimited right and is subject to many exemptions and limitations. The fair use defense, for example, allows people to use copyrighted works without permission and without paying for their use in certain circumstances, thereby preventing copyright from acting as a deterrent to free speech. The Supreme Court has stated that:

It should not be forgotten that the Framers intended copyright itself to be the engine of free expression and only if that engine is adequately fueled will public access to literary, musical and artistic creations be ensured.

Since the beginnings of copyright, a fundamental, philosophical debate has taken place involving whether copyright should be expanded to encompass new technologies so that authors and publishers can obtain the benefits of their works' value in the marketplace. Alternatively, should copyright be limited in order to insure that the public has free or at least inexpensive access to new works and new uses? This debate revolves around the issue of whether copyright should be viewed as an author's right (primarily benefiting authors) or a user's right (primarily benefiting consumers).

A. THE AUTHOR'S RIGHT PHILOSOPHY

Under the author's right (or natural right) philosophy, an author is believed to be morally entitled to control and exploit the products of the author's intellect. This includes the right to be credited as the author and the right to prevent the work from being changed substantially. The author's right philosophy extends copyright protection automatically, as a matter of principle, to every new form of artistic work. It is based on the idea that an author should be allowed to reap the fruits of his creation, to obtain the reward for his contribution to society and to protect the integrity of his creation as an extension of his personality. One of the earliest and most well known advocates of the author's right philosophy was the English philosopher John Locke. Locke believed that since authors own their bodies, they also own the labor of their bodies and the fruits of their labor. According to Locke, property in nature was given to man by God, but man acquired ownership of things by exerting labor and converting nature into something useful.[4]

Under the author's rights philosophy, a songwriter who composes a song should have the right to control the song's use and to be compensated for its sale, just as a farmer should be compensated for selling the crops he produces. Additionally, since the song has enriched society and may continue to do so in the future, the author should have the right to be compensated to the full extent of the song's success. While a piece of food has no further value after it is eaten, a song can be enjoyed by many people indefinitely. The author's right philosophy is followed, at least to some extent, by many European countries, some of which identify their copyright statutes as author's rights laws instead of copyright laws (e.g., droit d'auteur in France, Urheberrecht in Germany, and diritto d'autore in Italy).

Example 1.2:

According to the legislative record for the French copyright law, "[t]he most sacred, the most legitimate, the most unassailable, and, if I may say so, the most personal of all properties is the work, fruit of the thought of the writer."[5]

B. THE USER'S RIGHT PHILOSOPHY

The primary purpose of copyright law under the user's right (or utilitarian) philosophy is to encourage the widest possible production and dissemination of artistic works. Copyright law is designed to achieve this objective by granting property rights to authors that provide them with financial incentives to produce and distribute creative works. The user's right philosophy assumes that authors (as well as publishers who finance the creation and distribution of artistic works) will only invest sufficient resources in creating and publishing new works if they will have ownership rights that will enable them to control and profit from their works' distribution to the public. However, copyright law also recognizes that all creative efforts necessarily build on the creative efforts that precede them and if copyright law is to promote the dissemination of information, it must allow subsequent creators to draw on copyrighted works for their inspiration and education. Under a strict user's right approach, the public should be able to use works for free unless the author and publisher can prove that if they are not paid for the use, they will not have sufficient incentives to keep creating new works.

The free market economic system disfavors monopolies unless there is a compelling justification for them. Although copyright is a limited form of monopoly, its justification is that it is necessary to insure that creators have sufficient incentives to create. This results in a major difference between property rights in physical property and intellectual property. While the owner of physical property has absolute ownership rights to that property, intellectual property rights are not absolute. Copyright is a limited monopoly granted for a specified period of time. This limited copyright duration gives the copyright owner a chance to benefit financially from its property in order to recoup its investment and earn profits, thereby encouraging the creation and dissemination of new works of authorship. Since copyright ownership is limited in duration, all copyrighted works will eventually fall into the public domain where they will be free for all to use. Copyright is also limited in other ways—its scope is limited to original works of authorship, it protects only expression rather than ideas, and certain uses of copyrighted works are permitted without the copyright owner's consent.

Copyright law attempts to strike a balance between the incentives that authors and publishers need to produce original works and the freedom that creators need to draw on earlier copyrighted works. As stated by the Supreme Court:

The limited scope of the copyright holder's statutory monopoly, like the limited copyright duration required by the Constitution, reflects a balance of competing claims upon the public interest: Creative work is to be encouraged and rewarded, but private motivation must ultimately serve the cause of promoting broad public availability of literature, music and other arts.[6]

Under the user's right philosophy, the costs and benefits of extending copyright to a new type of work or a new type of use must be balanced against each other. A plausible argument can be made that copyright protection does not significantly affect the extent to which authors will create new works. It is certainly likely that some authors would still create works even knowing that they could not own them or profit by them. However, it is also conceivable that other authors would not.

Example 1.3:

Although writing this book has been somewhat a labor of love and I do not expect to earn a fortune from it, I probably would not have written it if there had been no possibility of receiving some compensation for my effort. I have spent a great deal of time and a fair amount of money creating this book. Like most authors, I hope that people will find my creation useful enough that they are willing to pay for it.

Another criticism that has been aimed at copyright law is that since it is often publishers rather than authors who end up owning copyrighted works, copyright law does not really provide much incentive for authors to create. However, it is the author's decision to transfer ownership of a copyrighted work to a publisher. In many situations, the only way the work will be made available to the general public is through a publisher's marketing and distribution. Even when an author transfers ownership to a publisher, the author will normally still receive royalties based on the publisher's distribution of the work so financial incentives still exist. Further, it certainly seems fair that publishers are compensated for taking the financial risk necessary to make works available to the public. Copyright is a necessary incentive for distributors of creative works such as publishers as well as authors.

Without the possibility of financial gain, publishers would certainly not be willing to invest the often substantial sums of money required to manufacture, market and distribute creative works. Without that investment by publishers, far fewer works would be likely to reach the public assuming that authors would still be willing to create them.

Copyright law involves striking a balance between providing sufficient incentives to authors to create works while also assuring that the public can have access to these works. The goal is to assure the greatest possible production of creative works. Eventually, all works will enter the public domain, where they will be free to all people to use.

American copyright law is based on the user's rights philosophy. In fact, Congress has specifically rejected the author's right philosophy as it recorded in the House Report on the 1909 Copyright Act:

The enactment of copyright legislation by Congress under the terms of the Constitution is not based upon any natural right that the author has in his writings . . . but upon the ground that the welfare of the public will be served and progress of science and useful arts will be promoted by securing to authors for limited periods the exclusive rights to their writings.

C. OTHER PHILOSOPHIES

The United States' economy and the economies of most Western nations are based on the free market system and the belief that profits are the just reward for labor expended in creative endeavors. However, some other countries are based on different economic foundations and have different viewpoints on the concept of authorship. Many eastern economies are related to the religions of Confucianism, Buddhism, and Islam, which are more communally oriented. According to these countries' economic systems, profits should be shared within society. Under the authorship philosophies of some Asian countries such as Korea, creative works have historically been viewed not as private property belonging to their authors but as goods for everybody to share freely. In these countries, cultural esteem rather than financial gain was the main incentive for creativity.

In feudal China, Confucian literary and artistic culture was based upon interaction with the past and discouraged bold innovation. Much of this background has survived in the People's Republic of China, which has been hostile to the concept of private ownership rights in intellectual property. However, China has been forced, due to foreign economic pressure, to adopt a copyright system highly similar to those of most Western nations. The forced nature of copyright is a probable reason for the enforcement problems that have been prevalent in China as well as other Asian countries.

In many cultures, copying of copyrighted works is tolerated to a much greater extent than in the United States. In Islamic countries, where piracy is rampant, the rationale is that copying of original material should not be prevented since the most widespread dissemination of knowledge benefits the public good. Similarly, in countries such as China, Taiwan, South Korea and Singapore, imitation and reproduction of ideas, art and scholarship are sometimes considered a token of honor and respect.

D. ECONOMIC RIGHTS PHILOSOPHY

American copyright law, although historically based upon the user's rights philosophy, also incorporates some of the author's rights philosophy. Actually, it may be more accurate to describe the current American copyright policy as an economic rights (or trade-based) philosophy. The United States is the world's largest producer and exporter of intellectual property. Copyrighted works account for over $457 billion (or 5.5%) of the annual gross domestic product in the United States. Copyright-related industries are also the fastest growing segment of the U.S. economy and employment in copyright related industries has grown at about three times the rate of employment growth in the economy as a whole in recent years, accounting for about 4.3 million jobs.[7] Copyrights bring more revenue into the United States than any other major industry, including aircraft, automobiles and agriculture.

As copyrighted works have become a larger part of international trade, they have also become one of the few positive components in the otherwise unfavorable United States trade balance (i.e., the U.S. imports more of just about everything than it exports). One major exception is copyrighted works, where the U.S. has a surplus trade balance with every country in the world. Although foreigners are not buying huge quantities of American physical products such as cars, stereos or computers, foreign sales of American intellectual property products such as music, movies, television programs and computer programs are substantial. Consequently, the United

States has taken a much more active role in expanding copyright's reach and enforcing copyright on an international basis, often without much consideration of either author's or user's rights. For example, the United States recently decided to extend the duration of copyright by twenty years. It seems unlikely that this additional twenty years of copyright protection will make authors more likely to create artistic works. In reality, the two primary motivating factors for the twenty year extension were: (1) to preserve many valuable copyrights (including the copyrights to several Disney characters such as Mickey Mouse and songs written by George Gershwin) that were about to expire; and (2) to bring the term of American copyright protection in line with many European countries.

Although these reasons may be important, they have little to do with encouraging authors to create new works. There was no evidence presented to suggest that authors would be less likely to create new works without the additional twenty years of protection and, in fact, this issue was not even considered by Congress. The passage of the term extension amendment was due primarily to the lobbying efforts of the copyright owners of some very valuable copyrighted works such as Disney and the Gershwin estate, with only token consideration given to providing incentives to authors or public access. This goes against the ideological basis for copyright, but reflects the reality of our political system.

III. Other Types of Intellectual Property

Many people confuse copyright with other types of intellectual property. Although copyright law is one category of intellectual property law, there are several others as well. Each category of intellectual property law is aimed at a particular type of intellectual property, but there is often a degree of overlap between these categories. For example, some patentable materials may be protected by trade secret law before a patent is granted, and although song titles are not protected under copyright law, they may be protected as trademarks under certain circumstances.

A. PATENTS

Patent law provides protection for certain inventions, discoveries and product designs. Patent protection is obtained by filing an application with the United States Patent & Trademark Office (PTO), which is a time consuming and often expensive process. The PTO examines the application to make sure that it complies with legal requirements and reviews prior patents and literature to determine whether the invention or design is eligible for patent protection. It is much more difficult to obtain patent protection than it is to obtain copyright protection because patent protection requires that the invention is novel and nonobvious while a copyright merely has to be original and fixed in tangible form.

B. TRADEMARKS

A trademark is any word, name, symbol or device, or any combination thereof, used to identify products or services and to distinguish them from those manufactured or sold by others.[8] Trademark law can be used to protect names, designs, logos, slogans, symbols, colors, packaging, containers and any other marks used by businesses to identify the source of their goods and services.

Trademark rights are acquired through use of a mark in commerce. In other words, the first person to use a mark will have rights in the mark, at least in the geographic area where the mark is used. Trademark rights last indefinitely as long as the mark is being used to identify a product or service.

A trademark owner has the exclusive right to use its mark to identify its product or service. This allows a trademark owner to prevent others from using the same or a confusingly similar mark to identify the same or similar products or services.

Although not required, trademarks can be registered with the federal government as well as state governments. A federal trademark registration is obtained from the United States Patent & Trademark Office. State registrations are generally obtained from the secretary of state's office. Federally registered trademarks must bear a notice using the symbol ® (which denotes a federally "registered" mark) in order to obtain certain benefits provided for by registration. The symbol ™ may be used for unregistered marks or marks covered by state registration.

C. TRADE SECRETS

A trade secret is any piece of business information that is kept secret and gives a business a competitive advantage. Trade secrets may include designs, devices, processes, databases, computer programs, formulas, and business plans. Some materials subject to protection as trade secrets, such as computer programs, may also be protected by copyright and patent law. There is no registration process for trade secrets. Instead, trade secret protection lasts as long as the information is kept secret.

D. RIGHT OF PUBLICITY

The right of publicity involves legal protection for an individual's name and image. Although the right of publicity applies to people in general, it is extremely important to famous people such as musicians and actors who rely on and use their names and image to earn a living.

The right of publicity gives people the right to prevent others from using their name and image for a commercial purpose without authorization. Some states have passed statutes dealing with the right of publicity while others recognize the right through common law. Either way, the degree of protection varies from one state to another. Generally, the right of publicity lasts for a person's lifetime, but the right is descendible (passed on to the person's heirs) in some states.

IV. Copyright's Importance to the Economy and the Music Industry

The United States economy has evolved from the industrial age to the post-industrial information age. In the industrial age, economic power was measured by the number of physical products a nation produced. In the information age, intellectual property is more important than any physical commodities. This is illustrated by the fact that the wealthiest individual in the world, Bill Gates, made his fortune from the intellectual property contained in Microsoft's computer software.

The importance of intellectual property has become even more apparent with the prevalence of digital technology and the Internet. As we begin the 21st century, intellectual property's importance is sure to increase. Property has always been equated with power, and in the 21st century, intellectual property such as that protected by copyright will be a crucial source of economic power and prosperity.

Copyright is vital to the existence of the music industry because it is based upon ownership of certain creative works, primarily songs and recordings. Since the rights provided by copyright law exist to protect creators and owners of original works of authorship, it is important to understand what these rights are, how they are exercised, and how they are enforced. This understanding will enable you to comprehend what ownership rights different parties in the music industry routinely have in different types of works. It will also enable you to know when certain rights are being violated and prevent you from violating other people's rights.

One of the criticisms leveled against copyright in recent years is that huge entertainment corporations use it to exercise control over content. Although it is certainly true that companies such as Universal, Sony, BMG, EMI and AOL/Time Warner (the five major record company conglomerates) own vast numbers of valuable copyrights, it is very inaccurate to imply that only these major companies benefit from copyright law. In reality, many people have jobs and make a living due to copyright law. Artists from Aerosmith (whose recordings are owned by Sony through their record label, Columbia Records) to Ani DiFranco (who owns and releases her recordings independently) are dependent on copyright law. In addition to famous musicians, there are also many behind-the-scenes individuals whose livelihoods are dependent on copyright law such as songwriters, record producers, recordings engineers, entertainment attorneys, etc.

Despite its critics, copyright law is here to stay. It is by no means a perfect system, but it has proven to be a fairly successful one. Its success is based on the fact that copyright law does provide incentives for authors to create new works that are generally made available to the public. Although the public is often forced to pay a price for access to these works, this price results in compensation to authors (and companies that finance author's creations) and that allows them to keep creating. Although copyright will remain with us, it is also certain to change. As discussed in the next chapter, copyright's history reflects a continuous evolution based on technological advancements. The challenge for copyright law is to accommodate technological advances while still guaranteeing that creators and producers have the right to control and to profit from the use of their creations.

1. "I Created Jazz in 1902, Not W.C. Handy," *Down Beat,* Aug.-Sept. 1938, reprinted in *Down Beat,* July 1994, at 10.

2. *Black's Law Dictionary, 6th ed.,* West Publishing Co. (1990).

3. International News Service v. Associated Press, 248 U.S. 215, 250 (1918).

4. J. Locke, *Second Treatise of Government,* Chapter 5 (1690).

5. *Le Moniteur Universal,* Jan. 15, 1971.

6. *Twentieth Century Music Corp. v. Aiken,* 422 U.S. 151, 156 (1975).

7. *Copyright Industries in the U.S. Economy: The 1998 Report,* prepared for IIPA by Economists, Inc.

8. 15 U.S.C. § 1127.

CHAPTER 2

The History of Copyright

▼

"The progress of copyright law does not take place by revolutions, but by successive stages. It resembles the growth of a city in which, as time goes on, some parts are torn down and others are devoted to new uses, while the plan remains the same and the great historic structures are preserved."[1]
Richard C. DeWolf

Although the main intention of this book is to discuss copyright law's current and future applications, before examining copyright law in the 21st century, it is first necessary to examine the evolution of copyright to the present. Many of the issues currently being raised about copyright law's application in the era of digital technology have been raised in the past in other contexts.

Copyright has existed in the United States since the nation's birth and in England since the beginning of the 18th century. Copyright has evolved over the past three centuries primarily due to new technologies that have resulted in new forms of creative expression and new media in which works are used. Consequently, the history of copyright law has involved the gradual expansion of the types of works protected by copyright as well as the rights encompassed by copyright. As advances in technology have expanded the range of economically valuable uses of copyrighted works, the types of works protected and the scope of exclusive rights in these works has also been expanded in order to enable copyright owners to realize the benefits of their works in these new mediums of expression.

I. The World Before Copyright

Prior to the 18th century, most creative workers were regarded as craftsmen who worked toward the creation of a product. At the beginning of the first millennium, a book trade in the Roman Empire developed. However, book manufacturing at this time consisted of slaves transcribing written works onto papyrus sheets that were then assembled into scrolls. More commonly, creative works were communicated orally. In the Greek states around the middle of the first millennium, authors read their works and musicians performed their works at public gatherings. Since there was no law protecting creative works of art, Greek states such as Athens relied on government sponsorship of the arts.

Example 2.1:

In the middle of the first millennium, in a precursor of many copyright disputes to come, the monk Columba transcribed the abbot Finnian's manuscript of the Psalms. Finnian objected to the unauthorized transcription and Celtic King Diarmait reportedly decided the dispute by stating "to every cow her calf, to every book its copy." Although copyright law did not yet exist, this was an early recognition of the idea that creative works should be treated as property.

Copyright's origins were in part a delayed response to technological advances. In 1436, Johannes Gutenberg invented the printing press. This innovation in technology made it possible to make cheap multiple copies of written works. One result of this invention was that many more literary works were made available to the public than ever before. Another result was that the issue of who would be entitled to own and profit from the production and distribution of these works arose.

During the 17th century, authors rarely owned or controlled the works they created. A book trade developed with printers owning the books they published. As the book trade grew, printers and distributors formed guilds to avoid competition. At the same time, governments engaged in censorship to avoid religious and political dissent. To do so, many European nations instituted monopolies for favored publishers who, in return for agreeing not to publish any heretical works, were able to prevent other publishers from competing with them.

Example 2.2:

Musicians were generally even worse off than their literary counterparts, mostly working in the streets or as servants. Classical composers such as Haydn and Mozart spent most of their lives working under the sponsorship of a monarch and received little compensation for their creations.

II. Copyright's English Origins

As a result of the competition among book publishers after the introduction of the printing press in England, the English Crown became concerned with the possibility of books being published that advocated religious heresy and political dissent. In 1534, to prevent such dissent, the Crown passed a law known as the Licensing Act requiring that anyone who wanted to publish written works must first obtain a license. The Licensing Act led to a publishing monopoly by a group of English printers and booksellers known as the Stationers' Company, which operated under the Crown's approval.

In 1557, a revised version of the Licensing Act was passed which required that all books had to be registered with the Stationers' Company, which recorded who owned the "copy-right" (i.e., the right to print copies of the work). The Licensing Act effectively gave the Stationers' Company a monopoly on printing. The Stationers' Company also had the authority to search out, seize and destroy any offending works, thereby operating as a form of censorship for the government. This precursor to copyright was a means of censorship rather than a means of protection for authors.

In 1694, the Licensing Act expired and the Stationers' Company started having competition from new printers who published cheaper versions of books previously published by the Stationers. The Stationers' Company lobbied in Parliament for legislative protection to maintain their monopoly. However, they made the fatal mistake of attempting to persuade Parliament that a law was needed, not solely to allow them to profit from publishing, but to provide authors with incentives to create new works. Their lobbying efforts eventually resulted in the world's first copyright statute, which was not the result that the Stationers had hoped for because, rather than recreating the monopoly the Stationers had previously enjoyed, it gave ownership rights to authors.

A. THE STATUTE OF ANNE

By the early 18th century, the mercantilist regimes that had dominated the previous century had given way to a less regulatory form of government. In this less regulatory environment, individuals became increasingly free to think, work and create without intervention. This environment led to the birth of copyright laws that recognized the importance of authorship. The notion that creators of artistic works should be accorded with ownership of the works they produced began to emerge. The idea that authorship justified ownership was based on the degree of originality involved in the creation of most artistic works.

In 1710, the English Parliament passed the Statute of Anne, which was formally titled "An Act for the Encouragement of Learning, by vesting the Copies of Printed Books in the Authors or Purchasers of such Copies, during the Times therein mentioned." The Statute of Anne stated its purpose as follows:

Whereas printers, booksellers, and other persons have of late frequently taken the liberty of printing, reprinting and publishing, or causing to be printed, reprinted and published, books and other writings, without the consent of the authors or proprietors of such books and writings, to their very great detriment, and too often to the ruin of them and their families: for preventing therefor such practices for the future and for the encouragement of learned men to compose and write useful books; may it please your Majesty, that it may be enacted . . . that the author of any book or books already composed, and not printed and published, or that shall hereafter be composed, and his assignee or assigns, shall have the sole liberty of printing and reprinting such books for the term of fourteen years, to commence from the day of the first publishing the same, and no longer...

Although the Statute of Anne confirmed the Stationers' copyrights in their existing books for a period of twenty-one years, it granted protection in new works to their authors. An author could obtain copyright protection by registering his work on the Stationers' register. Commonly, due to the high cost involved in printing and distributing books, authors sold their works to one of the Stationers for a lump sum payment. The Stationer then registered the work in its own name with no further compensation paid to the author.

The Statute of Anne provided that authors received a 14-year term of copyright protection with an additional 14-year term if the author was still alive. The reason for dividing the term of protection into two periods was that even if an author transferred his full copyright to a publisher, the copyright returned to the author at the end of the initial 14-year period. In order to receive protection, the copyright owner had to register the title of the book with the Stationers Company before publication. Infringement occurred when someone other than the author or owner printed, reprinted or imported a book without the author's permission. Once the copyright expired, anyone was free to copy the work and to distribute copies.

Copyright under the Statute of Anne was much more limited than modern copyright and applied solely to the printing, reprinting and selling of books. Copyright therefore covered the right to make copies by printing and to prevent others from making copies without permission. The Statute of Anne did not confer any protection on musical works. It was not until 1842 that the Victoria Statutes recognized the copyrightability of music in England,[2] although an earlier court case brought by the son of Johann Sebastian Bach had decided that the Statute of Anne was applicable to music.[3]

In the late 1720s, the Stationers once again petitioned Parliament for a return to the perpetual monopoly they had previously enjoyed. When Parliament once again refused, the Stationers decided to try to bypass Parliament by going through the common law court system. Andrew Millar, one of the Stationers, sued Robert Taylor, a bookseller who was not a member of the Stationers Company.[4] The dispute involved a popular poem called "The Seasons" by James Thomson, who in 1729 sold his copyright to Millar. By 1767, the statutory copyright in the poem had expired, and Taylor began printing and selling a cheap, competing edition. Millar claimed that Taylor's book was an infringement of the claimed common law right that Thomson had sold to him. The idea behind this claim was that regardless of the statutory copyright granted by the Statute of Anne, a perpetual common law copyright also existed. The ultimate issue was whether authors should have exclusive rights to their works and if so, whether these rights should be perpetual or limited in duration in order to provide enough incentive for authors to create new works. In other words, should copyright be an author's right or a user's right, allowing the public free use once authors and publishers have had an opportunity to recoup their investment in a work?

The Court held that a perpetual copyright existed at common law and that the Statute of Anne had not displaced that right (this decision was overruled in England five years later by *Donaldson v. Becket*, but the notion of common law copyright was later adopted in the United States). This decision was based on a theory of natural rights, which rests upon the belief that authors should receive protection for their creations, not because they need protection as an inducement for their efforts, but because they deserve protection as an inherent natural right attaching to the act of authorship. In endorsing this concept of natural rights, Chief Justice Mansfield stated that:

It is just, that an author should reap the pecuniary profits of his own ingenuity and labor. It is just, that another should not use his name, without his consent. It is fit, that he should judge when to publish, or whether he even will publish. It is fit he should choose not only the time, but the manner of publication; how many; what volume; what print. It is fit, he should choose to whose care he will trust the accuracy and correctness of the impression; in whose honesty he will confide; not to foist in additions; with other reasoning of the same effect.

III. Copyright in the United States

A. THE COLONIAL STATES

The development of copyright law in the United States was very similar to the evolution of copyright law in England. Several authors campaigned for copyright protection in the colonial states, including Noah Webster (author of the "Grammatical Institute of the English Language," which sold over 70 million copies) and Thomas Paine. The first state copyright statute was passed in 1783 by Connecticut and by 1786, twelve of the thirteen colonial states had passed copyright statutes.[5]

The preamble to the New Hampshire act is illustrative of the reasoning behind the passage of copyright laws:

As the improvement of knowledge, the progress of civilization, and the advancement of human happiness, greatly depend on the efforts of ingenious persons in the various arts and sciences; as the principal encouragement such persons can have to make great and beneficial exertions of this nature, must consist in the legal security of the fruits of their study and industry to themselves; and as such security is one of the natural rights of all men, there being no property more peculiarly a man's own than that which is produced by the labor of his mind.[6]

The fact that twelve of the thirteen colonial states each had their own copyright laws created problems with consistency and enforcement from one state to the next. Consequently, by the time of the Constitutional Convention, it had become apparent that a uniform, national copyright law was needed.

B. THE CONSTITUTIONAL COPYRIGHT CLAUSE

On March 10, 1783, the Continental Congress established a committee of three members to "consider the most proper means of cherishing genius and useful arts through the United States by securing to the authors or publishers of new books their property in such works." The representatives at the Constitutional Convention drafted a clause giving the federal government the authority to pass laws dealing with copyright, which passed unanimously. Article I, section 8, clause 8 of the Constitution, commonly known as the Copyright and Patent clause, states that Congress will have the power:

To promote the progress of Science and the Useful Arts, by securing for limited times to Authors and Inventors the exclusive right to their writings and discoveries.

At the time of the Constitution, the term "science" was much more general than its current meaning and included all knowledge. The Constitutional clause's language, "to promote the progress of science and the useful arts," established that the primary purpose of copyright law in the United States is to promote the creation and dissemination of creative works to the public. Copyright law in the United States is therefore supposed to primarily benefit the public rather than authors. Rewarding authors for their creations is only a secondary purpose. The rationale for rewarding authors is based on the idea that the best way to encourage people to create works of authorship is to provide financial incentives to do so. If no such financial incentives existed, people would be less likely to create new works. Over the years, courts have expressed this belief repeatedly. For instance, the Supreme Court has stated that:

[T]he encouragement of individual effort by personal gain is the best way to advance public welfare through the talents of authors.[7]

C. THE COPYRIGHT ACT OF 1790

In 1790, Congress exercised its right under the copyright clause of the Constitution and passed the first American copyright statute, which was largely based on the Statute of Anne and signed into law by President Washington. Copyright protection under the 1790 Act was limited to books, maps, and charts.

The 1790 Act provided for an initial term of copyright protection consisting of 14 years and a renewal term of 14 years, thus allowing for a maximum of 28 years of protection. Although the copyright clause of the Constitution clearly provides that copyright protection must be for limited duration, it applied only to the federal government and not to the states. The distinction between federal statutory copyright and common law copyright, previously debated in England, therefore arose in the United States. In *Wheaton v. Peters*,[8] the Supreme Court held that once a book was published, the Copyright Act displaced common law and became the exclusive source of rights in the published work. The United States therefore rejected the notion of natural rights that had been embraced in *Millar v. Taylor* in England.

D. THE COPYRIGHT ACT OF 1831

In 1831, the first general revision of the United States Copyright Act took place. The Copyright Act of 1831 changed the initial term of copyright protection to 28 years in order to give American copyright owners the same period of protection that many foreign authors enjoyed at that time. The 1831 Act also allowed the renewal right to pass to the author's widow or children if the author was not alive at the end of the initial term. The 1831 Act also included musical compositions as a class of copyrightable subject matter although a public performance right was not included until 1897.

E. THE COPYRIGHT ACT OF 1909

In 1905, President Theodore Roosevelt called for a complete revision of the Copyright Act in order to bring it in line with technological advances that had taken place. One of the main changes made by the 1909 Act was that, instead of individually specifying the types of works that can be subject to copyright, it simply stated that copyright protection is applicable to "all the writings of an author."[9] The term "writings" was interpreted by the Supreme Court to include works that are based upon the creative powers of the mind and are the fruits of intellectual labor and was therefore given a broad meaning which included most types of artistic works.

Under the 1909 Act, the renewal period of copyright protection was extended to 28 years, increasing the maximum period of copyright protection to 56 years (i.e., a 28 year initial period plus a 28 year renewal period). The 1909 Act protected only published works while leaving unpublished works protected by common law copyright.

One major shortcoming of the 1909 Act was that it failed to bring American copyright law in line with the terms required to join the main international copyright treaty (the Berne Convention) due to its insistence on formalities and shorter term of protection. Most foreign countries do not condition copyright protection upon any formalities such as registration and notice. However, the United States felt strongly that these requirements were necessary and the 1909 Act, like the copyright statutes before it, conditioned copyright protection upon these formalities.

A new and very important provision for copyright owners of musical works was incorporated into the 1909 Act. This provision created a compulsory mechanical license to reproduce and distribute sound recordings of musical compositions. It provided for a two-cent royalty to be paid to the copyright owner of a song for each record distributed containing that song, provided that the copyright owner had previously authorized the first recording and distribution of the song. In the early 1900s, the main formats in which recordings were reproduced were piano rolls, discs and cylinder recordings, which were all made mechanically. However, the mechanical license is now applicable to all types of reproduction regardless of the format that the recording takes. Consequently, the license required to record a copyrighted song, regardless of the type of recording (e.g., mechanical, analog, digital, etc.), is called a mechanical license *(see chapter 5 regarding the current compulsory mechanical license provisions)*.

Sound recordings were not protected under the 1909 Copyright Act, but in 1974 an amendment was passed giving a limited degree of copyright protection to sound recordings for the first time in the United States. This amendment prohibits the actual copying of a sound recording, but does not prohibit independently recording an imitation of a sound recording. It also did not include a right of public performance for sound recordings.

Although the 1909 Act has been replaced by the 1976 Act, it continues to be applicable in some respects for works created before January 1, 1978 (the date the 1976 Copyright Act became effective), subject to certain amendments that have since been passed.

F. THE COPYRIGHT ACT OF 1976

In 1955, Congress authorized a copyright revision project that, after 21 years of lobbying, studies and hearings resulted in the passage of a new and substantially revised copyright statute. The 1976 Copyright Act is a much more detailed statute than previous American copyright statutes. In many of its provisions, rather than specify general rules, the 1976 Act takes a much more regulatory approach, much of which resulted from extensive lobbying by special interest groups. The following are some of the more important changes made by the 1976 Copyright Act which are discussed in greater detail in subsequent chapters:

Protection: Copyright begins automatically when a copyrightable work is fixed in a tangible form *(see chapter 3)*.

Pre-emption: Section 301 of the 1976 Act states that since copyright applies to any works fixed in tangible form, there would no longer be any common law copyright for unpublished works. Any copyrightable work created on or after January 1, 1978, whether published or unpublished, is protected by the 1976 Copyright Act.

Subject Matter: Any original works of authorship can be protected by copyright. The 1976 Act specifies broad illustrative categories of the types of works that are copyrightable such as musical works and sound recordings *(see chapter 3)*.

Ownership: The 1976 Act made copyright divisible, meaning that a copyright owner can transfer less than its full ownership interest to other people. Copyrights can therefore be split up into many shares and in many different ways *(see chapter 4)*.

Duration: The 1976 Act changed the basic term of copyright protection to a period based on the life of the author plus 50 years which has since been increased to the life of the author plus 70 years *(see chapter 8)*.

Termination Right: The 1976 Act conferred a new right upon authors, allowing them to terminate transfers of copyright ownership and regain full ownership of their works *(see chapter 4)*.

Formalities: Copyright notice continued to be required for published works and registration and recordation of copyright transfers remained conditions to bringing suit for infringement although these formalities were later made optional *(see chapter 9)*.

Fair Use: The 1976 Act made the fair use doctrine, which had developed in common law, a part of the statute. Fair use is the broadest exception to the copyright owner's exclusive rights, giving others the right to use copyrighted works without permission in certain circumstances and for certain purposes *(see chapter 11)*.

Compulsory Licenses: The 1976 Act carried forward the 1909 Act's compulsory mechanical license, but provided for increases in mechanical royalty rates *(see chapter 5)*. It also added several other compulsory licenses which allow the use of copyrighted works upon compliance with certain procedures and payment of specified fees—cable television compulsory license, jukebox compulsory license and public broadcasting compulsory license.

Even though the 1976 Copyright Act was designed to be a flexible statute that could be applied to new types of works and new uses of copyrighted works, it has been amended over thirty times since its passage. The Copyright Timeline at the end of this chapter lists some of the more important of these amendments.

IV. International Developments

During the 19th century, the United States generally refused to give any copyright protection for foreign works and many American book publishers freely pirated English books. Similarly, the French book publishing industry was subject to rampant piracy in Belgium until the French government threatened trade reprisals. Eventually, France and Belgium entered into a treaty providing for copyright protection of each other's works. Other treaties between countries followed among various European nations resulting in a patchwork of laws providing for copyright protection among nations.

As the international market for copyrighted works increased, the system of bilateral treaties among individual countries made less and less sense. Instead, many countries started to realize that some type of uniform body of law binding as many countries as possible was needed. After years of negotiation, a small group of countries formed the Berne Convention in 1886. Under the Berne Convention, each member country agreed to give foreign works the same degree of protection as its law provided for domestic works. Over the next century, more countries gradually joined the Berne Convention. The United States however, resisted joining the Berne Convention until 1989.

Over the latter half of the 20th century, the importance of copyright has increased dramatically on an international basis. Virtually every country in the world recognizes some form of copyright law. Although copyright law varies from country to country, international treaties such as the Berne Convention guarantee at least certain minimum levels of copyright protection. For a more detailed explanation of international copyright law, see Chapter 14.

V. Summary

In the 16th and 17th centuries, governments attempted to combat piracy and exercise censorship by enacting legislation that limited the variety of works that reached the public. In the early 18th century, copyright laws began to develop which gave ownership rights to authors. Commonly, authors sold their right to publishers who manufactured, distributed and marketed their works. From the mid-19th century to the present, copyright has been adapted and expanded to accommodate many advances in technology.

In the 19th and early 20th centuries, new industries arose based on producing and distributing copyrighted works. Many of these industries (e.g., film, television and music) are highly cost-intensive, competitive and global in nature. Consequently, copyright has become increasingly important as a means of protecting the investment made by companies from piracy by others who wish to appropriate that investment without paying for it. In recent years, due to the ability to distribute copyrighted works worldwide, the importance of copyright has been increasingly recognized on an international scale. For an explanation of how copyright is currently affecting the music industry, see chapter 14.

1. *An Outline of Copyright Law* viii (1925)
2. 1842, 5 & 6 Vict., ch. 45, § 2.
3. *Bach v. Longman*, 98 Eng. Rep. 1274 (K.B. 1777).
4. *Millar v. Taylor*, 4 Burr. 2303, 98 Eng. Rep. 201 (K.B. 1769).
5. Delaware was the only state which had not passed a copyright statute.
6. Act of Nov. 7, 1783, ch. 1, 1783, 4th Sess., N.H. Laws (Vol. 4, at 521).
7. *Mazer v. Stein*, 347 U.S. 201 (1954).
8. *Wheaton v. Peters* involved an infringement suit brought by Henry Wheaton, the third Reporter of Decision for the Supreme Court against Richard Peters, the fourth Reporter. Peters authored a condensed version of Wheaton's reports summarizing Supreme Court decisions which were sold at considerably cheaper prices.
9. 17 U.S.C. § 4.

Table 2.1: Copyright Timeline

Year	Event
1436	Johannes Gutenberg invented the printing press, which made the mass production of written works possible.
1534	The English Crown passed the Licensing Act, which required that anyone who wanted to publish written works must first obtain a license. The Licensing Act led to a publishing monopoly by the Stationers' Company.
1557	A new version of the Licensing Act was passed which required that all books had to be licensed by registering them with the Stationers' Company which recorded who owned the "copy-right" (i.e., the right to print copies of the work).
1694	The Licensing Act expired and the Stationers' Company started having competition from new printers who published their own cheaper versions of books published by the Stationers.
1710	The English Parliament passed the Statute of Anne, the world's first copyright law.
1783	Connecticut passed the first copyright statute of the Colonial States.
1787	James Madison submitted to the framers of the Constitution a provision "to secure to literary authors their copyrights for a limited time."
1790	Congress passed the first United States Copyright Act, which protected books, charts and maps. The first copyrighted work to be registered in the United States was *The Philadelphia Spelling Book* by John Barry.
1831	The first general revision of the Copyright Act was made. Music was added to the types of works protected by copyright. The first term of copyright was extended to 28 years with a renewal term of 14 years.
1841	The case of *Folsom v. Marsh* introduced the concept of fair use into copyright law, which makes it possible to use copyrighted works without the copyright owner's permission in certain limited circumstances. For a more detailed explanation of fair use, see chapter 11.

1851	The first performing rights organization, Societe des Auteurs, Compositeurs et Editeurs de Musique (SACEM), was formed in France.
1856	Dramatic works were added to the types of works protected by copyright.
1865	Photographs were added to the types of works protected by copyright.
1870	The second general revision of the Copyright Act was passed. The responsibility for copyright formalities such as deposit and registration was centralized in the Library of Congress.
1877	Thomas Edison invented the phonograph.
1886	The Berne Convention became the first international copyright treaty. The United States did not join until 1989.
1891	The first U.S. copyright law authorizing the establishment of copyright relations with foreign countries was passed. The records of registered copyrights (the Catalog of Copyright Entries) were published in book form for the first time.
1897	The public performance right was made applicable to musical works. The Copyright Office was established as a department of the Library of Congress.
1908	In *White-Smith Music Publishing Co. v. Apollo Co.*, the Supreme Court held that player-piano rolls containing copyrighted musical compositions are not protected by copyright.
1909	The Copyright Act of 1909 was passed. Among other things, it extended copyright to player-piano rolls, reversing the Supreme Court's rule in the *White-Smith* decision.
1912	Motion pictures, previously registered as photographs, were added to the types of works protected by copyright.
1914	The American Society of Composers, Authors and Publishers (ASCAP), the first performing rights society in the United States, was formed.
1914	President Wilson proclaimed U.S. adherence to the Buenos Aires Copyright Convention of 1910, establishing protection between the United States and certain Latin American countries.
1940	Broadcast Music Incorporated (BMI), a performing rights organization, was formed to compete with ASCAP.
1955	The Universal Copyright Convention became effective in the United States.
1970	The World Intellectual Property Organization (WIPO) was established to protect creators and owners of intellectual property on an international basis.
1972	An amendment to the 1909 Copyright Act that provided limited copyright protection to sound recordings fixed and published on or after February 15, 1972 became effective.
1974	The United States became a member of the Convention for the Protection of Producers of Phonograms Against Unauthorized Duplication of Their Phonograms.
1974	The United States became a party to the 1971 revision of the Universal Copyright Convention.
1976	The fourth general revision of the United States Copyright Act was signed into law by President Ford.
1978	The 1976 Copyright Act became effective.
1982	§ 506(a) of the Copyright Act was amended to provide that persons who infringe copyright willfully and for purposes of commercial advantage or private financial gain shall be subject to criminal copyright infringement.
1984	The Record Rental Amendment became effective which granted the copyright owner of a sound recording the right to authorize or prohibit the rental, lease, or lending of phonorecords for direct or indirect commercial purposes.
1984	The Supreme Court ruled, in *Sony v. Universal*, that the videotaping of television shows using VCRs in order to watch the shows is fair use.
1989	The United States became a member of the Berne Convention (effective March 1, 1989). The Berne Convention Implementation Act made several changes to U.S. copyright law—Copyright notice was made optional rather than mandatory; the requirement of recordation of copyright transfers as a prerequisite for filing infringement actions was eliminated; and the compulsory jukebox license provision of § 116 was replaced by a voluntary license provision under § 116A (which was later renumbered as § 116).
1992	Renewal registration was made optional. Works copyrighted between January 1, 1964 and December 31, 1977 were automatically renewed even if renewal registration was not made.
1992	The Audio Home Recording Act was passed. This Act required serial copy management systems in digital audio recorders and imposed royalties on the sale of digital audio recording devices and media.
1993	The Copyright Royalty Tribunal Reform Act eliminated the Copyright Royalty Tribunal and replaced it with Copyright Arbitration Royalty Panels.

1993	The North American Free Trade Agreement (NAFTA) led to the addition of § 104A to the Copyright Act which permitted the restoration of certain foreign works which had entered the public domain in the United States due to failure to comply with the 1976 Act's notice provisions. NAFTA also created new rights and remedies against bootlegging of live performances.
1994	The Uruguay Round Agreements Act restored copyright to certain foreign works which were in the public domain in the United States and created legal measures to prohibit the unauthorized fixation and trafficking in sound recordings of live musical performances and music videos.
1995	The Performance Right in Sound Recordings Act was passed which provided for a limited performance right in sound recordings that applies to digital audio transmissions.
1996	The Anticounterfeiting Consumer Protection Act amended the Racketeer Influenced and Corrupt Organizations Act (RICO) to bring felony copyright infringement and music bootlegging within RICO's protection.
1997	The Technical Corrections Bill amended § 303 of the Copyright Act by adding subsection (b), which reversed the controversial decision of *La Cienega Music Co. v. ZZ Top. La Cienega* had held that a pre-1978 distribution of phonograph records without copyright notice resulted in a forfeiture of rights in the musical compositions contained on the records.
1997	The No Electronic Theft Act amended criminal copyright infringement provisions to permit the government to prosecute not only those who sell copies of copyrighted works without permission, but also individuals who merely give away copies. This reversed the decision of *United States v. La Macchia*, in which a bulletin board system operator was found not liable for unlicensed distribution by providing free pirated copies of copyrighted software.
1998	The Sonny Bono Copyright Term Extension Act was passed, increasing the term of copyright protection in the United States to the life of the author plus 70 years.
1998	The Fairness in Music Licensing Act was passed. It broadened the exemption to the public performance right in music for certain restaurants and other retail establishments depending on the size of the establishment and the number and size of speakers.
1998	Congress passed the Digital Millennium Copyright Act (DCMA), which implemented two international treaties designed to provide greater protection for copyrighted works in the digital environment.
1999	Congress passed the Digital Theft Deterrence and Copyright Damages Improvement Act of 1999, which increased the minimum statutory damages amounts under § 504(c) of the Copyright Act.
1999	Congress passed an amendment to the Copyright Act that added sound recordings to the classes of works that are eligible to be treated as specially ordered or commissioned works made for hire under § 101(2). This amendment provoked much criticism and was repealed the following year.

CHAPTER 3

The Subject Matter of Copyright

▼

*"In truth, in literature, in science and in art, there
are, and can be, few, if any, things, which, in an
abstract sense, are strictly new and original throughout.
Every book in literature, science and art, borrows,
and must necessarily borrow, and use much which
was well known and used before."*
Emerson v. Davies, 8 F. Cas. 615, 619
(C.C.D. Mass. 1845)

Many different types of creations are capable of being
protected by copyright. When the 1976 Copyright Act
was passed by Congress, it chose to adopt a very broad
definition of authorship, recognizing that authors are
constantly developing new ways to express themselves.
Generally, all forms of literary, musical and other artistic works can be protected by copyright if they fit the
requirements specified by the Copyright Act. Copyrightable works include, among other things, books,
magazines, newspapers, scripts, speeches, personal and
business correspondence (including e-mail), computer
programs, product packaging, musical compositions
(with or without lyrics), sound recordings, motion
pictures, videos, photographs, paintings, drawings and
sculpture.

It is important to understand that copyright
protection is not based on any aesthetic consideration
of the value of a work. Subjective judgments as to
whether a work is good or bad are irrelevant as far as
copyright protection is concerned. In a famous
Supreme Court opinion from 1903, Justice Holmes
stated that:

*It would be a dangerous undertaking for persons
trained only to the law to constitute themselves final
judges of the worth of pictorial illustrations outside of
the narrowest and most obvious limits.*[1]

Holmes was in effect saying that judges are not
necessarily the best qualified people to make judgments about the artistic value of creative works and
that, aside from determining whether the Copyright
Act's requirements for copyrightable subject matter
are met, courts should not have to evaluate the artistic
merit of works.

I. Requirements for Copyright

There are three basic requirements for a work to be
capable of copyright protection—originality, expression and fixation. Section 102(a) of the Copyright
Act specifies that copyright protection is available to:

*original works of authorship fixed in any tangible
medium of expression, now or later developed, from
which they can be perceived, reproduced, or otherwise communicated, either directly or with the aid of a
machine or device.*

A. ORIGINALITY

The first requirement that a work must satisfy in
order for it to be copyrightable is that the work must
be original. Although this requirement may seem
straightforward, the originality requirement is a common source of confusion. In the strictest sense of the
term, very little is totally original since virtually all

creativity draws on already existing elements. Composers, for example, select and arrange musical notes and rhythms that have existed for centuries.

How original does a work have to be in order to be entitled to copyright protection? The term "original" was purposely left undefined by the Copyright Act; Congress intended to let courts establish standards of originality and to allow the categories of copyrightable works to expand in response to technological advances. The first Copyright Act in the United States protected only books, charts and maps, but Congress has added other types of works over the years by passing amendments bringing works such as photographs and musical compositions within the scope of copyright. Rather than attempt to specify an all encompassing list of works protected by copyright, the 1976 Copyright Act provides copyright protection to all original works of authorship regardless of the type of work or form of authorship.

At its simplest, originality means that a work has been independently created by its author rather than copied from another work. Originality does not require any measure of novelty,[2] ingenuity or aesthetic merit. According to one court:

Originality is ... distinguished from novelty; there must be independent creation, but it need not be invention in the sense of striking uniqueness, ingeniousness, or novelty ... Originality means that the work owes its creation to the author and this in turn means that the work must not consist of actual copying.[3]

In *Sheldon v. Metro-Goldwyn Pictures Corp.*, Judge Learned Hand, who decided many important copyright cases, described the originality requirement stating that:

if by some magic a man who had never known it were to compose anew Keats's Ode on a Grecian Urn, he would be an 'author,' and, if he copyrighted it, others might not copy the poem, though they might of course copy Keats's.[4]

Substituting a song for Keats' Ode, if two different songwriters each composed exactly identical songs without copying from the other, each would own the copyright in their song. Although this situation would involve a very unlikely coincidence, it illustrates that originality is based upon independent creation.

In addition to independent creation, originality also requires a minimal amount of creativity. The reason for this requirement is that some works, although independently created, are too trivial or insignificant to justify copyright protection. The Supreme Court has held that, in addition to being independently created, a work must also possess "at least some minimal degree of creativity" although "the requisite level of creativity is extremely low" and "even a slight amount will suffice."[5] The Court went on to state, "the vast majority of works make the grade quite easily, as they possess some creative spark."

Although some degree of creativity is required, creativity is a subjective concept and courts have struggled with defining and measuring creativity. One thing that courts have agreed on is that the amount of creativity required is minimal. Courts have variously expressed the creativity requirement as requiring more than "merely trivial" variation,[6] a "modicum of creativity,"[7] a "touch of fresh authorship,"[8] and a "distinguishable variation."[9] Although none of these descriptions gives a bright line rule to determine exactly what degree of creativity is required, the rationale behind requiring a creativity threshold is possibly best explained by one author who stated that "to make the copyright turnstile revolve, the author should have to deposit more than a penny in the box."[10] Since the primary purpose of copyright is to encourage the production of the widest possible variety of literary and artistic expression, the low originality requirement helps to achieve that purpose by allowing protection for works that differ only minimally from earlier works.

The degree of originality required will vary somewhat for different types of works. Originality is easily found in highly artistic works such as literary works of fiction and musical works. In contrast, originality will be examined more closely in factual works (such as telephone directories) and functional works (such as accounting forms) since there is a limited amount of variation possible.

Example 3.1:

In *ZZ Top v. Chrysler Corp.*,[11] ZZ Top sued Chrysler over its use of the distinctive guitar riff from their song "La Grange" in a press conference to debut the Plymouth Prowler. Chrysler argued that the riff was substantially similar to riffs in earlier songs including "Boogie Chillen" by John Lee Hooker and "Spirit in the Sky" by

Norman Greenbaum. However, the court found the ZZ Top riff to be sufficiently original to be protected by copyright despite these similarities.

B. EXPRESSION

In actuality, no work is entirely original. All songs for instance are made up of notes, chords, and rhythms that have been used in many other songs before. This leads us to the second requirement for copyrightable subject matter, which is that a work must contain some original expression.

In order for a work to be copyrightable, it must include an author's expression rather than mere ideas, even if the ideas are totally original. This requirement is expressed in section 102(b) of the Copyright Act:

In no case does copyright protection for an original work of authorship extend to any idea, procedure, process, system, method of operation, concept, principle, or discovery, regardless of the form in which it is described, explained, illustrated, or embodied in such work.

The distinction between ideas and the expression of ideas is crucial to understanding copyright law. Whereas ideas are never protected by copyright, an author's expression of ideas may be protected. If an author expresses an idea in an original manner and fixes that expression in tangible form, the author's expression will be protected by copyright. However, the author's copyright will not prevent another person from using the same idea to create another original work since ideas are free for everyone to use. The expression requirement is therefore not the same as the originality requirement since some ideas will be original. However, even if an author comes up with an original idea, the idea will still not be entitled to copyright protection although the author's particular expression of that idea may be copyrightable.

The reason that copyright protection is limited to expression rather than ideas is totally consistent with the primary purpose behind copyright protection. In order to encourage the production of the greatest possible amount of artistic works, ideas must be free for use by all authors since they are the building blocks of creative expression.

Example 3.2:

Suppose I have the idea to write a song about love. Although I'm fairly sure that a few songwriters have already written songs about this topic, let's assume for argument's sake that I'm the first person to have this idea. It would be totally contrary to the rationale behind copyright law for me to have exclusive use of the idea of a song about love since I would have a monopoly on love songs and could prevent everyone else from writing love songs (or at least become very rich licensing my idea to others). The idea of writing a song about love is certainly a very general idea since there are obviously many different types of possible love songs and to allow any individual to monopolize that idea would hinder the creation of artistic works. Consequently, all songwriters are free to write love songs as long as their particular expression of the idea is original.

Distinguishing ideas from their expression is not always easy, but it is a distinction that must be made in order to know which elements of a work are unprotected and which elements are protected. In literary works, such building blocks would include the work's plot, stock characters and settings. As far as visual works of art are concerned, colors and shapes would certainly be considered unprotectible building blocks. For musical works, uncopyrightable building blocks will generally include a song's theme, individual words, individual notes, short musical phrases, rhythm and harmony.

What then constitutes expression rather than ideas? There are two basic guidelines that courts tend to follow in distinguishing ideas from expression. The first guideline involves a balancing of interests. Courts attempt not to draw the line so narrowly that authors will have no incentive to create original works. At the same time, courts also try not to draw the line so broadly that future authors will have a diminished base of ideas upon which to build their works. Second, in close cases, courts tend to find that a work contains protectible expression.

C. THE FIXATION REQUIREMENT

The third requirement for a work to be copyrightable is that the work must be fixed in tangible form. Section 102(a) of the Copyright Act, in addition to requiring originality, states that copyrightable works must be:

fixed in any tangible medium of expression, now known or later developed, from which they can be perceived, reproduced, or otherwise communicated, either directly or with the aid of a machine or device.

According to § 101's definition of fixation:

a work is fixed in a tangible medium of expression when its embodiment in a copy or phonorecord, by or under the authority of the copyright owner, is sufficiently permanent or stable to permit it to be perceived, reproduced, or otherwise communicated for a period of more than transitory duration.

At first, it might seem odd that although copyright protects intangible property, copyright protection is only available to works that are fixed in tangible form. Although a song is intangible, it must be produced in some kind of tangible form such as a recording or sheet music before it is capable of being protected by copyright. However, the reasoning for this requirement is simple practicality. If an intangible work was not made available in some tangible form, it could be very difficult to prove its existence.

The Copyright Act specifies two types of material objects that copyrighted works can be fixed in, copies and phonorecords. Both copies and phonorecords are physical objects from which a work can be perceived, reproduced or otherwise communicated. Section 101 of the Copyright Act defines "phonorecords" as:

material objects in which sounds, other than those accompanying a motion picture or other audiovisual work, are fixed by any method now known or later developed, and from which the sounds can be perceived, reproduced, or otherwise communicated, either directly or with the aid of a machine or device.

Phonorecords therefore encompass any type of recording such as cassette tapes, compact discs, digital audio tapes, digital video discs (DVDs), MP3 files, etc. A sound recording is fixed by definition since the recording process results in some type of phonorecord. Section 101 of the Copyright Act defines "copies" as:

material objects other than phonorecords, in which a work is fixed by any method now known or later developed, and from which the work can be perceived, reproduced, or otherwise communicated, either directly or with the aid of a machine or device.

Basically, copies encompass any material objects other than phonorecords. A musical work could be fixed in several different types of copies such as a lead sheet, written lyric, musical score, etc. Similarly, a literary work could be embodied in copies or phonorecords such as books, periodicals, microfilm, tape recordings, etc.

The language of § 102(a) states that fixation can be in a medium "now known or later developed." This is intended to include fixation in mediums brought about by technological advances. All that is required to satisfy the fixation requirement is that a work be embodied in some tangible medium. It does not matter what the form, manner or method of fixation may be—words, numbers, notes, sounds, pictures or any other graphic or symbolic indicia, as long as it is embodied in a physical object.

Example 3.3:

In 1908, the Supreme Court decided a case brought by the composer of "Little Cotton Dolly" and "Kentucky Babe."[12] The composer alleged that his songs had been infringed by a company that transcribed them onto perforated piano rolls used in player pianos, which were very popular at the time. Piano rolls operated by allowing air to rush through strategically-located perforations in the rolls, thereby placing pressure on the individual piano keys which played the song. The Copyright Act in effect at that time provided protection for musical works. The composer argued that copyright law protected all means of expression that could permit the song to be played and heard. The Supreme Court, however, took a narrow view and held that piano rolls were not copies since the musical compositions could not be visually perceived by looking at the rolls. Piano rolls could not be read and understood by most people and were part of a machine, rather than copies such as sheet music which was protected by copyright law. This decision was harshly criticized and overruled a year later by the 1909 Copyright Act, which included piano rolls and phonograph records as tangible objects which could contain copyrightable works. The 1909 Copyright Act, however, made both piano rolls and recordings subject to a compulsory license due to the concern that granting copyright protection to recorded music might result in a monopoly to one large, dominant player-piano manufacturer of the time.

II. Categories of Copyrightable Subject Matter

In addition to specifying the general requirements for copyrightable subject matter, Section 102(a) of the Copyright Act specifies eight specific categories of copyrightable works to illustrate the types of works that may be copyrightable. These categories are:

- *Literary works*
- *Musical works*
- *Dramatic works*
- *Pantomimes and choreographic works*
- *Pictorial, graphic, and sculptural works*
- *Motion pictures and other audiovisual works*
- *Sound recordings*
- *Architectural works*

These categories are not defined by the Copyright Act because Congress believed that they have commonly understood meanings. It is possible, in some circumstances, for a work to fit within more than one of these categories. For example, a sound recording could be part of a motion picture. The overlap may affect the particular rights in a work since § 106 specifies different rights for different categories of works and sections 108-120 specify limitations on some rights to certain categories of works.

It is also important to keep in mind that the eight categories specified by § 102(a) are not necessarily the only categories of copyrightable works. It is conceivable that some new type of work could be created which does not fit within any of the eight categories. The fact that the Copyright Act only lists eight categories does not imply that there cannot be additional categories. This is supported by § 102(a), which states that protected works of authorship "include" the eight listed categories. In § 101 the term "including" is defined as "illustrative and not limitative."

The next section will examine the eight different categories of copyrightable works, first examining the two categories of most importance to the music industry, musical works and sound recordings, then briefly the other categories of copyrightable works.

A. MUSICAL WORKS

Section 102(a)(2) of the Copyright Act specifies that "musical works, including any accompanying words" are protectible subject matter. Generally, a musical work consists of a combination of melody, harmony and rhythm, regardless of the material object in which it is embodied. Obviously, in order to be protected by copyright, musical compositions must be original, contain expression and be fixed in tangible form.

The term "musical works" includes songs consisting of music and lyrics as well as solely instrumental compositions. In the case of a musical composition that includes both music and lyrics, copyright will protect the combination of music and lyrics, the music alone and the lyrics alone. In one case, a court described this relationship between music and lyrics as follows:

The popularity of a song turns upon both the words and the music; the share of each in its success cannot be appraised; they interpenetrate each other as much as the notes of the melody, or separate words of the 'lyric.'[13]

Accordingly, if a person copies only the music or only the lyrics from a composition, he will be liable for infringement of the work to the same extent as if he had copied both the music and the lyrics.

(1) The Originality and Expression Requirements for Musical Works

Like any other type of work, musical compositions must be original and must contain expression. Musical compositions are generally comprised of several elements, which can include lyrics, melody, harmony and rhythm. Not every composition will contain all of these elements and the amount of originality and expression present in any of these elements will vary from one composition to the next.

(a) Lyrics

Some musical compositions contain lyrics as well as music. If a combination of words are created independently of music without any intention at the time of creation that they will be combined with music, the work will be considered to be a literary work. However, if created to be combined with music, the words will be part of a musical work.

Lyrics are one element of musical works that may be copyrightable if they contain original expression. This requirement prevents people from being able to claim copyright ownership in short and simple phrases.

For instance, in *Damiano v. Sony Music Entertainment, Inc. and Bob Dylan*,[14] the plaintiff alleged that the lyrics of various songs written by Bob Dylan infringed upon his copyrighted songs. The court, holding for the defendants, found that the lyric similarities alleged were not sufficiently original to be copyrightable stating that:

Plaintiff asks us to grant him a monopoly over the use of common combinations of words such as 'bell' and 'hell,' 'run' and 'hide,' or 'mind' and 'behind' merely because they are found together in a single song.

The court went on to say that copyright has no interest in "tying up random, fortuitous combinations of words" since this would not only stifle creativity, but would contravene the very policy behind copyright law. Similarly, in *O'Brien v. Chappel & Co.*, it was held that a phrase from the song "I've Grown Accustomed to Your Face" in the musical *My Fair Lady* was not an infringement. The phrase consisted of the lyrics "I've grown accustomed to the tune you whistle night and noon" while the plaintiff's song contained the following lyrics:

I've grown accustomed to the tune you whistle night and noon/Sharing My Dreams With a Star, asking the moon if it's soon/when you'll be mine, night and noon.

Although the plaintiff may have created a catchy lyrical phrase, the court refused to recognize any ownership rights in that phrase, stating that:

The plaintiff apparently thinks that he can get sole rights to the use of the phrase 'night and noon' no matter in what context the phrase is used. Such a common phrase in and of itself is not susceptible of copyright nor of appropriation by any individual. It is well established that copyright or literary rights do not extend to words or phrases isolated from their context, nor do they extend to abstract ideas or situations.

In another case, *Acuff-Rose Music, Inc. v. Jostens, Inc.*,[15] music publisher Acuff-Rose alleged that Jostens infringed upon its copyrighted song "You've Got to Stand for Something," which was written and recorded by country artist Aaron Tippin. The song is based on the theme of a father giving advice to his son to stand up for his principles. Jostens, a company that sells school rings, had developed an advertising campaign based on the slogan "If You Don't Stand for Something, You'll Fall for Anything." Even though the court believed that Jostens had copied its slogan from the song, it held that Jostens was not guilty of infringement since the lyrics involved lacked the requisite originality. The court noted that:

While especially creative phrases may be protected, there is nothing unique[16] about the use of standing/falling imagery to convey the importance of living a principled life.

It is possible that a musical composition containing music and lyrics that would not be sufficiently original or expressive to be copyrightable alone could be copyrightable when combined. In such a situation, a person who copied just the music or just the lyrics would not be liable for infringement of the work since he would only have copied unprotectible elements. It is also possible that a musical composition that contains music and lyrics may not be copyrightable at all due to lack of originality or expression.

(b) Melody
Melody has been defined as "a pleasing succession or arrangement of sounds" or "a rhythmically organized sequence of single tones so related to one another as to make up a particular phrase or idea."[17] At its simplest form, melody consists of the musical notes, the duration of these notes, and the order or arrangement of notes. For most musical compositions, melody is the most recognizable element. Although a melody must be original in order to be copyrightable, the components of melodic composition are very limited. First, melody is limited by the number of notes in the musical scale, which, as far as popular music is concerned, is twelve. Second, even though the twelve notes can be arranged in many different ways, the options are further limited by certain musical conventions. Composers seek to arrange these twelve notes in a way that conveys some emotional and artistic intent. In contrast, there are many more than twelve words commonly used in the creation of literary works. Consequently, it is generally a bit easier to find the requisite originality in literary works than in musical works.

Additionally, the distinction between ideas and expression is also important in the context of melody. Short musical phrases will usually be held to be ideas rather than expression and therefore not copyrightable in and of themselves.

In *Smith v. George E. Muehlebach Brewing Co.*, a jingle for a beer company which consisted of the phrase "Tic Toc, Tic Toc, Time for Muehlebach," scored to the notes "C" and "G" in the musical key of "C" to mimic the sound of a clock ticking was held not to be copyrightable.[18] According to the court, if all a composer does is "add a mechanical application of sound to a word that is itself not copyrightable, and adds the same to a descriptive phrase [Time for Muehlebach] already dedicated to the public domain, without the use of even the most simple harmonious chords, he has no musical composition subject to copyright."

Unfortunately, copyright law does not provide any strict rule to determine how long or creative a melody must be in order to be copyrightable. A common misconception among musicians sometimes referred to as the six bar rule is that any melody which lasts for less than six bars is not copyrightable. This misconception apparently developed in response to one particular court decision, *Marks v. Leo Feist, Inc.*[19] Marks was the copyright owner of a song entitled "Wedding Dance Waltz" and alleged that a song owned by Feist called "Swanee River Moon" infringed its copyright. The court held that there was no infringement even though "Swanee River Moon" contained six bars of music that were very similar to "Wedding Dance Waltz." The court stated that:

Musical signs available for combinations are about 13 in number. They are tones produced by striking in succession the white and black keys as they are found on the keyboard of the piano. It is called the chromatic scale. In a popular song, the composer must write a composition arranging combinations of these tones limited by the range of the ordinary voice and by the skill of the ordinary player. To be successful, it must be a combination of tones that can be played as well as sung by almost any one. Necessarily, within these limits, there will be found some similarity of tone succession. To constitute an infringement of the appellant's composition, it would be necessary to find a substantial copying of a substantial and material part of it. The exclusive right granted to the appellant by his copyright to print, reprint, publish, copy, and vend does not exclude the appellee from the use of 6 similar bars, when used in a composition of 450 bars."

The holding in *Marks* however, was limited to the particular factual situation and was not intended to set a limit as to how many bars of music are necessary to be copyrightable. In fact, other courts have held that as few as two to four bars of music may be protected by copyright.[20]

(c) Harmony

Harmony can be defined as "the structure, progression, and relation of chords."[21] The chord progression that makes up a harmony is, by definition, structured based on the melody. Since harmony is generally dictated by melody, harmony on its own will rarely be sufficiently original to be copyrightable. However, in a case involving an ownership dispute over a derivative version of the jazz classic Satin Doll, the court refused to say that harmony can never be copyrightable.[22] While recognizing that a melody usually implies a limited range of chords to accompany it, the court also believed that a composer may exercise creativity in selecting chords and that the choice of chords indicates the mood, feel and sound of the composition. Consequently, the court ruled that harmony may be capable of copyright protection in certain circumstances although it will not be in most circumstances. Although harmony by itself will rarely be copyrightable, it can certainly contribute to the copyrightability of a musical composition as a whole.

(d) Rhythm

The third basic element of musical composition is rhythm, which is "a regular pattern formed by a series of notes of differing duration and stress."[23] Simply put, rhythm is the beat that a musical composition follows. The vast majority of popular musical compositions have a steady, unvarying rhythm. Consequently, rhythm alone will rarely be sufficiently original to merit copyright protection. One court has stated that:

Rhythm is simply the tempo in which the composition is written. It is the background for the melody. There is only a limited amount of tempos; these appear to have been long since exhausted; originality of rhythm is a rarity, if not an impossibility.[24]

Although this court's view is perhaps a bit too limited, it is true at least with respect to popular music, that rhythm alone will usually not be copyrightable.

(e) Other Elements

Although lyrics, melody, harmony and rhythm are the main elements of musical composition, other elements may be present as well. For example, original expression may be found in a composition's accompaniment[25] or in a composition's fingering, dynamic marks, tempo indications, slurs and phrasing.[26]

In summary, the originality and expression requirement for musical works are usually satisfied due primarily to the composition's melody as well as the combination of melody, harmony, rhythm, lyrics and sometimes additional elements.

(2) The Fixation Requirement for Musical Works

Under the 1909 Copyright Act, musical compositions had to be reduced to readable form in order to be protected. In a case decided in 1908, the Supreme Court held that a perforated musical roll used in a player piano was not a "copy" of a musical composition and therefore could not infringe the right to make copies of the copyrighted composition since it was not "a written or printed record in intelligible notation."[27] However, under the 1976 Copyright Act, a musical composition may be fixed in either copies or phonorecords. Consequently, musical compositions can be fixed in the form of written musical notation or recorded on tape, disk or other mediums. According to the Copyright Office:

A musical composition would be copyrightable if it is written or recorded in words or any kind of visible notation, in Braille, on a phonograph disk, on a film sound track, on magnetic tape, or on punch cards.[28]

In fact, the majority of musical compositions registered with the Copyright Office are fixed in some type of recording rather than written musical notation.

B. SOUND RECORDINGS

It is very important to understand the distinction between musical works and sound recordings. Section 102(a)(7) of the Copyright Act includes sound recordings as one of the categories of copyrightable subject matter. Sound recordings are defined as:

Works that result from the fixation of a series of musical, spoken or other sounds, but not including the sounds accompanying a motion picture or other audiovisual work, regardless of the nature of the material objects, such as disks, tapes, or other phonorecords, in which they are embodied.[29]

Sound recordings are separate and distinct from the underlying musical, literary or dramatic works whose performance may be contained on the recording. For example, a recording of a song constitutes a sound recording, separately copyrightable from the song recorded. If the song is protected by copyright, the recording artist or record company must obtain a license from the copyright owner of the song to reproduce the song in phonorecords. If such a license is not obtained, the artist and record company will be liable for infringement of the song. Further, without such a license, the sound recording produced will not be protected by copyright since a sound recording is a derivative work and under § 103(a), protection for a derivative work utilizing "preexisting material in which copyright subsists does not extend to any part of the work in which such material has been used unlawfully."

The distinction between the copyright in sound recordings and the copyright in musical compositions is often difficult to comprehend since both the sound recording and the musical composition are fixed in the same physical object—a phonorecord. The copyright in the sound recording covers the rendition or performance of the musical composition rather than the composition itself. The copyright in the musical composition covers the sequence of musical notes and phrases, lyrics, and rhythm. The copyright in a sound recording covers the particular combination of sounds recorded rather than the musical work recorded or the physical object the sound recording and the musical work are embodied in (such as a compact disc, cassette or computer file).

Example 3.5:

Flautist James W. Newton sued the Beastie Boys for $150,000 for using a short sample from his musical composition "Choir" on their song "Pass the Mic." The Beastie Boys had obtained a license from Newton's record company to use the sound recording of Newton's performance, but had not obtained a license to use the musical composition owned by Newton. Since the sample used in the Beastie Boys' recording incorporates two separate copyrighted works (i.e., the musical composition and the sound recording), they were required to obtain licenses for both.

Sound recordings are not limited to recordings of musical compositions. A sound recording can consist of synthesized sounds, mechanical sounds or sounds that occur in nature (e.g., wind blowing, ocean sounds, etc.).

Example 3.6:

I own an album called Songs of the Humpback Whale, which is a recording of whales singing. Even though the performers were not human, this sound recording is just as copyrightable as a sound recording of Mozart symphonies or Madonna pop songs. Apparently, humpback whales are prolific songwriters; they supposedly compose new songs each year.

Sound recordings have not always been protected by copyright and still enjoy less protection than other types of works. Congress first granted copyright protection to sound recordings by passing an amendment to the 1909 Copyright Act that gave copyright protection to recordings fixed, published and copyrighted on and after February 15, 1972.[30] The 1976 Copyright Act incorporated this amendment into section 301(c).

Sound recordings fixed before February 15, 1972, although not protected under federal copyright law, may be protected under state statutory and common law.[31] In *Goldstein v. California*, the Supreme Court held that state laws prohibiting the copying of sound recordings fixed before February 15, 1972, were valid and enforceable.[32] However, since common law copyright generally lasts indefinitely, the 1976 Copyright Act imposed a time limitation on the duration of common law copyright for sound recordings fixed before February 15, 1972. Section 301(c) of the 1976 Act states that:

With respect to sound recordings fixed before February 15, 1972, any rights or remedies under the common law or statutes of any State shall not be annulled or limited by this title until February 15, 2067 . . . and the preemptive provisions of subsection (a) shall apply to any such rights and remedies pertaining to any cause of action arising from undertakings commenced on and after February 15, 2067.

Consequently, all sound recordings made prior to February 15, 1972 that are protected by common law copyright will enter the public domain on February 15, 2067. This expiration date insures that all such recordings will be protected for at least 75 years (i.e., 1972 to 2067).

Like all other types of copyrightable works, sound recordings must contain originality and expression. Congress has stated that copyrightable elements of sound recordings may include the contributions:

of the performers whose performance is captured and on the part of the record producer responsible for setting up the recording session, capturing and electronically processing the sounds, and compiling and editing them to make the final sound recording.[33]

Copyrightable elements of authorship in a sound recording can include the way the musical composition is sung by a vocalist, played by musicians, arranged by a musical director or producer, mixed by a recording engineer and so on. However, it is possible that only some of these individuals will contribute authorship. For instance, the record producer's contribution may be so minimal that the performance is the only copyrightable element in the work. In other situations, the record producer's contribution may be the only copyrightable contribution to a sound recording such as recordings of naturally occurring sounds (e.g., a thunderstorm, birdcalls, etc.). Since sound recordings often involve authorship by multiple individuals, determining who the authors and owners of the copyright are in a sound recording can be difficult. When sound recordings are made under a record contract between a recording artist and a record company, this difficulty is typically resolved through a contractual provision in which the various creators (artist, musicians and vocalists, producers, etc.) transfer any ownership interest they may have to the record company *(see chapter 4 for a more in-depth discussion of copyright ownership of sound recordings)*.

On occasion, some courts have been a bit too lenient in finding authorship in sound recordings. For example, one court held that merely providing the equipment and organizing the talent for a recording session was sufficient.[34] However, this result does not seem to satisfy the minimal level of creativity required for a work to be original. Drawing an analogy, if someone were to lock me in a room and provide me with a computer to work on writing this book, as much as I might need the forced discipline in order to be productive, it does not follow that this would entitle that person to claim authorship of the book.

In the context of sound recordings as well as all other copyrightable works, there must at least be some minimal degree of originality contributed—for example, by selecting the particular sounds to be recorded, selecting the specific point in time to record those sounds, and selecting the distance and angle between the microphone and the performers.

An important limitation on the copyrightability of sound recordings under §114(b) of the Copyright Act is that the reproduction right in sound recordings is limited to works "that directly or indirectly recapture the actual sounds fixed in the recording." In other words, the copyright in a sound recording only protects against actual copying of the recorded sounds and not against imitation of those sounds.

Example 3.7:

If I hired musicians to record a cover version of the song "Livin' La Vida Loca" imitating the musical performance of Ricky Martin, my recording, even if it sounded virtually identical to Ricky Martin's version, would not be an infringement of the Ricky Martin sound recording (owned by Sony). I would need a license to record the copyrighted song (which could be obtained under the § 115 compulsory mechanical license provision of the 1976 Copyright Act), but as long as I create my own recording rather than taking the sounds from the Ricky Martin recording, I would not have violated Sony's copyright in the sound recording. However, if I sold phonorecords of my recording, it is very likely that Ricky Martin would sue me for unfair competition and for violating his publicity rights. It is important to realize that copyright does not operate in a vacuum and even though I would not have violated copyright law, I probably would have violated other related laws.

C. LITERARY WORKS

Literary works are defined as "works, other than audiovisual works, expressed in words, numbers, or other verbal or numerical symbols or indicia, regardless of the nature of the material objects, such as books, periodicals, manuscripts, phonorecords, film, tapes, disks, or cards, in which they are embodied."[35] This category includes novels, magazine articles, poems, catalogs, directories, instructional works,

compilations of data, computer databases and computer programs, etc. For example, computer software programs such as the Wordperfect program used to write this book are classified as literary works since they are expressed in computer languages that use letters, words and numbers.

Generally, copyright protection in a literary work is based upon the arrangement of words that an author uses to express ideas. No individual words or ideas are copyrightable in and of themselves. Accordingly, copyright does not protect a literary work's theme, plot, or other common elements and ideas. Although copyright protection in literary works is based on the arrangement of words used by the author, this does not mean that a literary work can only be infringed upon by exact copying of the work. Even if a person paraphrases the work, he will still be liable for infringement if the paraphrase is based upon the work's expression rather than just its underlying ideas.

Example 3.8:

The book you are reading is a "copy" of a copyrighted literary work. Although you own the particular copy you are reading (assuming you acquired it lawfully), I, as the author, own the copyright. Accordingly, MixBooks (which I have a contract with to publish this book) is the only party that has the right to manufacture and sell the book. If you were to photocopy this book and give the photocopy to a friend, you would have committed copyright infringement. Although I own the copyright in this book, that does not prevent anyone else from writing his own book about copyright. It does, however, prevent them from taking the copyrightable expression from my book.

D. DRAMATIC WORKS

Section 102(a)(3) specifies that "dramatic works, including any accompanying music" may be copyrightable works. Although the Copyright Act does not define the term, dramatic works must tell a story through action, dialog and narration. A dramatic work may also include music such as the musical play *West Side Story*.

There is often a degree of overlap between a dramatic work and other types of works. First, since dramatic works are generally expressed using words, they may also qualify as literary works. Dramatic works may also be expressed by the use of actions and may therefore also qualify as pantomimes or choreographic works. If a dramatic work is fixed in an audiovisual medium such as film or videotape, it may also qualify as a motion picture. Finally, since the Copyright Act states that dramatic works may include "any accompanying music," parts of dramatic works may also qualify as musical works.

E. PANTOMIMES AND CHOREOGRAPHIC WORKS

Pantomimes and choreographic works are generally expressed by movement (such as dance) or physical attitudes and are usually fixed in videotape or film. However, a dance routine could also be fixed in a written description. Pantomimes comprise a drama presented by gestures and action without words. Choreographic works consist of recorded or notated movements of a dancer. Although choreographic works can include dance routines, dance steps and simple dance routines are not copyrightable due to lack of sufficient originality or expression.

F. PICTORIAL, GRAPHIC AND SCULPTURAL WORKS

Pictorial, graphic, and sculptural works are defined as "two-dimensional and three-dimensional works of fine, graphic, and applied art, photographs, prints and art reproductions, maps, globes, charts, diagrams, models, and technical drawings, including architectural plans."[36] A simple photograph for instance will generally qualify as a pictorial work since, as one court observed, "no photograph, however simple, can be unaffected by the personal influence of the author."[37] However, individual elements of a pictorial, graphic or sculptural work such as color, perspective and shapes will be considered ideas rather than expression and will be unprotectible unless combined and arranged in a way that constitutes expression.

Visually depicted characters, such as cartoon characters, may be protectible as pictorial, graphic or sculptural works.[38] Several cases have involved the Superman character and have held that although the character itself is copyrightable, this does not prevent others from creating characters possessing similar attributes such as feats of miraculous strength, flight, X-ray vision, and imperviousness to bullets.[39]

G. MOTION PICTURES AND OTHER AUDIOVISUAL WORKS

Section 102(a)(6) includes motion pictures and other audiovisual works as copyrightable works. Audiovisual works are "works that consist of a series of related images which are intrinsically intended to be shown by the use of machines or devices such as projectors, viewers, or electronic equipment, together with accompanying sounds, if any, regardless of the nature of the material objects, such as films or tapes, in which the works are embodied."[40] Motion pictures are "audiovisual works consisting of a series of related images which, when shown in succession, impart an impression of motion, together with accompanying sounds, if any."[41]

Audiovisual works may embody other types of copyrightable works. For instance, a musical composition contained in an audiovisual work is considered part of the audiovisual work rather than a musical work under § 102(a)(2).[42] Consequently, a song included in an audiovisual work such as a movie or music video will not be subject to the compulsory license provisions of § 115 since it has only been embodied in a copy rather than a phonorecord as required under § 115(a)(1).

Another important distinction involves motion picture soundtracks. The definition of a sound recording under § 101 excludes "the sounds accompanying a motion picture or other audiovisual work." However, the recorded sounds contained in the soundtrack to a motion picture are copyrightable as part of the motion picture. Due to the limited rights afforded to sound recordings, a recording that is part of a motion picture soundtrack will have greater rights than a sound recording. Specifically, the sounds contained in a soundtrack will be subject to the full performance right and the right against imitation as well as against dubbing.

III. Compilations

Section 103 of the Copyright Act provides that compilations may be copyrightable subject matter. Compilations are special types of works that overlap the classes of subject matter specified in section 102(a). Consequently, they may be literary, musical, dramatic or other categories of works. Section 101 defines a compilation as:

A work formed by the collection and assembling of preexisting materials or of data that are selected, coordinated, or arranged in such a way that the resulting work as a whole constitutes an original work of authorship.

Like all copyrightable works, compilations are subject to the requirements of originality, expression and fixation. They differ from other types of works due to the fact that they are based upon preexisting material. Consequently, the requisite originality and expression must be found in the selection and arrangement of the preexisting materials.

There are two very important rules concerning compilations. First, under § 103(b), the copyright in a compilation:

extends only to the material contributed by the author of such work, as distinguished from the preexisting material employed in the work, and does not imply any exclusive right in the preexisting material. The copyright in such work is independent of, and does not affect or enlarge the scope, duration, ownership, or subsistence of, any copyright protection in the preexisting material.

Second, under section 103(a), "protection for a work employing preexisting material in which copyright subsists does not extend to any part of the work in which such material has been used unlawfully."

The copyright in a compilation results from the selection, coordination and arrangement of the preexisting materials in such a way that the resulting work constitutes an original work of authorship. The term "selection" refers to the choice of material, regardless of whether it is taken from one source or from multiple sources. The terms "arrangement" and "coordination" refer to the ordering or grouping of material which must be more than mere mechanical grouping of data, such as alphabetical or chronological listings of data. The copyright in a compilation protects the author's original expression and not any of the ideas or materials compiled.

Although a compilation may consist of individually copyrighted works (such as a compilation of songs), a compilation may also consist of preexisting material that is not protected by copyright. A famous Supreme Court case dealing with compilations involved a dispute over telephone directories. In *Feist Publications, Inc. v. Rural Telephone Service Co.*, Rural published white and yellow page telephone directories for its service area. Feist published an area-wide telephone directory that covered eleven different telephone service areas including Rural's. Feist requested a license from Rural to copy its white page listings and was denied. Feist, however, went ahead

and copied Rural's listings. Feist's directory differed from Rural's, but 1309 of Feist's 46,878 listings were identical to Rural's, including four fictitious listings included by Rural to detect copiers.

Both the district and appellate courts found in favor of Rural since it was clear that Feist had copied Rural's listings. The Supreme Court, however, reversed this decision, holding that although Feist copied Rural's listings, those listings were not copyrightable. The reasoning for its decision was based on the rule that facts such as names and telephone numbers are not original and therefore not copyrightable.

According to the Court, facts themselves can never be copyrightable although compilations of facts may be. The originality requirement is the key to the different treatment between facts and factual compilations. The distinction is between creation and discovery—facts are discovered while compilations of facts are created. If the creation of a compilation possesses the requisite originality, the compilation will be copyrightable. Originality in a compilation is found in the materials selected by the author and the way in which those materials are arranged. However, in *Feist*, the selection or arrangement was not original since it consisted of the residences in Rural's telephone service area arranged in alphabetical order. The Court stated that "there is nothing remotely creative about arranging names alphabetically in a white pages directory."

The Court also rejected what had become known as the "sweat of the brow" theory for copyright protection that some lower courts had recognized. The Court's ruling means that regardless of the time and effort spent in researching and accumulating information for a compilation, the research and accumulation will not qualify the results for copyright protection. A compilation will only be copyrightable if it contains originality of expression.

Example 3.9:

In *Consolidated Music Publishers, Inc. v. Ashley Publications, Inc.*,[43] the plaintiff sued to prevent the defendant from manufacturing and distributing a compilation of sheet music entitled *World's Favorite Classic To Contemporary Piano Music* which the plaintiff alleged was an infringement of its compilation entitled *Easy Classics to Moderns*. Both compilations consisted entirely of public domain musical compositions. The plaintiff's compilation was originally published in 1956 and contained 142 compositions. The defendant's compilation was published in 1961 and contained 83 compositions, 29 of which were contained in the plaintiff's compilation. Additionally, the defendant's compilation contained editorial material allegedly copied from the plaintiff's and there were several errors common to both works. The court found that the plaintiff's compilation exhibited originality in the fingering, dynamic marks, tempo indications, slurs and phrasing as well as the selection and arrangement of the compositions. The court consequently held that the defendant was guilty of infringement since it utilized the same titles arbitrarily chosen by the plaintiff for several compositions, duplicated a selection already in its book under a different title; misspelled an author's name in the same manner as the plaintiff and repeated another notational error made by the plaintiff. It is important to note that the court's ruling does not mean that no one else can create a compilation using the same compositions. However, it does mean that one cannot merely copy parts of the plaintiff's compilation that exhibit originality and are therefore copyrightable.

> **Tip:** The following conditions are necessary in order to have a copyrightable compilation:
> 1. Collection and assembly of pre-existing material or facts.
> 2. Selection, coordination and arrangement of those materials.
> 3. Creation, through the selection, coordination and arrangement, of an original work of authorship.

(1) Collective Works

A collective work is a type of compilation and is defined as "a work, such as a periodical issue, anthology, or encyclopedia, in which a number of contributions, constituting separate and independent works in themselves, are assembled into a collective whole." In other words, a collective work is a compilation of copyrighted works. As with other types of compilations, originality in a collective work will usually be found in the author's selection and arrangement of the works included. If the method of arrangement is very simple or is dictated by function (such as alphabetical arrangements and chronological order), the collection may not be copyrightable due to its lack of originality.

A songbook containing a group of previously existing copyrighted songs such as the top 10 songs of 1999 would be a collective work. In order to compile such a work, the author of the collective work must have print licenses from the copyright owners of each of the songs in the songbook. If, however, the songbook contained 10 public domain songs such as the top 10 songs of 1899, no licenses would be required. Whether the songbook contained copyrighted or public domain songs, the copyright in the resulting compilation would only cover the author's particular selection and arrangement of songs (assuming such selection and arrangement is original) and would not give the author any rights in the individual songs. Similarly, a record album consisting of 10 individual copyrighted master recordings is a collective work although such works are commonly called compilation albums.

IV. What Is Not Protected by Copyright?

A. THE PUBLIC DOMAIN

Creative works that are not protected by copyright are considered to be in the public domain. A work that is in the public domain is not owned by anyone. Any member of the public is free to use the work without having to obtain permission and without having to make any payment for the use. Since virtually all authorship borrows to some extent from prior works of authorship, without the public domain, it would be almost impossible for authors to create new works without violating someone's copyright. As stated by one legal scholar:

Transformation is the essence of the authorship process. An author transforms her memories, experiences, inspirations, and influences into a new work. That work inevitably echoes expressive elements of prior works.[44]

There are several ways by which a work can enter the public domain. First, when the copyright to a work expires, the work enters the public domain. Additionally, some works published before 1964 that were not renewed are in the public domain. Some works for which the author did not take the proper steps to secure copyright such as works published before March 1, 1989 without copyright notice may be in the public domain. Finally, a work may enter the public domain due to the copyright owner's abandonment of the work.

B. IDEAS VERSUS EXPRESSION

Section 102(b) of the Copyright Act provides that ideas, procedures, processes, systems, methods of operation, concepts, principles and discoveries are not copyrightable and are therefore part of the public domain. The notion that ideas cannot be copyrighted is fundamental to copyright law since to allow authors to monopolize ideas would inhibit authorship rather than encourage it. Instead, copyright protection is limited to an author's particular expression of ideas. Although anyone is free to use an author's ideas, they are not free to copy the author's expression of an idea. Legal disputes usually arise over where to draw the line between a work's expression and its underlying ideas.

C. FACTS

Copyright law does not protect facts of any kind. The reason is similar to the distinction between ideas and expression. Like ideas, if the first author to write about a specific fact could gain a monopoly over that fact, the creation of other works of authorship using the same fact would be severely restricted. A further reason for not allowing facts to be copyrightable is that facts, although they may be discovered by an author, are not created by an author.

D. NAMES, TITLES, SLOGANS AND SHORT PHRASES

Although there can be creativity and originality in names, titles, slogans and short phrases, these materials are not generally subject to copyright protection.[45] This is because names and titles usually consist of short phrases which are either unoriginal or constitute ideas rather than expression. However, although rare, it is conceivable that some titles might be sufficiently original and expressive to qualify as copyrightable literary works.

Example 3.11:

A court indicated that the song title "Supercalafajali-stickespeealadojus" was capable of being protected by copyright.[46] Although the music and lyrics of the songs were not at all similar, the court held that since the title was so unique, it could be protected. This is a questionable decision since uniqueness is not a requirement for copyright protection. A better way of achieving the same result might have been to recognize that such a unique and recognizable title could be protected by trademark rather than copyright law.

Example 3.12:

There are at least 129 songs entitled "Love Is a Wonderful Thing" registered with the Copyright Office (two of which were the subject of a lawsuit by the Isley Brothers against Michael Bolton, discussed in Chapter 10). Although all of these songs are protected by copyright, none of the copyright owners of these songs has any copyright ownership in the title itself.

Although names, titles and slogans are generally not protected by copyright, they may receive protection under trademark and unfair competition laws. These types of protection are essentially based on use of the name, title or slogan (legally known as the "mark") in commerce and prevent uses that are likely to cause confusion among consumers as to the source of goods or services.

Example 3.13:

Short phrases and slogans such as "just do it" as used by Nike are not protected by copyright. Similarly, the often-used blues lyrical phrase "got my mojo working" was held not to be copyrightable.[47] However, slogans can be protected by trademark law if they become closely associated with a product or service. Nike has trademark rights in the slogan "just do it" because it has spent millions of dollars advertising its products using that slogan, and consequently developing a close association among consumers between the slogan and Nike products.

E. UNFIXED WORKS

Since fixation in tangible form is one of the requirements for copyright protection, any work not fixed in tangible form will not be protected by copyright.

Although most musical works are fixed in tangible form as part of the creation process, there are some musical works created without fixation. For example, works that are improvised during a performance are not ordinarily fixed in tangible form unless the performance is recorded. An improvised work is by definition actually created spontaneously during a performance. Improvisation therefore combines the activities of authorship and performance, which, for most musical works, are done separately. Improvisation is one of the defining compositional elements of jazz and there are consequently many improvised musical compositions by jazz artists that are not protected by copyright.[48]

Although improvisation and other unfixed works are not protected under copyright law, they can be protected under other legal doctrines. For instance, some states protect works that are not fixed in tangible form. Although states are prevented from passing laws affecting the rights protected by federal copyright law under the doctrine of preemption, since unfixed works are not protected by copyright, preemption is not applicable. California, however, is the only state that has enacted a statute providing for protection for improvised works. This statute states that "the author of any original work of authorship that is not fixed in any tangible medium of expression shall receive exclusive ownership in the representation or expression thereof."[49]

One way for improvisational authors to protect themselves is to record their performances, thereby fixing an improvisational performance in tangible form as it occurs. This gives the performer a copyright in the underlying musical composition as well as the sound recording of the performance. However, if someone other than the performer also records the performance at the time it takes place, would this be an infringement of the underlying musical composition? Since the other person did not copy the performer's sound recording, there is clearly no infringement of the copyright in the performer's sound recording. Further, since the underlying musical composition is merely in the process of being fixed when being copied, it is uncertain whether the underlying musical composition is protected by federal copyright at this point in time. However, the Copyright Act's definition of the term "fixed" states that "[a] work consisting of sounds, images, or both, that are being transmitted, is 'fixed' for purposes of this title if fixation of the work is being made simultaneously

with its transmission." This part of the definition was intended primarily to address the problem of taping of live broadcasts of sporting events, but applies equally to live musical performances.[50] The person recording a performance of a previously unfixed work would therefore be guilty of copyright infringement.

Another source of protection for unfixed works is found in section 1101 of the United States Code, commonly referred to as the anti-bootlegging statute. This provision prohibits the unauthorized fixation of "sounds or sounds and images of a live musical performance" and was intended to provide protection to performers rather than authors by prohibiting the bootlegging of live performances. Although it does not give a performer of an improvisational work a copyright in the improvised musical composition, it does have the practical effect of preventing bootlegger's recordings, which also indirectly protects against unauthorized reproduction of the underlying musical composition.

F. WORKS OF THE UNITED STATES GOVERNMENT

Under § 105 of the Copyright Act, copyright protection is not available to works created by the United States Government. A work of the United States Government is defined as a work prepared by an officer or employee of the United States Government as part of that person's official duties. This means that government works such as federal judicial opinions and legislative enactments are part of the public domain and can be used freely by all. Additionally, all publications of the Copyright Office, the Trademark Office and the IRS are in the public domain.

It is important to note that § 105 applies only to the federal government and does not prevent states from claiming copyright ownership of works created by state employees. Further, § 105 does not prevent the United States Government from owning copyrights that are transferred to it rather than created by the federal government.

1. *Bleistein v. Donaldson Lithographing Co.,* 188 U.S. 239 (1903).

2. Although novelty is not required, its existence can be used to help prove that a work is original.

3. *Batlin & Son, Inc. v. Snyder,* 536 F.2d 486, 490 (2d Cir. 1976).

4. 81 F.2d 49, 54 (2d Cir.).

5. *Feist Publications, Inc. v. Rural Telephone Service Co.,* 499 U.S. at 345.

6. *Alfred Bell & Co., Ltd. v. Catalda Fine Arts, Inc.,* 191 F.2d 99, 103 (2d Cir. 1951).

7. *Universal Athletic Sales Co. v. Salkeld,* 511 F.2d 904, 908 (3d Cir. 1975).

8. *Kuddle Toy, Inc. v. Pussycat-Toy Co.,* 183 U.S.P.Q. 642, 663 (E.D.N.Y. 1974).

9. *L. Batlin & Sons, Inc. v. Snyder,* 536 F.2d 486, 490 (2d Cir. 1976).

10. B. Kaplan, *An Unhurried View of Copyright* 46 (1966).

11. 54 F. Supp. 2d 983.

12. *White-Smith Music Publishing Co. v. Apollo Co.,* 209 U.S. 1 (1908).

13. *Edward B. Marks Music Corp. v. Jerry Vogel Music Co.,* 140 F.2d 266 at 267 (2d Cir. 1944).

14. 975 F. Supp. 623 (1996).

15. 45 U.S.P.Q. 2d (BNA) 1452 (1997).

16. Although the court's reasoning is correct, it's use of the word "unique" is unfortunate since copyright only requires originality rather than uniqueness.

17. *The American Heritage Dictionary of the English Language, Third Edition,* Houghton Mifflin Company (1992).

18. *Smith v. George E. Muehlebach Brewing Co.,* 140 F. Supp. 729 (W.D. Mo. 1956).

19. 290 F. 959, 960 (2d Cir. 1923) ("The exclusive right granted to the appellant by his copyright to print, reprint, publish, copy and vend does not exclude the appellee from the use of 6 similar bars, when used in a composition of 450 bars.").

20. *Boosey v. Empire Music Co.,* 224 F. 646, 647 (S.D.N.Y. 1915).

21. *The American Heritage Dictionary of the English Language, Third Edition,* Houghton Mifflin Company (1992).

22. *Tempo Music, Inc. v. Famous Music Corporation v. Gregory A. Morris,* 838 F. Supp. 162 (1993).

23. *The American Heritage Dictionary of the English Language, Third Edition,* Houghton Mifflin Company (1992).

24. *Northern Music Corp. v. King Record Distrib. Co.,* 105 F. Supp. 393, 400 (S.D.N.Y. 1952).

25. See, e.g., *Fred Fisher, Inc. v. Dillingham,* 298 F. 145, 147 (S.D.N.Y. 1924).

26. See, e.g., *Consolidated Music Publishers, Inc. v. Ashley Publications, Inc.,* 197 F. Supp. 17, 18 (S.D.N.Y. 1961); Desclee & Cie., S.A. v. Nemmers, 190 F. Supp. 381, 388 (E.D. Wis. 1961).

27. *White-Smith Music Publishing Co. v. Apollo Co.,* 209 U.S. 1, 17 (1908).

28. See Register's Supplementary Report, 4.

29. 17 U.S.C. § 101.

30. Pub. L. No. 92-140, 85 Stat. 391 (1971), as amended, Pub. L. No. 93-573, 88 Stat. 1873 (1974).

31. For example, California enacted a statute protecting sound recordings created prior to February 15, 1972. CAL. CIV. CODE § 980.

32. 412 U.S. 546, 178 (1973).

33. The House Report on the 1976 Act at 56.

34. *Shaab v. Kleindienst,* 345 F. Supp. 589 (D.D.C. 1972).

35. 17 U.S.C. § 101.

36. 17 U.S.C. § 101.

37. *Jeweler's Circular Publishing Co. v. Keystone Publishing Co.,* 274 F. 932, 934 (S.D.N.Y. 1921).

38. See, e.g., *Walt Disney Prods. v. Air Pirates,* 581 F.2d 751, 756, 199 U.S.P.Q. 769 (9th Cir. 1978); *Detective Comics, Inc. v. Bruns Publications, Inc.,* 111 F.2d 432, 433-434 (2d Cir. 1940).

39. See, e.g., *Warner Bros., Inc. v. American Broadcasting Cos.,* 720 F.2d 231, 243 (2d Cir. 1983); *Detective Comics, Inc. v. Bruns Publications, Inc.,* 111 F.2d 432, 433 (2d Cir. 1940); *DC Comics, Inc. v. Unlimited Monkey Business, Inc.,* 598 F. Supp. 110, 118-119 (N.D. Ga. 1984).

40. 17 U.S.C. § 101.

41. 17 U.S.C. § 101.

42. *WGN Continental Broadcasting Co. v. United Video, Inc.,* 693 F.2d 622, 627 (7th Cir. 1982).

43. 197 F. Supp. 17 (1961).

44. Litman, "The Public Domain," 39 Emory Law Journal 965 (1990).

45. 37 C.F.R. §202.1(a) (1993).

46. *Life Music, Inc. v. Wonderland Music Company,* 241 F. Supp. 653 (1965).

47. *Stratchborneo v. Arc Music Corp.,* 357 F. Supp. 1393 (S.D.N.Y. 1973).

48. See H.R. Rep. No. 94-1476, at 52 ("an improvisation ... would not be eligible for Federal statutory protection under section 102").

49. Cal. Civ. Code 980(a)(1).

50. H.R. Rep. No. 94-1476, at 52 (1976).

CHAPTER 4

Ownership of Copyright

▼

*"The songs I create mean many things to me.
Foremost among them is my goal, and I think the
goal of every artist, to connect with and communicate my thoughts, emotions and beliefs to my
audience . . . But, my songs also are my livelihood.
If I can't earn a living from them, I'll have to do
something else . . . I love what I do. But this is a
tough business. And to illustrate that, I would ask
each of you on this distinguished committee to
think about this question: Have you ever seen in
the classified section of any newspaper an ad which
reads: "Songwriter wanted. Good salary. Paid vaca-
tion. Health benefits and many other perks." I'm
sure you haven't. Most songwriters are lonely entre-
preneurs trying again and again for that hit which
will help them take care of their families and keep
them writing in the hopes of another hit down the
road, so that songwriting can be a career, not a
part-time unpaid struggle. However, success would
be meaningless without strong copyright laws ...
For it is only through the protection of the copyright law . . . that our right to earn a living from
our creative work is assured."*[1]
Lyle Lovett, testifying before the House
Subcommittee on Courts, the Internet and
Intellectual Property, May 17, 2001

Like any other type of property, a copyright can be
owned by one or more people and can be transferred
from the owner to another party. Just as a car owner
can sell her car, a copyright owner can sell its copyright. A major difference is that when an author sells

a copyrighted work, the author usually retains a right
to receive income from uses of the work. In many
situations, in order to earn income from their copyrighted works, authors must transfer their copyrights
to publishers so that the publisher can exploit the
work. Primarily due to the fact that copyright is
intangible property, there are some strict rules for the
transfer of copyright that must be followed.

It is crucial to understand the difference between
ownership of copyright as opposed to ownership of
physical objects that copyrighted works may be
embodied in. Section 202 of the Copyright Act provides that:

*Transfer of ownership of any material object, including
the copy or phonorecord in which the work is first
fixed, does not of itself convey any rights in the copyrighted work embodied in the object.*

For example, the transfer of ownership of a
compact disc would not constitute a transfer of copyright ownership. The purchaser of the compact disc
owns the physical object embodying the copyrighted
works contained on the compact disc, but does not
acquire any ownership rights in the copyrighted
works themselves.

I. Initial Ownership

Copyright ownership arises from and begins upon
creation of a work. Many people confuse copyright
ownership with copyright registration and assume
that you have to register a work in order for it to be

copyrighted. In fact, a work is automatically protected by copyright from the moment it is created as long as it satisfies the requirements for copyrightable subject matter discussed in the previous chapter. Although registration of a work does provide certain benefits to the copyright owner, copyright ownership is not conditioned upon registration.

Section 201(a) of the Copyright Act provides that the author of a work is the initial owner of the copyright. Although in most situations it is obvious who the author of a work is, there are some situations where this is not totally clear such as when there is more than one author and when one person creates a work on behalf of another. In general, the author of a work is the person who creates the work or translates an idea into fixed, tangible expression. The Supreme Court has stated that the term "author" should be interpreted in a broad sense and defined an author as "he to whom anything owes its origin."[2]

Example 4.1:

If I wrote a song, I would be the author and the copyright owner of that song (assuming that the song is original and fixed in tangible form).

The owner of a copyrighted work may exercise any of the rights provided by copyright law or may authorize others to exercise any of those rights. The owner may also transfer copyright ownership to others.

Example 4.2:

As the copyright owner of the song from the previous example, I could reproduce, adapt, distribute and publicly perform my song or I could allow others to do any of these things. If I wanted to, I could sell my song to a publisher who would then become the owner of the song.

Obviously, knowing the identity of the author of a work is extremely important since all rights initially belong to the author. An author, however, does not necessarily have to perform all of the tasks involved in the creation of a work. For instance, copyright ownership in a sound recording may belong to the producer who directs and supervises the recording process as well as the performers themselves.

II. Joint Ownership

It is not uncommon for more than one person to contribute to the creation of a work. In fact, as far as songs are concerned, it is rare for a single individual or entity to own the whole copyright to a song. One reason for this split ownership is that songwriters often collaborate in the creation of songs.

Example 4.3:

If a song is written by a band consisting of five individuals with all five members contributing to its authorship, the copyright will be split among five co-owners. Ownership may be further divided due to transfers of ownership by the authors. If three of the band members have co-publishing contracts with three different music publishers, there would be eight co-owners (i.e., the five band members and three additional publishing companies).

Even if a song is written by one author, copyright ownership may still be split among several parties. For instance, if a songwriter writes a song and pitches it to a record producer, the producer might insist on partial ownership in return for getting an artist to record it. Sometimes artists as well as record companies will similarly insist on partial ownership of a song in return for recording it. The result is that a song written by one person may end up being owned by several different publishing companies.

Section 101 of the Copyright Act defines a joint work as a work prepared by two or more authors with the intention that their contributions be merged into inseparable or interdependent parts of a unitary whole.[3] Under § 201(a), the authors of a joint work are considered co-owners of the copyright in the work.

A. REQUIREMENTS FOR JOINT OWNERSHIP

There are two requirements necessary for the creation of a joint work. First, two or more authors must contribute to the creation of the work. Second, each of the co-authors must make their contributions with the intention that their contributions be combined to form a single work.

(1) Intent Requirement

In order for a work to qualify as a joint work, its authors must intend to combine their contributions into a unitary whole. The authors' intent to combine their contributions must exist at the time their contributions are created. When two or more co-authors work together at the same time and in the same place to create a work, it will be fairly obvious that they intend their contributions to be combined.

Example 4.4:

Many publishers in Nashville have "writer's rooms" where songwriters get together to collaborate on new songs. Songs created in this manner will clearly be joint works as long as each collaborator has made an independently copyrightable contribution. Similarly, when members of a band write songs together, the songs will be joint works.

It is not necessary, however, that authors work together at the same time and place or that they even know each other as long as each intends that their contribution will be combined with someone else's contribution to form a single work.

Example 4.5:

In one case, a songwriter sold lyrics he had written to a music publisher who then had another writer compose music for the lyrics. The court held that the resulting song was a joint work, stating that "It makes no difference whether the authors work in concert, or even whether they know each other; it is enough that they mean their contributions to be complementary in the sense that they are to be embodied in a single work to be performed as such."[4] In another case, a composer and a lyricist wrote a song together and later, a different lyricist, with the consent of the composer, wrote new lyrics for the song. This court held that the song resulting from the music and lyrics contributed by the second lyricist was a new joint work.[5]

There are however, situations in which separate works may be combined to form a single work and the resulting combination is not a joint work. For example, if one person writes a poem he intends to be complete as is and later, another person writes music to accompany the poem, the resulting song would not be a joint work since the intent to combine the poem with the music did not exist at the time the poem was composed. Instead, the song would be a derivative work based on the poem.

In one case, commonly referred to as the 12th Street Rag case, a court took the position that a joint work could be created even though the authors did not intend that their contributions would be combined. This case involved an instrumental composition to which lyrics were added four years later. The court held that the song was a joint work even though the composer of the instrumental version had no intention that lyrics would be added. However, the 12th Street Rag case is very much a minority position and it is unlikely that it would be followed today.

In order to determine whether authors possessed the intent to create a joint work, courts will generally look at several different factors. First, a court will examine the conduct of the contributors and any statements they may have made indicating their intent. Additionally, courts may consider the quality and quantity of the contribution. If the quality and quantity of a contribution is great, it is likely that a joint work was intended. On the other hand, the fact that someone contributed a relatively small amount to a work indicates that joint authorship was probably not intended. Finally, if the copyright to a work has been registered, courts will presume that the information identifying the authors in the registration application are accurate and someone claiming to be an author who is not identified as such in the registration application will have the burden of proving that he is in fact a co-author.

(2) Copyrightability of Individual Contributions

In addition to having the intent to create a joint work, each of the contributors must contribute original expression that would be copyrightable on its own. This requirement results from section 101's definition of a joint work, which specifies that the work must be prepared by two or more "authors." In other words, each contributor must contribute copyrightable authorship in order to have a joint work.

Example 4.6:

If I added a few words to a song's lyrics, I would not be a joint author since my contribution would not be copyrightable on its own. Similarly, if I have an idea for a song, but since I have no talent as a songwriter, I tell someone else my idea and they write the song, I would not be a joint author. My idea, no matter how important it is to the song, is not a copyrightable contribution.

Although uncopyrightable contributions will not qualify a contributor as an author, a contributor could still be a co-owner of the resulting work's copyright. For instance, if I have an idea for a song and want someone else to write a song based on my idea, I could require the songwriter to sign a contract giving me partial copyright ownership in the song in return for the idea. In this situation, I would have acquired my ownership from a transfer of ownership rather than from being an author. Sometimes, individuals who have not contributed authorship to a song will still be credited as authors. In some situations this results merely because the parties involved are not aware of the legal requirements for joint authorship. In other situations, the parties may agree to treat someone as a co-author even though they know that the person is not really an author such as when a recording artist is credited as a co-author of a song when the artist merely makes some minor, uncopyrightable lyric changes.

Although each co-author's contribution must be independently copyrightable, it is not necessary that each contribution be equal. In other words, it is possible for one author to contribute much less to the creation of a work than another, but still be a co-author.

B. RIGHTS AND DUTIES OF JOINT OWNERS

The Copyright Act provides some rules governing joint ownership of copyright. These rules can be thought of as default rules that apply unless the co-owners make up their own rules. Co-owners are free to agree to any other ownership rules as long as they put their agreement in writing. However, if they do not agree otherwise in writing, the Copyright Act's rules apply.

(1) Equal, Undivided Ownership Interests

Section 201(a) provides that joint authors of a copyrighted work are co-owners of the copyright in equal, undivided interests. This means that each co-author owns an equal share of the entire work. For instance, if two songwriters collaborate in the creation of a song, each will own a 50 percent interest in the entire song. This is true regardless of the contributions made by the individual authors. Even if one author composes the music while the other writes the lyrics, both authors will own a 50 percent interest in the entire song rather than one owning the music and the other owning the lyrics. The same rule holds true even if one songwriter contributes 90 percent of the song and the other only contributes 10 percent.

The joint work provisions operate under the assumption that co-authors contribute relatively equal portions and deserve an equal share of any profits derived from the work. There are two main reasons for this assumption. First, courts should not be put in the position of having to make subjective judgments about the relative value of co-authors' contributions. Second, in reality, co-authors rarely discuss how ownership should be shared prior to collaborating in the creation of a work. In many co-writing relationships between songwriters, it is assumed that each co-writer will own an equal share in the song. However, co-authors are perfectly free to alter this assumption of equality and agree upon any ownership split they choose as long as they put their agreement in writing.

Example 4.7:

Papa-June Music v. McLean[6] involved an ownership dispute between co-authors of songs. In 1989, Ramsey McLean sent some poems he had written to Harry Connick, Jr., who added music to them and recorded the resulting songs on an album. Connick and McLean entered into a co-publishing contract which provided that copyright ownership of the songs would be split 70 percent to Connick and 30 percent to McLean. Several years later, McLean sent Connick some new poems that Connick added music to and recorded on another album. McLean then notified Connick that he wanted a 50/50 ownership split. Connick however thought the 70/30 split previously agreed to should apply. The court held that McLean was a joint owner of the copyrights for the songs and since the parties did not have a written agreement specifying a different arrangement for these songs, McLean and Connick each owned 50 percent under § 201(a) of the Copyright Act. This result illustrates the importance of having a written agreement if co-owners intend to share ownership in anything other than equal shares.

Tip: In my experience as an entertainment attorney, I have advised many songwriters and publishers regarding decisions involving ownership of their songs. Yet I have very rarely come across situations where co-writers had any written agreement (or even any discussion) regarding ownership of songs they write together. I also know through experience that many disputes arise over ownership of songs. In fact, this is one of the most common reasons for disputes between band members. Many of these disputes could be avoided by the authors having a simple, written agreement. In an effort to avoid some potential future disputes, I have put together a very basic songwriter collaboration agreement that can be downloaded from my web site at **musiccopyright.net**. Although there are much more elaborate collaboration agreements that can be used and which may be needed in certain situations, this agreement can be used in most circumstances to specify the basic rights and responsibilities of co-authors.

(2) Right to License

Since each joint owner of a copyrighted work owns an equal, undivided interest in the work, each joint owner has the right to use the work or to authorize others to use the work. This rule applies regardless of whether the author authorizing the use has the consent of the other authors. For instance, if three songwriters collaborate in the creation of a song, each would be free to record the song themselves. Further, each of the songwriters would be free to issue mechanical licenses authorizing someone else to record the song. The only exception is that a joint owner cannot grant an exclusive license since that would prevent its co-owners from granting licenses. Practically, this rule can present licensing problems, but, as with all of the joint ownership rules, co-owners are free to agree otherwise in writing. Even though one joint owner can grant non-exclusive licenses, many licensees will want to obtain a license from all joint owners. Contrary to American copyright law, many foreign countries require all joint owners to consent to the issuance of a license.

(3) Duty to Account to Co-Owners

Although joint owners have the right to use and to authorize others to use the copyrighted work, they are required to account to their co-owners for their share of any profits derived from the use. Unless the co-owners have agreed otherwise in writing, each co-owner is entitled to an equal share of any income generated by a jointly owned work.

Example 4.8:

Jerry Vogel Music Co. v. Miller Music, Inc.[7] involved the song "I Love You California." It was composed by two authors, each of whom assigned their ownership interest to a different publisher. Universal Pictures asked Jerry Vogel Music Co. for a license quote for the use of the song in a movie and Vogel quoted a fee of $1000. Universal then obtained a license from Miller Music for $200. Vogel demanded half of the license fee and after Miller refused, sued for an accounting. The court held that co-owners have a duty to account for profits from licensing to third parties. The court recognized that not having a duty to account to co-owners would lead to competition among co-owners for a low bid and encourages waste of copyrighted works. In other words, one co-owner cannot underbid another co-owner and keep the entire amount of income generated from the low bid.

(4) Duty Not to Destroy Copyright

Some courts have indicated that if a co-owner's use of a copyrighted work will deplete or destroy the work's value, that co-owner should be accountable to his co-owners for destruction of the copyright. Under modern case law, since co-owners have a duty to account to other co-owners for profits earned from their use of a copyrighted work, depletion of a copyright's value will probably not be an issue too often. However, there may be exceptions where one co-owner licenses the use of a work at a rate that is much lower than standard license rates for the particular type of use.

Example 4.9:

If a co-owner of a copyrighted song issues a synchronization license for the use of the song as the title theme for a $100 million major motion picture for a fee of $100, he may be liable to other co-owners for depleting the copyright's value since the standard fee for such a use would be much higher.

(5) Joint Authorship Problems

Problems frequently arise with respect to joint authorship of copyrighted works. Usually these problems are the result of authors who collaborate in the creation of a work, but fail to discuss what their ownership interests will be. Disputes also tend to arise when songs are composed or worked on during recording sessions.

Example 4.10:

In 1999, Sarah McLachlan was sued in a Canadian court by a musician named Daryl Neudorf who was hired by McLachlan's record company to work on the pre-production of her first album. Neudorf claimed during this working relationship, he co-wrote four songs with McLachlan that were included on her album. McLachlan contended that Neudorf only provided services as a musician and producer and that his contributions to the songs did not constitute authorship. The court found that although Neudorf did make contributions to the songs, his contributions to three of the songs were not sufficient to constitute original expression. However, even though the court believed that Neudorf had contributed original expression to the fourth song, it held the song was not a joint work since Neudorf failed to prove a mutual intent to co-author the song with McLachlan. The problem that arises from this decision is that, regardless of the extent of a musician or producer's songwriting contributions, a recording artist could always defeat the musician or producer's joint authorship claim by simply intending not to treat that person as a co-author. Instead, the artist could claim that any contributions the musician or producer may have made to songs were merely part of the services they were hired to perform. The only practical solution is for the co-authors to have a written collaboration agreement for any co-written songs.

In recent years, the distinction between songwriters, musicians and producers has become blurred. This is especially true in musical styles such as hip-hop, rap, and electronica, which are largely dependent on beats and samples as opposed to more traditional melody and lyric based songs. In these types of music, the distinction between the creation of a song and a recording is often also blurred.

Example 4.11:

In 1998, 4 individuals who worked on Lauryn Hill's album, *The Miseducation of Lauryn Hill*, sued Hill claiming that they were co-authors of several songs on the album. Hill contends that she was the sole writer of the songs. Interestingly, the album's liner notes credit the individuals as performers, producers or contributors of "additional music or lyrics," arguably indicating that they are co-authors. This lawsuit has reportedly been settled with the terms of the settlement confidential.

C. COMMUNITY PROPERTY

Nine states, including California, have community property laws specifying that property acquired while people are married belong to both spouses equally.[8] In such states, if a wife were to compose a musical composition, the copyright ownership in that composition would belong jointly to the husband and wife unless they agree otherwise. A California court has held that a copyright acquired by one spouse during marriage is community property.[9] The other community property states have not yet considered whether copyrights are community property, but it is likely that they would conclude that they are. Property acquired before or after marriage is not considered community property.

Under community property laws, either spouse would be entitled to sell a jointly owned copyright without the other's consent. Any income from such a sale would have to be shared jointly. However, a spouse cannot give away community property without the other spouse's consent. When one spouse dies, the other spouse would not necessarily inherit a copyright owned as community property since the deceased spouse may convey its share of the copyright by will to anyone. Upon divorce, the spouses are free to divide their jointly owned property in any way they choose. However, if they cannot agree, a court may end up splitting up the property. In such a situation, the judge could award a copyright entirely to one party and award the other cash or other property of equal value or could award each spouse half of the copyright.

Tip: An author or other copyright owner who is planning on getting married in a community property state and does not want to share ownership of copyrighted works can enter into a prenuptial agreement specifying that copyrights will be owned individually by the author. Even in non-community property states, it might be a good idea to enter into such an agreement to protect against a judge awarding a spouse ownership of community property in a divorce settlement. Such an agreement can be entered into before or during marriage.

III. Works Made for Hire

In some situations, the person who creates a work will not be considered the work's author and therefore not the initial copyright owner. Such situations occur when a person creates a work on another's behalf. The work for hire doctrine is an exception to the general rule that copyright ownership vests initially in the work's creator. Instead, the person or party on whose behalf the work is created is considered to be the author and initial copyright owner. Section 201(b) of the Copyright Act provides that:

In the case of a work made for hire, the employer or other person for whom the work was prepared is considered the author for purposes of this title, and, unless the parties have expressly agreed otherwise in a written instrument signed by them, owns all of the rights comprised in the copyright.

Under the work made for hire doctrine, an author does not have to be a human being. A corporation or other business entity can qualify as an author under certain circumstances. The copyright owner of a work made for hire, whether an individual or a business, will have the same rights in the work that any author would have with a few exceptions (such as the duration of copyright protection) and can exercise any of the exclusive rights or authorize others to do so. The actual creator of a work made for hire has no ownership rights in the work.

A work's classification as a work made for hire is important for several reasons. First, the initial ownership of a work made for hire belongs to the employer or commissioning party rather than the person who actually creates the work. Second, works made for hire have a different copyright term than other works (95 years from publication or 120 years from creation, whichever expires first). Third, there is no termination right applicable to works made for hire.

A. TWO CATEGORIES OF WORKS MADE FOR HIRE

There are two different types of situations in which a work made for hire will result. The first involves works made by an employee as part of the employee's employment. The second involves certain types of works which are specially ordered or commissioned.

(1) Works Prepared by Employees Within the Scope of Employment

Under the work for hire definition of § 101(1), if an employee creates a copyrightable work as part of his or her job, the employer will own the copyright to the work. It is not necessary for the employer to tell employees that such works will be works made for hire nor is it necessary to have a written contract stating so (although it may be advisable to do so).

(a) Who Is an Employee?

In order to determine whether a work is made for hire, a determination must first be made as to whether the creator of the work is an employee rather than an independent contractor. Although the Copyright Act does not define the term "employee," the Supreme Court has held that a person is an employee if the party on whose behalf the work is performed has the right to control the manner and means by which the work is performed. This rule will be applicable regardless of how the parties classify their relationship. For instance, the fact that two parties have a written contract stating that a work created by one party is a work made for hire does not necessarily make it so. It also generally does not matter whether control is actually exercised by the employer as long as it has the right to control.

In *Community for Creative Non-Violence v. Reid*,[10] the Supreme Court held that a sculptor who was hired to create a sculpture was an independent contractor rather than an employee. The Court considered a group of factors in reaching its conclusion to determine whether a person is an employee or an independent contractor. The following factors should be evaluated to determine whether the hiring party has the right to control the work of the hired party:

- The skill required to do the work

- The source of tools and materials used to create the work

- The location of the work performed

- The duration of the relationship between the parties

- Whether the hiring party has the right to assign additional projects to the hired party

- The extent of the hired party's discretion over when and how long to work

- The method of payment for the work

- Which party decides whether assistants will be used and which party pays them

- Whether the work is part of the regular business of the hiring party

- Whether the party creating the work is in business for itself

- Whether the hired party receives employee benefits from the hiring party

- The tax treatment of the hired party

In *Reid*, the Court evaluated these factors as follows: Reid was a sculptor which is generally regarded as a skilled occupation; Reid supplied his own tools; Reid worked in his own studio; He was retained for less than two months; CCNV had no right to assign additional projects to Reid; Reid had control over when and how long he worked; CCNV paid Reid a $15,000 lump sum rather than a salary; Reid had authority to hire and pay assistants; Creating sculptures was not part of CCNV's regular business; CCNV did not pay payroll or social security taxes; and CCNV did not provide any employee benefits to Reid.

Many of the *Reid* factors are quite broad and courts have a good deal of discretion in how they are weighed. Although none of the factors are individually determinative, three factors have generally weighed heavily in courts' evaluations. These are: (1) whether the worker is paid a salary; (2) whether the hiring

party provides employee benefits; and (3) whether the hiring party pays the worker's social security taxes. The reason for the importance of these factors is that it would be unfair for a company to be allowed to treat a worker as an independent contractor for tax purposes and as an employee for copyright ownership purposes. It is usually safe to assume that an employment relationship exists when an employee is paid a salary, provided with benefits and the employer pays social security taxes for the employee.

> **Tip**: Some states such as California require that employers who obtain copyright ownership from their employees as works made for hire must pay worker's compensation, unemployment insurance and disability insurance.[11]

(b) When Is a Work Prepared Within the Scope of Employment?

After determining that an employment relationship exists, a determination must be made as to whether the work was created by the employee within the scope of employment. Generally, a work will be considered to be made within the scope of employment if: (1) it is the type of work that the employee is paid to perform; (2) the work is performed substantially within work hours at the work place; and (3) the work is performed, at least in part, to benefit the employer.[12]

Any works created outside of the scope of an employment relationship will not be works made for hire unless the parties have a written agreement stating otherwise and the work fits within certain specified categories. An employer and employee are also free to agree that the employee will own the copyright in a work created within the scope of employment. To do so, there must be a written agreement transferring copyright ownership to the employee since the employer would still be considered to be the author of the work. In situations where it is uncertain whether an employment relationship exists, it is a good idea to have a written contract giving the hiring party ownership or the specific rights in the copyrighted work that are needed.

Some music publishers, in exclusive contracts with songwriters, state that songs will be considered to be works made for hire. However, regardless of what a contract says, whether songs are works made for hire depends on whether the relationship between the publisher and songwriter is an employment or independent contractor relationship. If the songwriter is an employee, any songs written by the songwriter would be works made for hire and the publisher would be considered the author. If the songwriter is an independent contractor, the songwriter would be considered the author although the contract would provide that copyright ownership is transferred by the songwriter to the publisher. Although either way, the publisher will own the copyrights to the songs, there are some important differences. For example, the duration of copyright protection will differ. Also, the author's termination right does not apply to works made for hire. In the vast majority of situations, songwriters will not be considered employees of publishers. Analyzing the Reid factors: songwriting is generally regarded as a skilled occupation; songwriters generally work at times and places of their own choosing; songwriters are not usually paid a salary (although they may receive advances); publishers do not normally pay payroll or social security taxes; and publishers do not normally provide any employee benefits to songwriters.

(2) Specially Ordered or Commissioned Works
If an employment relationship does not exist and one party hires another to create a copyrightable work, the work may still be a work made for hire if it is one of the types of specially ordered or commissioned work specified in § 101(2). A specially ordered or commissioned work is created when the hiring party is the motivating factor in the creation of the work. In many circumstances, payment to the creator from the hiring party is considered to be the motivation for the creation of a work. Specially ordered or commissioned works can be works made for hire if the parties agree in writing and the works fits one of the following nine categories:

• A contribution to a collective work (e.g., an article in a magazine)
• A part of a motion picture or other audiovisual work (e.g., a screenplay)
• A translation

• A supplementary work—a work prepared for publication as a secondary part of a work by another author such as a foreword, pictorial illustration, musical arrangement, bibliography, appendix, etc.
• A compilation
• An instructional text (e.g. a manual for stereo equipment)
• A test (e.g., ACT, LSAT)
• Answer material for a test
• An atlas

A movie producer hires a composer to write the soundtrack music for a motion picture. In order for the music to be a work made for hire, the producer and composer must enter into a contract stating that the music is created as a work made for hire. Since the music is to be a part of a motion picture (which is one of the nine specified categories), it would qualify as a work made for hire under § 101(2).

In order for a work to be considered a work made for hire under § 101(2), it must fit strictly within one of the nine specified categories. For example, one court held that advertising jingles did not fit the audiovisual works category since they did not have a visual component.[13] Instead, the jingles were sound recordings and therefore could not be works made for hire under § 101(2).

If a work made for hire relationship does not exist, the party commissioning a work can have the creator assign the copyright to the commissioning party under a written contract. The only major disadvantage is that the creator will have the right to terminate the assignment.

IV. Beneficial Ownership

When an author of a copyrighted work such as a songwriter transfers ownership to a publisher, the publisher obtains legal title or ownership of the copyright. Frequently however, the author will have the right, under its contract with the publisher, to receive royalties based on the commercial use of the song. Although the author no longer owns the copyright, the author is said to have a beneficial interest in the copyright due to its right to receive royalties. A beneficial owner, as well as the legal owner of a copyright, may sue for copyright infringement in order to protect his or her economic interest in the copyright.

Example 4.14:

A somewhat unusual situation arose in *Fantasy, Inc. v. Fogerty*, [14] where a court held that it is possible for one song by a songwriter to infringe upon another song by the same songwriter. In 1970, John Fogerty wrote the song "Run through the Jungle," which he transferred to a company that was acquired by Fantasy. In 1984, Fogerty wrote "The Old Man Down the Road," which he recorded and released on Warner Bros. Records. Fantasy sued Fogerty and Warner Brothers alleging that "The Old Man Down the Road" was merely "Run through the Jungle" with new words. Since Fogerty had transferred copyright ownership in "Run through the Jungle," he no longer owned the song. However, he was still a beneficial owner of the copyright since he had the right to be paid royalties under his publishing contract. Fogerty argued that he could not infringe upon a song he was a beneficial owner of since co-owners of a copyright cannot infringe upon the copyright. The court, however, disagreed since beneficial owners do not have the right to use or license the use of the copyright and can therefore infringe upon the copyright owner's exclusive rights. The court held that Fantasy could sue Fogerty for infringement, and if "The Old Man Down the Road" was found to be a derivative work based on "Run through the Jungle," Fogerty would be guilty of infringement. However, it was decided that "The Old Man Down the Road" did not infringe upon "Run through the Jungle" even though they were similar sounding songs.

In addition to authors who have transferred ownership, beneficial owners can include copyright owners that have used their copyright as collateral or security for a debt. Performing rights organizations can also be considered beneficial owners since songwriters give them the right to enforce their public performance rights against infringers, especially when it would be too expensive for an individual member to pursue an infringer. However, a person who creates a work as a work for hire cannot be a beneficial owner even if he or she is paid a royalty based on sales of the work, since such a person never actually owned the copyright to the work he or she created.

V. Transfer of Copyright Ownership

Like any other type of property, copyright ownership can be transferred. As defined in § 101, a transfer of copyright includes:

an assignment, mortgage, exclusive license, or any other conveyance, alienation, or hypothecation of a copyright or of any of the exclusive rights comprised in a copyright, whether or not it is limited in time or place of effect, but not including a nonexclusive license.

Example 4:15:

Songwriters often transfer copyright ownership of songs they write to music publishers in return for the publisher's efforts at exploiting the songs and the contractual right to receive royalties from any such exploitation.

The two most common types of transfers are assignments and exclusive licenses. An assignment occurs when a copyright owner transfers its entire ownership interest in a copyrighted work. An exclusive license occurs when a copyright owner transfers one or more of its exclusive rights, but retains one or more rights as well. An exclusive licensee owns the rights transferred to it and therefore, unless the license provides otherwise, has the right to sue infringers of its rights and to transfer its rights to others. Nonexclusive licenses, on the other hand, do not involve a transfer of ownership. Instead, a nonexclusive license gives someone the right to exercise one or more of the copyright owner's rights, but does not restrict the copyright owner from letting others exercise the same right. Both exclusive and nonexclusive licenses may be limited in scope. For instance, a license can be limited in terms of duration, territory or type of use.

Under the 1909 Copyright Act (which still applies to transfers made before January 1, 1978), copyright ownership was indivisible, meaning that a copyright owner's interest could not be divided. The 1976 Copyright Act changed this rule, making copyright ownership divisible. This means that a copyright can be divided without restriction. Consequently, a copyright owner can transfer its ownership interest in full or in part. Section 201(d)(1) provides that the author of a work may, as the initial owner of copyright, transfer his copyright by assigning all rights in the work and his assignees and their assignees may similarly assign all rights in the work. Alternatively, under section 201(d)(2), the author and any assignees may transfer any one or more of the exclusive rights specified in § 106. Finally, the author and any assignees may make transfers of subdivisions of the exclusive rights. It is also possible to transfer individual exclusive rights and to transfer different rights for different territories.

Example 4.16:

Since copyright ownership is divisible, a songwriter can transfer partial ownership of songs he writes to a publisher, retaining partial ownership (and a greater percentage of income earned). This type of arrangement between a songwriter and publisher is known as a co-publishing agreement and is quite common for successful songwriters. Alternatively, a songwriter could grant copyright ownership to different publishers for different territories of the world, although this is not common.

A. THE WRITING REQUIREMENT

The Copyright Act requires that transfers of copyright ownership must be made in writing. Section 204(a) provides that:

A transfer of copyright ownership, other than by operation of law, is not valid unless an instrument of conveyance, or a note or memorandum of the transfer, is in writing and signed by the owner of the rights conveyed or such owner's duly authorized agent.

Exclusive licenses, since they involve a transfer of ownership, must be made in writing except when made by operation of law. For example, if author dies without a will, the law of the state where he lives will transfer copyright to the author's heirs without a written document. Nonexclusive licenses do not have to be made in writing, but it is a good idea to do so anyway to specify the exact terms and rights involved.

The Copyright Act imposes the writing requirement to ensure that creators will not give away their copyright ownership inadvertently. It also forces someone who wants to use a copyrighted work to negotiate to determine precisely what rights are to be transferred and at what price.

(1) What Kind of Writing Is Required?

Courts have tended to be very liberal in their interpretation of what form of writing is required to transfer copyright ownership. For example, courts have held that endorsed checks can fulfill the writing requirement. Obviously, it is better to use a clearly written document to avoid misunderstanding, but a complicated contract is not necessarily needed. Often, a simple letter or memo will be sufficient as long as the terms of the transfer are specified. At a minimum, any transfer document should be in writing, signed by the owner of the rights being transferred, specify the particular rights being transferred, specify who is acquiring the rights transferred and the duration of the transfer. Additionally, a license should always state whether it is exclusive or nonexclusive.

Example 4.17:

In *Ballas v. Tedesco*, a ballroom dancer (Ballas) wanted to record a compact disc containing music from the movie *Titanic* to be used at dance competitions. Ballas negotiated a deal through e-mail correspondence with a producer (Tedesco) to produce the compact disc. Ballas agreed to pay Tedesco $15,000 for making musical arrangements, producing, mixing and mastering the CD. Ballas was to have the exclusive right to manufacture 5,000 copies of the CD for sale. Although they exchanged drafts of a proposed written agreement through e-mails, due to disagreements, the parties' relationship ceased and negotiations ended. Tedesco registered the copyright for the sound recordings embodied on the CD and began marketing it at dance competitions. Ballas sued claiming that Tedesco had breached the parties' contract. The court held that there was no written agreement evidencing any transfer of ownership to Ballas as required by § 204(a) of the Copyright Act. The court disagreed with Ballas' contention that the exchange of e-mails satisfied the writing requirement since the e-mails were not signed by Tedesco. Tedesco was therefore the sole owner of the recordings.

Tip: It is a good idea to sign three copies of any transfer document—one for the transferor, one for the transferee and one for recordation with the Copyright Office.

B. RECORDATION OF TRANSFERS

Any document pertaining to a copyright may be recorded in the Copyright Office.[15] This includes transfers of ownership, exclusive or nonexclusive licenses, wills, contracts, etc. When a transfer is recorded, a copy is placed in the Copyright Office's files which is indexed and available for public inspection. This is similar to the process for recording the deed to a house with a county recorder's office. The Copyright Office will also send a certificate of recordation to the recording party.

> **Tip**: Recordation, the process of recording transfers of copyright ownership, is not the same thing as copyright registration, which is the process for recording claims of copyright ownership (see chapter 9 for a discussion of copyright registration). In a perfect world, the author of a work would register the copyright shortly after its creation and any transfers of ownership would be recorded promptly after they occur. In the real world, which is far from perfect, many authors and copyright owners neglect to register their copyrights and record transfers of ownership. This often makes it difficult to determine who actually owns a copyrighted work.

Although recordation is not mandatory, there are several important benefits gained by recordation. Since copyright is intangible property that can be transferred without possession of any physical object, it is easy for unscrupulous copyright owners to attempt to make multiple transfers of the same copyright interest. Recordation protects purchasers by establishing rules of priority between transferees when a copyright owner makes multiple transfers of the same interest. Most importantly, recordation gives constructive notice to the world of the facts specified in the recorded document. Constructive notice means that everyone is deemed to have knowledge of the transfer regardless of whether they actually have knowledge or not. The reasoning is that once a transfer is recorded, anyone can check the Copyright Office records and find out about it.

(1) Priority Rules for Transfers

The Copyright Act provides the following rules regarding priority of copyright transfers:

- If there are conflicting transfers of copyright ownership of a registered work, the first transfer takes priority of over any subsequent transfers if it is recorded first.

- If a subsequent transfer is recorded first, the first transfer will still take priority over the subsequent transfer if the first transfer is recorded within one month after it is made (or two months if the transfer was made outside of the United States).

- If the first transfer is not recorded or is recorded more than one month after it is made (or two months if outside of the United States), the transfer that is recorded first will take priority even if it is made subsequent to another transfer. There are two limitations to this rule. First, it is not applicable if the transfer was a gift or is inherited by will. Second, it is not applicable if the subsequent transferee had knowledge of the earlier transfer.

Example 4.18:

Sammy Sleazeball writes a song, registers it with the Copyright Office and then transfers it to Honest Abe's Music on March 1st in return for a $1000 advance. A week later, after spending the $1000, Sammy attempts to transfer the same song to Trustworthy Tunes for another advance.

Who owns the copyright to the song if Honest Abe's records its transfer agreement on March 3rd? Honest Abe's since the first transfer will always prevail if it is recorded first.

Who owns the copyright to the song if Honest Abe's records its transfer agreement on March 31st? Honest Abe's since it has 30 days to record its transfer and still have priority over any subsequent transfers.

Who owns the copyright to the song if Honest Abe's records its transfer agreement on April 31st, but Trustworthy Tunes records its transfer agreement on April 30th? Trustworthy as long as it did not know of the previous transfer to Honest Abe. If, however, Trustworthy was not really trustworthy and knew of the previous transfer to Honest Abe's, Honest Abe's would own the copyright regardless of when it recorded its transfer.

(2) How to Record a Transfer

In order to record a transfer document, you must fill out a Document Cover Sheet form, which can be obtained from the Copyright Office. If the work has not previously been registered, a registration form should be filed as well. The Document Cover Sheet specifies basic information about the transfer document such as the names of the parties (assignor and assignee), the titles of the works transferred, the number of copyrighted works included in the recorded document (which is used to determine the filing fee), and the date the document was signed or became effective. Additionally, include the address where the Copyright Office should send the certificate of recordation at the bottom of the page.

The Copyright Office currently charges $50 for the first title and $15 for each group of up to 10 additional titles. For example, if a document contains 30 titles, the fee will be $95. When you have filled out the Document Cover Sheet, send the original and one copy along with the recordation fee and the document to be recorded to Documents Unit, LM-462, Cataloging Division, Copyright Office, Library of Congress, Washington, DC 20559. Within two to three months, you should receive a certificate of recordation along with the original transfer document.

VI. Termination of Transfers

A. RATIONALE FOR THE TERMINATION RIGHT

Although American copyright law has given authors the right to transfer copyright ownership, Congress has at the same time tried to protect authors from transfers that turn out to be bad deals for the author. Congress has provided this protection first with the renewal provisions of the 1909 Copyright Act and then with the termination provisions of the 1976 Act.

The renewal system under the 1909 Copyright Act was designed to allow authors and their heirs to regain ownership of copyrighted works that the author had previously transferred. Section 24 of the 1909 Act provided for an initial period of copyright protection lasting for 28 years from the date of the work's first publication. Section 24 also provided for a second 28 year period of protection for works which were renewed. The renewal right belonged to the author or to the author's heirs if the author died prior to the 28th year of the initial period. The rationale for having a renewal period was described by Congress as follows:

It not infrequently happens that the author sells his copyright outright to a publisher for a comparatively small sum. If the work proves to be a great success and lives beyond the term of twenty-eight years, your committee felt that it should be the exclusive right of the author to take the renewal term.[16]

Unfortunately, the renewal provision was largely unsuccessful in accomplishing its intended purpose. The 1909 Act did not address the question of whether an author could assign its rights to the renewal term. In *Fred Fisher Music Co. v. M. Witmark & Sons*,[17] the authors of the song "When Irish Eyes Are Smiling" assigned both the initial term and the renewal term to a music publisher. The Supreme Court ruled that the renewal term was assignable during the original copyright term, provided that the author survived beyond the end of the original term. In a subsequent case, *Miller Music Corp. v. Charles N. Daniels, Inc.*,[18] the Supreme Court held that when the author died before the 28th year of the initial term, the renewal right belonged to the author's heirs, regardless of any assignment to another party.

Many authors did not have the opportunity to take advantage of the renewal period since publishers routinely required authors to assign their rights in the renewal term to the publisher. Consequently, if the author was alive at the time for renewal, the renewal right belonged to the publisher rather than the author.

The 1976 Copyright Act did away with the renewal system, but added provisions designed to accomplish a similar result. The 1976 Copyright Act gives authors the right to terminate transfers of copyright after a certain period of time. This is a highly unusual right and is unique to copyright law. For instance, when you sell any other kind of property such as a car, you have no right to take back that property at some future point in time. According to Congress:

A provision of this sort is needed because of the unequal bargaining position of authors, resulting in part from the impossibility of determining a work's value until it has been exploited.

There are two different provisions in the 1976 Copyright Act dealing with termination.

Section 203 governs terminations of transfers made beginning in 1978 and § 304 governs terminations of transfers made before 1978. Unlike the renewal right under the 1909 Copyright Act, the termination right cannot be waived by an author. In other words, even if a songwriter agrees in a contract with a publisher that he will not exercise his right to terminate, such a contractual agreement is not legally valid and the author can still terminate the transfer. Works made for hire are not subject to termination since the rationale of protecting authors from unremunerative transfers does not really apply to employers.

The termination provisions are very detailed and complex and it is important that they be fully complied with since the failure to do so can result in a loss of the termination right. In addition to the rules specified by sections 203 and 304 of the Copyright Act, the Copyright Office is authorized to proscribe additional regulations that are included in the U.S. Code of Federal Regulations, 37 C.F.R. § 201.10.

B. TRANSFERS MADE ON OR AFTER JANUARY 1, 1978

The termination right under § 203 applies to any "exclusive or nonexclusive grant of a transfer or license" of a copyright or any right under copyright that is made by the author on or after January 1, 1978. For purposes of the termination right, it does not matter when a work was created. Instead, the important date is the date when a transfer of rights is made. For instance, if a song was composed in 1960 and transferred by its composer to a publisher in 1978, the transfer is subject to the composer's termination right. The fact that the song was created prior to 1978 does not matter as long as the transfer took place on or after January 1, 1978.

(1) Who Can Terminate?

The termination right can be exercised by the author or the author's successors as specified by § 203. Section 203 provides a succession hierarchy which works basically as follows:

- If the author dies and is survived by a spouse, but no children or grandchildren, the spouse gets the termination right.

- If the author dies and is survived by a spouse and children or grandchildren of a deceased child, the spouse gets half of the termination right and the surviving children and grandchildren share the other half. Grandchildren get the share their deceased parent would have had.

- If the author dies and is survived by children & grandchildren of deceased children (but no spouse), the children and grandchildren get the termination right in equal shares.

- If the author dies leaving no surviving spouse, children or grandchildren, the author's executor (as appointed by the author's will) gets the termination right.

- A majority of the persons who hold the termination interest is required to exercise the termination right. If a work has more than one author, termination can be made by a majority of the authors or their successors.

Example 4.19:

Peter, Paul and Mary, joint authors of a song called Blowing in the Wind, transfer the song to Dylan Music. If Peter dies, leaving a wife and two children, the termination can be made by either: (1) Paul and Mary; or (2) Paul or Mary and at least two out of Peter's three successors.

(2) When Can the Termination Right Be Exercised?

Termination can be made at any time during a 5 year time period between 35 and 40 years after the date of transfer. However, if a transfer includes the right of publication (as most do), termination may be made during the 5 year period beginning at the end of 35 years from publication or 40 years from the transfer date, whichever is earlier. Since most works are published shortly after they are transferred, 35 years from publication will usually be the beginning of the termination period rather than 40 years from the transfer date. The first terminations to be made under § 203 will occur in 2013 (35 years after 1978).

Example 4.20:

Tommy Tunesmith wrote a song and transferred the copyright to Deaf Mute Music in 1980. Tommy could terminate the transfer during the 5-year period beginning in 2015 and ending in 2020.

---

(3) What Must Be Done to Exercise the Termination Right?

In order to effectuate a termination, the terminating party must give written notice, signed by the terminating party (or his or her agent) to the transferee. If the transferee has transferred the copyright to another party, the termination notice must be sent to that party if the terminating party knows of that party's identity. Before sending a termination notice, it is advisable to check the Copyright Office records as well as the records of the performing rights organizations (for musical compositions) to verify who the current owner is. The notice must state the intended termination date and may be sent at any time between 2 to 10 years before the termination date. A copy of the notice must also be filed with the Copyright Office.

Example 4.21:

To effectuate the termination right for the previous example in 2016, Tommy could send notice to Deaf Mute Music at any time from 2006 to 2014. If Tommy waited until 2015, the termination could not take place in 2016 although it could still take place during the remaining 4 years of the 5-year termination period. If Deaf Mute Music had sold the copyright to Omniversal Music in 1990, the notice must be sent to Omniversal

although it couldn't hurt to send a copy to Deaf Mute as well if they are still in business.

(4) What Happens After Termination?

Once a termination takes place, the copyright reverts to the author or the author's successors. If there are more than one author, even authors or successors who did not join in signing the termination notice, will co-own the copyright.

An owner of a copyright acquired by termination has the same rights as any copyright owner, including the right to sell and license the work. However, these rights cannot be exercised prior to termination even if a termination notice has already been made. In other words, an author who sends a termination notice, cannot assign his rights to a new transferee before the termination becomes effective. There is one exception to this rule that provides that a new transfer may be made to the original transferee or the successor of the original transferee.

Example 4.22:

Using the information from the previous example, if Tommy gives proper notice to terminate the transfer effective as of 2016, he cannot make a new transfer to anyone except Deaf Mute Music (or its transferee) before 2016. Beginning in 2016, Tommy can transfer or license the copyright to anyone.

> **Tip:** Publishers or other transferees who receive termination notices for valuable works may attempt to convince the author (or other terminating party) to re-transfer the copyright to them before the termination takes place. In order to do so, they will probably have to offer the author a better deal than the one under which they originally acquired the copyright (e.g., higher royalty rates, additional advances, co-publishing rights, etc.).

C. Transfers Made Before January 1, 1978

The termination provisions of § 304 govern transfers made before 1978 and allow the author or the author's successors to recapture the 39-year extension provided by the 1976 Act and the Term Extension Act of 1998. The provisions of § 304 are very similar to those of § 203 although there are a few important differences. One difference is that in addition to transfers made by authors, the termination right under § 304 also applies to transfers made by the author's beneficiaries who are entitled to a renewal right under the 1909 Copyright Act (i.e., the author's spouse, children, executor, or next of kin). The 5-year termination period begins 56 years after copyright is secured. Additionally, if an author fails to terminate during that period, they have a second chance during the 5-year period beginning 75 years after the copyright was secured under the Term Extension Act of 1998.

Example 4.23:

Theresa Tunesmith writes a song and registers the copyright in 1940. If the copyright was transferred by Theresa before 1978, she could terminate the transfer during the 5-year period from 1996 to 2000. If Theresa failed to exercise this termination right, she or her successors have a second chance to terminate from 2016 to 2020.

Tip: Since music publishers are subject to termination rights of songwriters, it is important that any subpublishing and administration agreements they enter into acknowledge that songs may be subject to termination.

D. The Derivative Works Exception

Even if a transfer is terminated, a derivative work made before termination can continue to be used by the transferee. This derivative works exception applies to transfers made before and after 1978 and states that:

A derivative work prepared under authority of the grant before its termination may continue to be utilized under the terms of the grant after its termination, but this privilege does not extend to the preparation after the termination of other derivative works based upon the copyrighted work covered by the terminated grant.[19]

Example 4.24:

A record company which received a license from a publisher to make sound recordings of a song is allowed to continue to sell sound recordings containing that song after the songwriter terminates its transfer to the publisher. Although the termination allows the author to recapture ownership of the song, the author cannot prevent the continued exploitation of derivative works (such as sound recordings) based on the song.

The rationale for the derivative works exception is that a substantial investment may be made in some derivative works and it would be unfair to prevent someone who has made that investment from being able to continue using the derivative work. The exception only allows continued use of derivative works made before termination. It does not allow a transferee to make any derivative works after termination.

Tip: It is quite possible that transferees that receive termination notices will have derivative works created based on the work to which the termination applies. For instance, a music publisher might have a derivative musical composition made based on a musical composition to which its rights are to be terminated and then attempt to exploit the derivative composition as much as possible instead of the original composition. It does not appear that there is any way authors can prevent this practice (unless they have a contractual right of approval over derivative works) although they may be able to limit it by giving termination notices close to the latest possible date allowed (i.e., 2 years prior to termination).

VII. Ownership of Sound Recordings

Determining who the authors of a sound recording are can often be a complicated matter. Generally, the recording artist whose performance is recorded would be considered an author. In addition, the record producer (and/or recording engineer) who is responsible for setting up the recording sessions, capturing and electronically processing the sounds, and compiling and editing them to make the final recording may also be an author.[20] However, in some situations, the record producer's contribution may be so minimal that the recording artist's performance is the only copyrightable element in the work. In other situations, the record producer's contribution may be the only copyrightable contribution to a sound recording such as recordings of naturally occurring sounds (e.g., a thunderstorm, birdcalls, etc.).

Regardless of who the authors of a sound recording are, sound recordings made by artists under contract to record companies are virtually always owned by the record company. This result is not usually due to the record company being considered an author, but is accomplished contractually by transfers of ownership from the authors to the record company.

Disputes arise fairly frequently when an investor pays for recording studio time to enable an artist to make a recording. Often, the investor believes he or she owns the copyright in the recording produced simply because he or she paid for it. However, if the investor did not contribute any original material to the sound recording, he or she would not be legally entitled to claim authorship unless the recording was a work made for hire. Sometimes an investor will require the artist to sign a contract stating that the recordings produced will be works for hire. Regardless of what a contract says, such recordings will not usually qualify as works made for hire. Consequently, an investor would be better off having a contract under which the artist transfers ownership to the investor until the investor is paid back.

A recent controversial issue involves whether sound recordings can qualify as works made for hire. Most recording contracts provide that recordings made under the contract will be considered to be works made for hire. However, due to the uncertainty as to whether sound recordings qualify as works made for hire, recording contracts also usually provide that if the recordings are not works made for hire, the artist transfers its copyright ownership to the record company.

In November of 1999, the Recording Industry Association of America (RIAA), a trade organization which represents record companies, got an amendment included in an appropriations bill (which otherwise had nothing to do with copyright) which added sound recordings as a ninth category of works eligible for treatment as works made for hire under the specially ordered or commissioned works category of § 101(2). Congress passed the bill without any debate or hearings on the issue.

Although the RIAA described the amendment as a technical clarification of existing law, it has extremely severe implications on recording artists and producers. Under copyright law prior to the amendment, artists (and possibly producers and other contributors to the creation of sound recordings) who signed contracts with record companies beginning in 1978 will quite likely have the right to terminate the transfer of sound recording copyrights to record companies 35 years after the transfers were made. For commercially valuable recordings, the artist would be in much better bargaining position after termination than when the original transfer was made. The artist could sell or lease the sound recording back to the record company for a much greater share of the recording's revenue, sell or lease it to a different record company, or retain ownership and sell the recording to the public itself. However, the amendment, by allowing sound recordings to be treated as works made for hire, eliminated the possibility of termination by artists since the termination right is not available for works made for hire.

After the amendment's passage, when it first became common knowledge, several entertainment attorneys, artist managers, and journalists began to voice their objections to it. Some prominent recording artists such as Don Henley and Sheryl Crow also started to speak out about the amendment's impact on artists as well as the way it was surreptitiously passed into law. Due to these efforts, Congress repealed the amendment and the law goes back to what it was prior to the amendment's passage. Accordingly, the status of sound recordings as works made for hire is still unclear since it is still possible that sound recordings could be considered to be works made for hire under § 101(2) under the categories of compilations and collective works. It is virtually certain that there will be litigation to resolve this issue in the near future. Lawsuits over this issue could be filed as early as 2003 since that will be the first year in which termination notices can be sent.

> **Tip:** In my opinion, sound recordings will not qualify as works made for hire in the vast majority of circumstances since they are not usually created under an employment relationship and since they probably do not fit within any of the nine categories of specially ordered or commissioned works that can be works made for hire. Consequently, transfers of copyright ownership of sound recordings will probably be subject to termination rights. Some artists are very excited about this since they believe it will allow them to regain copyright ownership of valuable sound recordings. However, other individuals (producers, engineers, musicians, etc.) may have termination rights in addition to artists in some circumstances. This may result in situations where multiple parties attempt to terminate transfers of copyright ownership in a single sound recording. Problems arising from such situations will include determining which parties are actually authors and have termination rights, determining how many of these parties are necessary to effectuate termination (since a majority is legally required), and determining how a sound recording can be exploited after termination when it is co-owned by multiple terminating parties.

1. Testimony On the Internet Uses of Music Before the House Subcommittee on Courts, the Internet and Intellectual Property, May 17, 2001.

2. *Goldstein v. California,* 412 U.S. 546, 561 (1973) (quoting *Burrow-Giles Lithographic Co. v. Sarony,* 111 U.S. 53, 58 (1884)).

3. The difference between inseparable and interdependent is that the contributions are inseparable when they have little or no independent meaning standing alone and interdependent when the parts have some significant meaning alone, but achieve their primary significance because of their combined effect. For example, the music and lyrics of a song would be interdependent.

4. *Edward B. Marks Music Corp. v. Jerry Vogel Music Co.,* 140 F.2d 266, 267.

5. *Shapiro, Bernstein & Co. v. Jerry Vogel Music Co.,* 161 F.2d 406, 409 (2d Cir. 1946).

6. 921 F. Supp. 1154 (1996).

7. 73 F. Supp. 165, 168 (S.D.N.Y. 1947).

8. Other states that have community property laws include Arizona, Idaho, Louisiana, Nevada, New Mexico, Texas, Washington and Wisconsin.

9. *Marriage of Worth,* 195 Cal. App. 3d 768 (1987).

10. 490 U.S. 730, 753 (1989).

11. CAL. LAB. CODE § 3252.5.

12. *Miller v. CP Chemicals, Inc.,* 808 F. Supp. 1238 (D.S.C. 1992) (quoting Restatement of Agency).

13. *Lulirama Ltd. v. Axcess Broad. Servs., Inc.,* 128 F.3d 872 (5th Cir. 1997).

14. 654 F. Supp. 1129 (N.D. Cal. 1987).

15. 17 U.S.C. § 205.

16. H.R. REP. NO. 2222, 60th Cong., 2d Sess. 14 (1909).

17. 318 U.S. 643 (1943).

18. 362 U.S. 373 (1960).

19. 17 U.S.C. § 203(b)(1) and 304(c)(6)(A).

20. The House Report on the 1976 Act at 56.

CHAPTER 5

The Reproduction Right

▼

"We think of copyright as a bundle of rights—the reproduction right, the distribution right, and the performance right—and the reason for thinking that way is historical. In the beginning, when people copied manuscripts by hand, we had a "copy" right, which gradually evolved over time to encompass newer technologies. The key idea behind all of these rights is giving copyright owners the ability to meaningfully exploit their works."
Shira Perlmutter, Former Associate Register for Policy and International Affairs, United States Copyright Office

I. Introduction—Exclusive Rights

Section 106 of the Copyright Act provides for six exclusive rights that copyright owners may have depending on the type of work involved. The exclusive rights have been referred to as a "bundle of rights" that may overlap, be subdivided, and be owned and enforced separately. These exclusive rights are the essence of copyright law since they allow the copyright owner to control the use of his work. The copyright owner can exercise any of the rights himself or authorize others to do so. Generally, no one other than the copyright owner can exercise any of the exclusive rights without obtaining the copyright owner's permission. If someone other than the copyright owner exercises one or more of the exclusive rights without the copyright owner's permission, that person has committed an infringement unless the use is permitted by any of the defenses to copyright infringement.

Tip: Permission to use a copyrighted work is normally granted by a license. A license is an agreement in which one party (the copyright owner or "licensor") gives another party (the "licensee") permission to do something (e.g., use a copyrighted work in a specified manner), usually for some type of compensation (i.e., a fee or royalty). There are different types of licenses for different uses of music, the most common of which are as follows:

Mechanical license: Allows the licensee (record company or recording artist) to reproduce and distribute a copyrighted musical work in recordings such as compact discs and cassettes in return for a royalty (a percentage of the sale price) on recordings sold.
Performance license: Allows the licensee (radio or television station, concert venue, business establishment, etc.) to publicly perform a copyrighted musical work in return for a royalty.
Synchronization license: Allows the licensee (movie or television producer, etc.) to reproduce and distribute a copyrighted musical work in audiovisual recordings such as movies, television and videocassettes in return for a flat fee and/or a royalty.
Print license: Allows the licensee to reproduce and distribute a copyrighted musical work in printed form such as sheet music in return for a royalty.

It is important to realize that the exclusive rights are not absolute and are subject to various exemptions, compulsory licenses and defenses. In fact, while the exclusive rights are all specified in one section of the Copyright Act (i.e., § 106), the limitations on the exclusive rights are specified in many sections (i.e., §§ 107 through 120), some of which are quite lengthy and detailed.

II. The Reproduction Right

Section 106(1) gives the copyright owner the exclusive right to reproduce, and to authorize others to reproduce, the copyrighted work. Reproduction involves producing a material object in which the copyrighted work is contained or embodied. The Copyright Act specifies two categories of material objects in which copyrighted works can be embodied—copies and phonorecords (as discussed in chapter 3).

Example 5.1:

Copyrighted works such as songs and sound recordings can be embodied on material objects such as recording tape or compact discs among other things. Although the copyrighted work cannot be directly perceived, reproduced or communicated merely by possession of the object itself, it can be perceived, reproduced and communicated with the aid of a machine or device such as a stereo system.

A. REPRODUCTION OF MUSICAL WORKS

(1) The Compulsory Mechanical License
The most important limitation on the reproduction right for musical works is the compulsory mechanical license. A mechanical license gives the licensee (a record company or artist) permission to reproduce and distribute a copyrighted musical work in recordings. In most situations, licenses are negotiated and if a copyright owner does not want to issue a license, it is free to decline to do so. However, the compulsory mechanical license provision says that under certain circumstances, a mechanical license can be obtained regardless of whether the copyright owner gives permission or not.

The compulsory license was introduced in the 1909 Copyright Act in order to prevent a monopoly from arising in the manufacture of piano rolls.[1] Although piano rolls are no longer used for the mechanical reproduction of music, the compulsory license still serves its purpose by insuring that no company (not even the major recording and publishing companies) can have a monopoly on the recording of musical compositions.

The compulsory license provision was contained in § 115 of the 1976 Copyright Act and provides that once a musical composition has been distributed in phonorecords in the United States with the copyright owner's permission, anyone may reproduce the composition. This means that the copyright owner has absolute control over the first recording of its song. However, once that first recording has been distributed, the copyright owner cannot prevent anyone else from recording their own version of the song. Distribution of phonorecords includes distribution of audio recordings of any type (cassette, compact disc, etc.), but does not include audiovisual works since audiovisual works are embodied in copies rather than phonorecords.

Example 5.2:

A song contained in the soundtrack to a motion picture will not be subject to a compulsory license unless it is also contained on a phonorecord such as a soundtrack album that is distributed to the public.

The compulsory license only applies to non-dramatic musical works (i.e., musical compositions or songs). Accordingly, if you want to record a literary work or a dramatic musical work, the compulsory license is not available and you must obtain the copyright owner's permission.

Example 5.3:

Martin George, an aspiring producer, wants to record the Beatles' song "Yesterday." He can obtain a compulsory license since "Yesterday" is a non-dramatic musical composition which has been previously recorded and distributed. However, he cannot copy the Beatles sound recording of "Yesterday" under the compulsory license. Instead, he would have to hire singers and musicians to record a new sound recording of the song. To use the Beatles recording, he would have to obtain a license from the copyright owner of the sound recording (Capitol Records), referred to as a master-use license, as well as a mechanical license from the copyright owner of "Yesterday" (Sony Music).

a. Obtaining a Compulsory License

In order to obtain a compulsory license, you must comply with the provisions of § 115 of the Copyright Act as well as the applicable regulations of the Copyright Office. The following are the basic conditions required in order to obtain a compulsory license:

The primary purpose for making your recording must be to distribute it to the public for private use. If you intend to make a recording of a song which will be sold on cassettes, compact discs or some other audio-only recording format, that is exactly what the compulsory license is intended for. In contrast, if you intend to make a recording primarily to broadcast it or use it in connection with background music services such as Muzak, you cannot obtain a compulsory license. Instead, you would have to request a license directly from the copyright owner (which the copyright owner could refuse to grant).

You are allowed to make an arrangement of the copyrighted musical composition to the extent necessary to conform the work to the style or manner of interpretation of your performance. This arrangement privilege is very limited and does not allow you to change the basic melody or fundamental character of the work. Minor changes to the work are permitted such as recording the work in a different key than it was written in or changing pronouns from masculine to feminine or vice versa. If the changes are major, the result would be considered a derivative work which cannot be made without the copyright owner's consent.

You must file a Notice of Intention to Obtain Compulsory License with the copyright owner. This notice must be made no later than thirty days after making your recording and before distributing it. If you fail to give this notice, you cannot get a compulsory license and, unless you have a negotiated license from the copyright owner, subjects you to liability for infringement.

> **Tip:** If the copyright owner of a song you want to record is unknown and the Copyright Office records do not identify the owner, you can file the notice with the Copyright Office. If the copyright owner later registers its copyright, you only have to pay mechanical royalties for records sold after the registration was made.

You must pay the statutory mechanical royalty rate for each record made and distributed. This rate applies to each song contained on a recording, so if your recording contains more than one song, you would pay a royalty for each song. At the time of this book's writing, the statutory royalty rate is 8 cents per song or 1.55 cents per minute, whichever is greater. The statutory rate is adjusted every other year based on changes in the consumer price index. Until recently, the adjustments were made by copyright arbitration royalty panels appointed by the Copyright Office.[2] However, beginning in 1998, representatives from the music publishing and record industries negotiated a ten-year schedule for increases. A summary of the statutory mechanical royalty rate is shown is Table 5-1.

Royalties must be paid on a monthly basis by the 20th day of each month and must include all royalties for the previous month. Monthly royalty statements accompanied by any applicable royalty payments must be made under oath and in addition, an annual statement of account certified by a certified public accountant must be made. If you fail to make the required royalty payments or to file the required monthly and annual statements of account, the copyright owner can send you notice of termination of the license. After termination, the making or distribution of all phonorecords for which the royalty has not been paid will be considered acts of infringement.

Table 5-1: Statuatory Mechanical Royalty Rates

Year	Per-song Rate	Per-Minute Rate
1909	2 cents	None
1976	2.75 cents	.5 cents
1980	4 cents	.75 cents
1984	4.5 cents	.8 cents
1986	5 cents	.95 cents
1988	5.25 cents	1 cent
1990	5.7 cents	1.1 cents
1992	6.25 cents	1.2 cents
1994	6.6 cents	1.25 cents
1996	6.95 cents	1.3 cents
1998	7.1 cents	1.35 cents
2000	7.55 cents	1.45 cents
2002	8 cents	1.55 cents
2004	8.5 cents	1.65 cents
2006	9.1 cents	1.75 cents

Out-Of-Tune Records obtains a compulsory license to record one song on an album. Out-Of-Tune must pay the copyright owner(s) of that song 8 cents for each record made and distributed. If the album sells 100,000 units, Out-Of-Tune would pay the copyright owner $8,000. If the same album sold 500,000 units, Out-Of-Tune would pay the copyright owner $40,000. However, if the song was over 5.3 minutes in length, Out-Of-Tune would have to pay the per-minute rate (i.e., 8.68 cents) for each record since it would be a greater amount than the per-song rate. (Note: The copyright owner will often be a publishing company which will normally be contractually obligated to pay the songwriters of the song half of what it receives).

If the album released by Out-Of-Tune Records in the previous example contained ten copyrighted songs and Out-Of-Tune obtained compulsory licenses for all of these songs, it would pay 80 cents in mechanical royalties for each album distributed to the copyright owners of the songs. If 100,000 albums were sold, Out-Of -Tune would owe $80,000 in mechanical royalties. If one million albums were sold, Out-Of -Tune would owe $800,000 in mechanical royalties.

(2) Negotiated Mechanical Licenses

Despite the existence of the compulsory mechanical license, it is rarely used since its requirements are very strict and a bit impractical. For example, record companies do not want the administrative burden of accounting for and paying mechanical royalties on a monthly basis. Consequently, mechanical licenses are usually negotiated between the record company making the recording of a song and the copyright owner of the song to be recorded (a music publisher or an agency representing the music publisher such as the Harry Fox Agency).[3]

Even though the compulsory license provision is rarely used, many of its terms are used in negotiated licenses. However, negotiated licenses do not have to contain the terms prescribed by the compulsory license provision. In practice, mechanical licensing is usually a simple process in which very little negotiation takes place. It is common in negotiated licenses for royalties to be paid on a quarterly rather than monthly basis with no annual accounting required. Royalty payments are usually required to be paid only on records sold rather than merely distributed which allows record companies to hold a portion of royalties as a reserve against returns. Finally, the royalty paid under a negotiated mechanical license will be either the statutory rate or a reduced rate agreed upon by the publisher and record company. Reduced rates are usually specified as a percentage of the statutory rate, most commonly 75 percent of the statutory rate. Reduced rates are commonly granted for records sold through record clubs, record sold at less than normal prices and for songs written by a songwriter who is subject to a controlled composition clause in a record contract.[4]

Mucho Music is the copyright owner of a song entitled "InnaGaddaLaVidaLoca." Mucho issues a negotiated mechanical license to LaBomba Records to use a song at a rate of 75 percent of the statutory rate. Mucho will receive 6 cents (75 percent of 8 cents) from LaBomba for each record sold. If an album containing this song sold 100,000 copies, Mucho would receive $6,000, half of which would be paid to the songwriter(s) of the song.

Sometimes the rate to be paid under a negotiated license will be limited to the statutory rate in effect at the time the license is issued, thereby preventing the record company from having to increase its payments each time the statutory rate is increased. A publisher, on the other hand, would prefer to get the benefit of increases in the statutory rate and might use language specifying that the rate will be increased in proportion to increases in the statutory rate. Finally, the per-minute rate is rarely used in negotiated licenses, regardless of the duration of the song.

(3) Mechanical Royalty Collection Agencies

Many publishers do not issue mechanical licenses themselves. Instead, they use a mechanical licensing agent to do so on their behalf. Many American publishers use the Harry Fox Agency to issue mechanical licenses and to collect mechanical royalty payments for them. In 2000, the Harry Fox Agency collected $570 million in mechanical royalties. The Harry Fox Agency charges a 4.5 percent fee which makes it a cost effective alternative for publishers since it would probably cost them more to issue licenses and collect mechanical royalties themselves. Another important benefit to publishers in using the Harry Fox Agency is that it periodically conducts audits of all of the major record companies and distributes any recovered monies among publishers in proportion to their earnings.

The Harry Fox Agency also provides a benefit to record companies since they don't have to request mechanical licenses from each individual publisher. Instead, when a record company is going to record an album, it merely sends mechanical license requests for the songs to be recorded to the Harry Fox Agency which will issue mechanical licenses for all the songs except any songs not owned by a publisher affiliated with the Harry Fox Agency. The Harry Fox Agency also has agreements with foreign agencies allowing American publishers to collect foreign mechanical royalties through the Harry Fox Agency. Some important limitations on Harry Fox Agency licenses are: (1) It will only cover records manufactured and distributed in the United States; and (2) It will not give you the right to print song lyrics on album liner notes (you must obtain permission from the publisher that owns the song for this).

Tip: You can obtain mechanical license request forms from the Harry Fox Agency's web site at **www.nmpa.org/hfa/mechanical.html.** If you are going to make up to 2500 recordings, you can obtain a license by filling out a form online at SongFile.com (you must be willing to pay the statutory royalty rate for 2500 recordings by credit card in order to use this service).

Although the Harry Fox Agency is the largest mechanical rights agency in the United States, there are some other companies that perform similar functions such as Copyright.net in Nashville. Additionally, foreign countries have mechanical rights collection agencies that issue licenses and collect royalties in their territories.

(4) Foreign Mechanical Royalty Rates

The United States and Canada are the only countries that have a statutory mechanical royalty rate. Mechanical royalty rates in other countries are based on either a percentage of the retail sales price or the wholesale price that the records sell for. For instance, if the royalty rate was 8 percent of the retail sales price and a compact disc sold for $16, the mechanical royalties would be $1.28 which would be divided by the number of songs contained on the CD (if 10 songs, each would be allocated 12.8 cents).

An advantage that percentage-based systems of foreign countries have over the U.S. system is that the mechanical royalty will automatically increase as the price of recordings increases. A potential disadvantage is that the total mechanical royalties per album will be the same regardless of the number of songs contained on the album. However, mechanical royalties tend to be higher in most major foreign countries than the U.S. statutory rate.

(5) Digital Phonorecord Deliveries

Through the combination of digital technology and the Internet, it has become possible to reproduce musical works without copying the work onto a traditional physical object such as a compact disc. When a musical work is downloaded, the recording of the work is transmitted in digital form over the Internet. However, downloading music still involves reproduction of the musical work. Instead of being reproduced onto a compact disc, the music is reproduced onto a computer hard drive or other storage device.

The Digital Performance Right in Sound Recordings Act was passed by Congress in 1995 and amended § 115(c) of the 1976 Copyright Act. This amendment states that the compulsory mechanical license is applicable to the distribution of phonorecords of musical works "by means of a digital transmission which constitutes a digital phonorecord delivery." The Copyright Act defines a "digital phonorecord delivery" as:

each individual delivery of a phonorecord by digital transmission of a sound recording which results in a specifically identifiable reproduction by or for any transmission recipient of a phonorecord of that sound recording, regardless of whether the digital transmission is also a public performance of the sound recording or any nondramatic musical work embodied therein.[5]

The Digital Performance Right in Sound Recordings Act specifies a procedure for setting the royalty rate for digital phonorecord deliveries. Until the end of 1997, the rate was set at the same amount as the statutory mechanical royalty rate. Beginning in 1998, the rate was to be reached through negotiation between the music publishing and recording industry. If a negotiated rate could not be reached, the rate is to be determined by a copyright arbitration royalty panel. A two-year agreement was negotiated specifying that the rate would continue to remain the same as the statutory rate. It was also agreed that no royalties would be payable for digital phonorecord deliveries of music lasting for less than thirty seconds for promotional purposes.

At the end of 1999, when the initial negotiated agreement expired, the publishing and recording industries were unable to reach a new agreement. The music publishers' position is that the digital phonorecord delivery rate should remain at the statutory rate. However, Internet music companies argue that certain digital transmissions of music (such as streaming transmissions) do not result in a reproduction on the recipient's hard drive and should therefore not be subject to mechanical royalties at all. At the time of this book's writing, a copyright arbitration royalty panel has been appointed to set the new rate. It is possible, although by no means certain, that the panel may set two different rates—one for transmissions which result in a copy of the musical work on the recipient's hard drive (probably at the statutory rate) and another for transmissions which do not result in a copy of the musical work on the recipient's hard drive (probably at a rate lower than the statutory rate).

Just as it is permissible for a mechanical license to make a recording to be negotiated and the terms of the compulsory license provision varied, it is also permissible to negotiate licenses for digital phonorecord deliveries. If the copyright owner of a musical work is willing to do so, it could license digital phonorecord deliveries at a rate lower than the rate to be set by the copyright arbitration royalty panel.[6]

B. REPRODUCTION OF SOUND RECORDINGS

In the United States, federal copyright law did not protect sound recordings until 1972 although sound recordings were protected under some state laws. However, even though sound recordings are now protected under the Copyright Act, they still receive a lesser degree of protection than other types of copyrightable works.

(1) The Dubbing Limitation

An important limitation on the reproduction right regarding sound recordings is that the right extends only to works "that directly or indirectly recapture the actual sounds fixed in the recording."[7] In other words, the copyright in a sound recording only protects against copying of the actual recorded sounds and not against imitation of those sounds. This limitation is sometimes referred to as the "dubbing limitation" since the reproduction right for sound recordings only prohibits dubbing (re-recording from an existing recording) and does not prevent making an independent recording of other sounds, even if those sounds imitate the sounds from a copyrighted sound recording. *(See example 3.7)*

(2) Home Taping

The reproduction or copying of copyrighted works by people in their homes has been prevalent since home recording equipment first became available. It is a common practice for people to make copies of recordings on home audio recording equipment. Sometimes such copying is done in order to listen to a recording on different devices (e.g., copying a CD onto cassette to play in a car cassette deck). Other times, people make copies of recordings and give away or sell the copies. Obviously, this poses a problem for copyright owners of musical works and sound recordings since each home copy potentially displaces a sale.

With analog recording technology, a first generation copy made from an original recording would lose some degree of sound quality during the copying process with the result being that the copy would not be quite as good as the original. Additionally, each successive generation of copying resulted in a further loss of sound quality. For instance, if you make a cassette copy of a CD, the sound quality of the cassette is not quite as good as the CD. If you then made a second cassette copy from the first cassette copy, the sound quality of the second copy will be a bit worse than the first copy.

Beginning in 1986, digital audio tape recording technology was introduced to the consumer marketplace. Digital audio tape (DAT) provides the ability to make copies of recordings with no loss of sound quality. Due to the preservation of sound quality from one copy to the next, digital audio technology also gave consumers the ability to make high-quality copies from copies (serial copying). Unlike analog recording technology, digital audio recording allows consumers to make near perfect fidelity copies and therefore poses a more serious threat to the music industry.

The music industry had tried on several occasions to secure some type of legal protection and compensation for the losses it incurred due to unauthorized home taping of copyrighted musical compositions and sound recordings. However, the consumer electronics industry strenuously resisted these efforts. Finally, after an attempted legislative solution stalled in 1990, a group of songwriters and music publishers brought a class-action lawsuit against Sony Corporation.

In *Cahn v. Sony Corp.*,[8] a group of songwriters and publishers alleged that manufacturers, importers, and distributors of digital audio tape recording equipment and blank digital audio tapes were guilty of contributory and vicarious copyright infringement. The alleged contributory and vicarious infringement resulted from the direct infringement by consumers who used the defendants' equipment to make unauthorized recordings of copyrighted works. This lawsuit could have resulted in an important legal decision since no United States court has ever ruled on whether unauthorized home audio taping is illegal.[9] However, no decision was made by the court since the parties reached a settlement which provided that the defendants would support legislation that would provide for royalties to compensate for losses incurred by copyright owners due to home taping. The contemplated legislation was passed as the Audio Home Recording Act of 1992.

(3) The Audio Home Recording Act

The Audio Home Recording Act (AHRA) added Chapter 10 to the Copyright Act and is designed to allow consumers to copy recordings of copyrighted music for private, noncommercial use while also compensating copyright owners for lost income due to such copying. The AHRA applies to "digital audio recording devices" which are defined as devices that are designed or marketed primarily for making digital audio recordings for private use. Devices that do not fit the definition of digital audio recording devices include professional recording equipment, analog recording equipment, audiovisual recording equipment and computers. The AHRA contains three main sets of provisions.

a. Royalty System

Sections 1003 and 1004 of the AHRA establish a royalty system under which manufacturers and distributors of digital audiotape recorders and digital audio tapes are required to pay a royalty on sales. The royalty is 3% of the wholesale price of digital audio tape and 2% on the wholesale price of digital recording equipment with a minimum of $1.00 and a maximum of $8.00 for digital recording equipment. The royalties are collected by the Copyright Office and are distributed based on record sales and radio airplay. However, in order to be eligible to receive these royalties, one must file a claim with the Copyright Office.[10]

The royalties collected are divided into two funds. One-third goes to the "Musical Works Fund" which is split equally between songwriters and music publishers. The remaining two-thirds goes to the "Sound Recordings Fund." The Sound Recordings Fund is split up with 4% paid to nonfeatured performers (background musicians and vocalists). The remainder is split between featured performers who receive 40% and sound recording copyright owners (typically record companies) who receive 60%.

It is important to note that the royalty provisions of the Audio Home Recording Act only apply to digital recording equipment and tape. In contrast, many foreign countries including Australia, Germany and France impose a royalty on analog as well as digital recording equipment and tape.

b. Copy Protection

The AHRA also requires that manufacturers and importers of digital audio recording equipment must incorporate technology that prevents serial copying (i.e., making copies from copies).[11] A specific technological protection system called the serial copy management system (SCMS) is specified by the AHRA, although other systems may also be used.

Example 5.7:

If a consumer buys a digital audio tape recorder equipped with SCMS and wants to copy a CD, the consumer could make an unlimited number of digital audio tape copies from the CD (first generation copies). The consumer could not, however, make additional copies from the digital audio tape copies (serial copies) since the SCMS would prevent this.

c. Infringement Exemption

In return for the protections given to copyright owners by the AHRA, the Act exempts consumers from liability for direct copyright infringement for home taping of copyrighted works.[12] An important qualification for this exemption is that the home taping must be for a noncommercial use although the AHRA neglects to define noncommercial use.

When Congress passed the AHRA, it indicated that it only intended to allow consumers to copy authorized commercially released compact discs or other digital recordings.[13] Under this reasoning, it would not be permissible to make copies from copies or to make copies from unlawfully acquired recordings.

Example 5.8:

Harry Hometaper, a high school student, receives a CD as a Christmas present. If Harry makes a copy of the CD in order to listen to it in his car, he is exempt from liability for copyright infringement under the AHRA. However, if Harry made copies of his CD and sold the copies to others, the home taping exemption would not apply since this is a commercial use. Even if Harry gave a copy to a friend, the home taping exemption might not apply since the potential displacement of a sale to the friend might be considered a commercial use.

---

d. The Diamond Rio Case

The AHRA was at the heart of one of the first highly publicized lawsuits involving digital music. On October 9, 1998, the Recording Industry Association of America (RIAA) filed a lawsuit against Diamond Multimedia, a company that made a portable MP3 player called the Rio.[14] The RIAA alleged that the Rio violated the AHRA because it did not contain SCMS copyright protection technology and because Diamond did not pay royalties on sales of the Rio.

The resolution of this dispute turned on two very technical definitions provided in the AHRA. A "digital audio recording" is defined as a material object upon which digital music is fixed such as a compact disc or a digital audio tape (DAT). A "digital audio recording device" is defined as a device that creates digital musical recordings or copies of digital musical recordings such as a compact disc recorder (CD-R) or a DAT recorder.

Both the District Court and the Court of Appeals denied the RIAA's request to issue a preliminary injunction to prevent Diamond from selling the Rio. The Court of Appeals ruled that the Rio was not a digital audio recording device and was therefore not subject to the AHRA. The court based its decision on the fact that the Rio does not actually record anything directly, but simply accepts the transfer of files from a computer's hard drive to make them portable. It is not possible to make a digital audio recording from a Rio since the Rio's output signal is analog. Because the Rio is incapable of creating digital audio recordings, it could not be considered a digital audio recording device. Further, when the AHRA was passed, the computer industry managed to get an exemption for copying from computer hard drives since their primary purpose is not to record digital audio. The RIAA argued that MP3 files did not qualify for this exemption since the exemption was not intended to exempt all files stored on a computer, but only computer programs with incidental audio files such as a computer game with audio sound effects. The court however disagreed with the RIAA, finding that the exemption applies to all files contained on a computer.

Although the court correctly applied the provisions of the AHRA, the result is probably not at all what Congress intended the AHRA to achieve. When the AHRA was enacted in 1992, it is unlikely that anyone expected computers to be used to copy music files to the extent that they are today. The exemption for computer hard drives has made the AHRA almost worthless since, once a music file is stored on a computer hard drive (regardless of where it came from or how it got there), it is exempt from the AHRA. The district court recognized the irony of this result, stating that the exemption for computers "would effectively eviscerate the Act" since:

any recording device could evade regulation simply by passing the music through a computer and ensuring that the MP3 file resided momentarily on the hard drive. While this may be true, the Act seems to have been expressly designed to create this loophole.

Although the AHRA provides some protection against piracy using digital audio tape recorders (which in 1992 were envisioned as the next consumer recording technology), it provides no protection against copying from computers (which has become much more common). In order to correct this inequity, Congress would have to amend the AHRA to include all digital recording technologies rather than narrowly defined technologies.

Manufacturers of DAT recorders and digital audio recording tape must comply with the AHRA by using the SCMS copyright protection system and paying royalties on sales of the recorders and tape. This limits unauthorized copying as well as compensates for unauthorized copying that does occur. However, manufacturers of computers do not have to comply with the AHRA even though they are much more commonly used to make copies of illegal music files.

In another bit of irony, in the copyright infringement lawsuit filed against Napster, one of the defenses asserted by Napster was that the AHRA exempts its users from liability for home taping of copyrighted works. However, based on a strict interpretation of the AHRA and the *Diamond* decision, this defense is meritless as the Napster courts have recognized. The home taping liability exemption applies only to devices covered by the AHRA (i.e., digital audio recording devices). Since computers are expressly excluded, the exemption from liability does not apply to infringements made using file-sharing services such as Napster, which allow users to trade music files stored on computers.

In the *Diamond* case, the court also concluded that although the Rio could be used to store and play illegal MP3 files, it could also be used for legitimate purposes. One such legitimate purpose was what the court referred to as "space-shifting" which involves copying a legally obtained music file from one medium (such as a computer hard drive) to another (such as a Rio player) to be able to listen to the music in other locations.

Example 5.10:

You may purchase and download an MP3 file and copy it onto a Rio player since the copying would be considered space-shifting, but you cannot resell or give away any copies of that file.

(4) Sampling

In simple terms, the concept of sampling involves using part of an existing work in order to create a new work. Musicians and composers have always borrowed, at least to some degree, from prior works. For instance, some French composers in the 1940s developed a style of music called musique concrete which combined musical and nonmusical sounds into a collage by cutting, splicing and manipulating pre-recorded tapes.

In the 1980s, sampling started to become much more prevalent in American music with the advent of digital technology, especially in rap and hip hop music. Digital technology allows analog sound waves to be converted into digital code by breaking the waves into small bits represented by a digit. The digital code can then be electronically manipulated or combined with other digital recordings by using a machine with digital data memory capabilities such as computer or computerized synthesizer.

Two of the most successful songs in 1990 were based on sampled material. M.C. Hammer's "U Can't Touch This" contained a sample from the Rick James recording "Super Freak." Although the Rick James sample was licensed,[15] many artists released recordings containing samples of copyrighted material without obtaining licenses. The 1990 hit "Ice Ice Baby" by Vanilla Ice sampled the melody line from a recording of the song "Under Pressure" by Queen and David Bowie. The sample was used without permission, but the subsequent threat of a copyright infringement suit prompted a settlement for an undisclosed amount of money.

Up until the early 1990s, it was not totally certain that unauthorized sampling was illegal since there had not been any cases involving sampling. However, this uncertainty was resolved in 1991 by *Grand Upright Music Ltd. v. Warner Bros. Records.*[16] *Grand Upright* involved a copyright infringement suit brought against rap artist Biz Markie over a song on his album *I Need a Haircut,* which contained a sample from "Alone Again Naturally," written and recorded by Gilbert O'Sullivan. Biz Markie's song "Alone Again" sampled the first eight bars and the three-word lyric phrase "alone again naturally," which consisted of about 10 seconds of music. However, this relatively short sample was looped throughout the recording so that the same 10 seconds of music are heard repeatedly.

After recording the song but before its release, Biz Markie's attorney sent a copy of the recording to O'Sullivan's manager requesting permission to use the sample. Before receiving a response, Warner Bros. Records released Biz Markie's album. O'Sullivan's manager then responded with a letter demanding that the song be deleted from the album or that the album be withdrawn from distribution. Biz Markie's attorney sent a letter expressing Biz Markie's "sincere regrets that the new composition was released" without permission, but asserted that based on their previous negotiations, O'Sullivan had impliedly agreed that permission would be granted for a price to be agreed upon.

The court did not seem to be impressed with Biz Markie's implied license argument. Setting an ominous tone, the court began its written opinion by quoting the 7th commandment—"thou shalt not steal." To the court, sampling a copyrighted work without permission quite simply equaled theft and since Biz Markie had admitted using the sample, he had admitted infringement.

The court issued a preliminary injunction ordering Warner Bros. to stop selling recordings containing the infringing song. Warner placed an ad in Billboard magazine asking retailers to return any copies of the Biz Markie album not yet sold and had the song deleted from subsequent pressings of the album. Two weeks after the court's decision, a confidential settlement was reached which reportedly included a substantial cash payment.

Shortly after the *Grand Upright* decision, several other copyright infringement suits were brought involving the use of samples. For instance, Tuff City Records sued Sony Music and the Sony-distributed label Def Jam alleging that rap producer Marley Marl had illegally sampled drum sounds from a 1973 sound recording by The Honeydrippers called "Impeach the President" and incorporated them into two recordings by rapper LL Cool J. This case, as were most of the subsequent sampling claims, was settled out of court.

After *Grand Upright* was decided, record companies became much more stringent in making sure that samples were properly licensed. Although record contracts routinely provide that the recording artist is responsible for clearing samples, in practice, it is often the record company that obtains clearances. There are also several clearance agencies that specialize in obtaining sampling licenses for record companies and artists. The compensation a copyright owner receives for licensing the use of a sample ranges from a flat fee (i.e., $250—$10,000 and up)[17] to a royalty (i.e., 1-5 cents per record sold) often with an advance, to an ownership interest in the new work.

It is important to realize that sampling usually involves the use of two separate copyrighted works, a sound recording and the underlying musical composition embodied in the sound recording. Consequently, an artist or record company wanting to use sampled material must normally negotiate two separate licenses with two different copyright owners (i.e., a record company and a music publisher).

Example 5.12:

Many famous recording artists have had their music sampled. For instance, one of my favorite artists, Steely Dan, has had their music sampled on several occasions. Rapper De La Soul used a sample from Steely Dan's "Peg" in his recording "Eye Know." Another Steely Dan sample involved the unauthorized use by rappers Lord Tariq and Peter Gunz of part of Steely Dan's "Black Cow" on their song "Deja Vu." After the threat of a copyright infringement lawsuit, the rappers' record company ended up paying $105,000 for the sample, which was more than three times the standard rate. The two rappers didn't make any money from their recording (since their royalties went to pay back the sample fee in addition to other costs traditionally recouped from the artist's royalty). The morale of this story for copyright purposes is that it is almost always better to obtain a license for a sample before using the sample than afterwards.

Although using samples of copyrighted material without permission will normally be infringement, there are some defenses that may be applicable in rare circumstances. First, if a sample is so small that it is unrecognizable, a court might find it to be a de minimis use (i.e., too small to be important). However, there is no clear rule as to how much is de minimis. Arguably, a sample containing only a note or two would be de minimis. However, since most sampling artists want the samples to be recognizable, the de minimis defense will rarely be applicable. Additionally, it is possible that sampling could be considered fair use if it was transformative (i.e., if significant original contributions were added to create a new work) and did not affect the market for the sampled work.

An interesting lawsuit involving sampling was brought by rock group U2 against a little-known group called Negativland. Negativland is a group that creates recordings by mixing their own music with samples from various sources, a process they refer to as musical collage. However, Negativland received much more publicity from a sampling controversy than it has ever generated from its music. Negativland, through its former record label SST Records, released a single called U2 which contained a sample from U2's recording "I Still Haven't Found What I'm Looking For." U2's record label, Island Records, demanded that SST stop selling the record and threatened an infringement suit. Negativland contended that its sampling constituted fair use because it was made for purposes of parody and cultural criticism, stating that:

Our single deals, in part, with our perception of the group U2 as an international cultural phenomenon, and therefore particularly worthy of artistic comment and criticism. Island's legal action thoroughly ignores the possibility that any such artistic right or inclination might exist.

Although this controversy may have presented a good opportunity for a court to interpret the applicability of the fair use defense to sampling, Negativland agreed to recall and destroy all copies of the record, claiming that they could not afford to pursue their fair use claim in court. Instead, Negativland has pursued its claim in the media and online (**www.negativland.com**) by becoming vocal critics of copyright law and proponents of expanded fair use rights.

1. *White-Smith Music Publishing Company v. Apollo Company*, 209 U.S. 1 (1908).
2. The mechanism for adjusting the statutory mechanical royalty rate has changed several times. The 1976 Copyright Act created a Copyright Royalty Tribunal which was to periodically adjust the statutory royalty rates under the four compulsory licenses created by the Act (for cable retransmissions, mechanical reproduction of musical compositions, jukebox performances and public broadcasting). In 1993, the Copyright Royalty Tribunal was eliminated and replaced with copyright arbitration royalty panels appointed by the Librarian of Congress at the Register of Copyrights' recommendation. Copyright arbitration royalty panels consist of three arbitrators and are convened whenever it is necessary to adjust any of the compulsory license rates. However, in 1998, an agreement was reached establishing a ten year schedule for increases. By 2008, either a new agreement will have to be reached or a copyright arbitration royalty panel will be appointed to adjust the rate.
3. The Copyright Act provides that copyright owners and licensees can vary the terms of mechanical licenses from the terms of the compulsory license provision. See 17 U.S.C. § 115(c)(3)(E).
4. Controlled composition clauses are commonly contained in record contracts between artists and record companies. Under such a clause, the artist guarantees the record company that it will be able to obtain mechanical licenses for any songs written, owned, or controlled by the artist at reduced rates.
5. 17 U.S.C. § 115(d). It is important to note that the term "transmission" is used instead of distribution since distribution requires the transfer of a physical object which does not occur in the context of digital downloads.
6. 17 U.S.C. § 115(c)(3)(E)(i). An exception to the right to modify the rate for digital phonorecord deliveries applies in situations where reduced rates are specified by controlled compositions clauses in record contracts. In such situations, the copyright owner must be paid the full statutory rate unless: (1) the contract containing the controlled composition clause was entered into before June 22, 1995; or (2) the contract containing the controlled composition clause is entered into by an artist/songwriter who retains his music publishing rights and the contract is entered into after the songs have been recorded.
7. 17 U.S.C. § 114(b).
8. No. 90 Civ. 4537 (S.D.N.Y. July 11, 1991).
9. In 1984, the Supreme Court held that private home taping of television broadcasts for purposes of viewing the shows at a later time was a fair use. *See Sony Corp. v. Universal City Studios, Inc.*, 464 U.S. 417 (1984). However, that decision did not specifically address home audio taping.
10. 17 U.S.C. § 1007.
11. 17 U.S.C. § 1002.
12. 17 U.S.C. § 1008.
13. S. Rep. No. 294, 102d Cong., 2d Sess. 18 (1992).

14. *Recording Indus. Ass'n of Am. v. Diamond Multimedia Sys., Inc.*, 29 F. Supp. 2d 624 (C.D. Cal. 1998), aff'd, 180 F.3d 1072 (9th Cir. 1999).

15. Reportedly, M.C. Hammer agreed to split copyright ownership of the song 50/50 with Jobete Music, the publisher of *Super Freak*.

16. 780 F. Supp. 182 (1991).

17. Supposedly, the rap group 2 Live Crew paid about $100,000 to include sampled dialogue from the movie *Full Metal Jacket* in their single *Me So Horny*.

CHAPTER 6

The Derivative and Distribution Rights

▼

*"Of course, the law is not the place for
the artist or poet." Oliver Wendell Holmes.*

I. The Derivative Right

A. WHAT IS A DERIVATIVE WORK?

Section 106(2) of the 1976 Copyright Act gives copyright owners the exclusive right to prepare derivative works based upon the copyrighted work. A derivative work takes a preexisting work and adapts it in some way in order to create a new work. Consequently, the right to make derivative works is often referred to as the adaptation right. The Copyright Act defines a derivative work as:

a work based upon one or more preexisting works, such as a translation, musical arrangement, dramatization, fictionalization, motion picture version, sound recording, art reproduction, abridgment, condensation, or any other form in which a work may be recast, transformed, or adapted.[1]

Derivative works have not always received protection under copyright law. In the 19th century, English courts were unwilling to grant protection to derivative works based on music in the public domain. One court decision stated that while an original work requires "genius for its construction, a mere mechanic in music can make the adaptation or accompaniment."[2] Courts in the United States have also been reluctant to recognize copyright in some derivative musical works.

| Example 6.1: |

In 1885, Gilbert and Sullivan's *Mikado* was held to have entered the public domain in the United States.[3] British composers Gilbert and Sullivan owned the copyright to the opera in England and wanted copyright protection in the United States as well. Since the United States did not recognize foreign copyrights at the time, Gilbert and Sullivan hired an American musician, George Tracey, to create a piano arrangement from the original score. When an unauthorized performance of Tracey's arrangement took place, Tracey sued to enforce his copyright. The court, however, ruled that an arrangement could not be an original work since an arranger "originates nothing, composes no new notes or melodies, and simply culls the notes representing the melodies and their accompaniments."

The 1909 Copyright Act was the first United States copyright statute to allow for copyright in derivative works and the 1976 Copyright Act continued the recognition of copyright in derivative works.

B. REQUIREMENTS FOR A COPYRIGHTABLE DERIVATIVE WORK

An otherwise copyrightable work must satisfy two requirements to constitute a derivative work. First, the work must borrow from another work. Second, the work must recast, transform or adapt the work upon which it is based.

Woods v. Bourne[4] involved a dispute over different versions of the 1926 hit song "When the Red, Red Robin Comes Bob-Bob-Bobbin' Along." Bourne was a publisher that had acquired copyright ownership of the song from its composer Harry Woods. Woods' heirs contended that they were entitled to royalty payments from several arrangements made by Bourne. Bourne argued that since Woods had only turned in a lead sheet (i.e., the melodic line with the lyrics written under it) to the original publisher in 1926, every version of the song published since then were derivative works. The court disagreed, holding that the modifications to a work must be an original work of authorship in order for the resulting work to be a derivative. The court stated that: "In order therefore to qualify as a musically 'derivative work,' there must be present more than mere cocktail pianist variations of the piece that are standard fare in the music trade by any competent musician. There must be such things as unusual vocal treatment, additional lyrics of consequence, unusual altered harmonies, novel sequential uses of themes—something of substance added making the piece to some extent a new work with the old song embedded in it but from which the new has developed. It is not merely a stylized version of the original song where a major artist may take liberties with the lyrics or the tempo, the listener hearing basically the original tune. It is, in short, the addition of such new material as would entitle the creator, to a copyright on the new material."

Derivative works are therefore created by taking existing material and adding new original material to it, thereby transforming it into new work. If the existing material used to create a derivative work is protected by copyright, the author of the derivative work must obtain permission to use the existing work (the exception to this rule is if the derivative work is a fair use).

C. TYPES OF DERIVATIVE WORKS

There are many different types of derivative works, some of the most common of which are as follows:

Editorial Revisions: A work that revises an earlier work.

At some point in the future it will become necessary to revise *Music Copyright for the New Millennium* to incorporate developments in copyright law that take place after its publication. The new edition would be a derivative work based on the original edition of the work.

Fictionalizations: The transformation of a preexisting nonfiction work into a fictional work such as a novel or screenplay.

Dramatizations: The transformation of a preexisting work into a work that can be performed on stage.

Andrew Lloyd Webber and Trevor Nunn composed the musical Cats based on poems contained in *Old Possum's Book of Practical Cats*. The preexisting material (the poems) were combined with music and used as the basis for the derivative dramatic work.

Translations to New Language: Translating a work from one language into another language. Although it may not seem that simply translating a work into another language creates a new work, translation typically involves some creative choices by the translator that enable the translation to make sense in the new language. These creative choices may satisfy the requirements of originality and expression necessary for a derivative work.

When an English language song is translated into another language, the translation will often qualify as a derivative work.

Translations to New Medium: The transformation of a work from one medium into another medium

Virtually all sound recordings are derivative works since their creation typically involves transforming a song into a recorded medium.

Abridgements and Condensations: The transformation of an existing work into a shorter version (such as an abridged version of a novel).

D. DEGREE OF PROTECTION IN DERIVATIVE WORKS

Although derivative works can be copyrightable, it is important to understand that the copyright in a derivative work extends only to the original material contributed by the author of the derivative. According to § 103(b) of the Copyright Act:

The copyright in a compilation or derivative work extends only to the material contributed by the author of such work, as distinguished from the preexisting material employed in the work, and does not imply any exclusive right in the preexisting material. The copyright in such work is independent of, and does not affect or enlarge the scope, duration, ownership, or subsistence of, any copyright protection in the preexisting material.

The copyright in a derivative work does not affect the copyright in the original work upon which it is based. If an existing work is protected by copyright, it is still protected to the same extent after the creation of a derivative work. If an existing work is not protected by copyright, its public domain status will not be changed by the creation of a derivative work. Anyone is free to make derivative works based on works that are in the public domain. However, if you want to make a derivative work based on a copyrighted work, you must obtain the copyright owner's permission. If you use a copyrighted work to create a new work without the copyright owner's permission, you will not have a copyrightable derivative work since copyright protection does not extend to any part of a derivative work in which preexisting material is used without permission.

Example 6.7:

The song "Love Me Tender" is credited as being written by Elvis Presley and Vera Matson. It was derived from a public domain song called "Aura Lee" written in 1861. No permission was required to make a derivative work based on "Aura Lee" since it was in the public domain. Puff Daddy's song "I'll Be Missing You" is a derivative musical composition based on Sting's "Every Breath You Take." Because "Every Breath You Take" is a copyrighted song, Puff Daddy had to obtain Sting's permission to use it and Sting consequently ended up owning the derivative as well as the original song and earning a lot more money from an already lucrative song.

E. DERIVATIVE MUSICAL ARRANGEMENTS

Derivative works are generally held to a slightly higher standard of originality than works in general. This is particularly important in the case of musical arrangements. Commonly, when a recording artist is going to record a musical composition, an arrangement of the composition will be made of the composition to be recorded. Whether an arrangement is copyrightable as a derivative work depends on the amount of original expression that has been added by the arranger. Since musical composition is based on a fairly limited musical vocabulary, arrangements must contain substantial variations in order to be copyrightable as derivative works.

Example 6.8:

In *Shapiro, Bernstein & Co. v. Jerry Vogel Music Co.,* a court ruled that a derivative musical composition was not copyrightable since the only new elements added to the original work were a change in rhythm and accompaniment.[5] Similarly, in *McIntyre v. Double-A-Music Corp.,* a court refused to recognize copyright in an arrangement of a Bing Crosby song, stating that the arrangement involved merely "melodic and harmonic embellishments" that "are frequently improvised by any competent musician."[6]

Conversely, if an author makes substantial variations to an existing work, the resulting work will be a copyrightable derivative work.

Example 6.9:

In *Wood v. Boosey,*[7] a court ruled that a piano arrangement of an opera qualified as a derivative work. The court decided that the arrangement, by translating a score for many instruments into a piece for only piano, constituted a significant departure from the original, and was therefore worthy of protection as a derivative work.

In one very interesting case, an artist recorded an arrangement of a popular song. The arrangement added an introduction, handclapping, choral responses, and additional instrumentation to the original song. Later, another artist made its own arrangement of the song, based in part on the first artist's arrangement. The record company that owned the first artist's recording sued the record company which owned the second artist's recording for infringing the copyright in its arrangement. Without determining whether the defendant had copied the plaintiff's arrangement, the court examined the plaintiff's arrangement and concluded that it was not copyrightable since the techniques used in the plaintiff's arrangement were very common and not sufficiently original. The court stated that a musical arrangement will not be protected by copyright unless it has "a distinctive characteristic . . . of such character that any person hearing it played would become aware of the distinctiveness of the arrangement."

F. ARRANGEMENTS UNDER THE COMPULSORY MECHANICAL LICENSE

As discussed in chapter 5, § 115 of the Copyright Act provides for a compulsory license to record musical compositions and distribute those recordings without the copyright owner's permission. When an artist makes a recording of a musical composition, it will usually be necessary to make some changes to the composition in order to fit the artist's performance style. Accordingly, the compulsory license provision, in § 115(a)(2), provides for a limited arrangement privilege, stating that:

the compulsory license includes the privilege of making a musical arrangement of the work to the extent necessary to conform it to the style or manner of interpretation of the performance involved.

It is important to understand that this arrangement privilege is quite limited and allows only minor changes to be made. Under § 115(a)(2), the "arrangement shall not change the basic melody or fundamental character of the work." Finally, § 115(a)(2) provides that an arrangement:

shall not be subject to protection as a derivative work under this title, except with the express consent of the copyright owner.

Although § 115(a)(2) gives some general rules for the arrangement privilege under the compulsory mechanical license, applying these rules to specific

situations can be problematic. Determining what changes are minor and thus permitted as opposed to changes that affect the basic melody or fundamental character of a composition are to some degree subjective. It is helpful, however, to keep the purpose of the limited arrangement privilege in mind when making such determinations. For instance, if an artist recorded a song in a different key from the key in which it was written, the change has probably been made to fit the artist's performance style and would be permitted. Similarly, if a male artist wanted to record a song written from a female perspective, it might be necessary to make some minor lyrics changes such as changing pronouns from feminine to masculine or vice versa (e.g. "I love him" to "I love her"). On the other hand, if an artist wanted to change more than a very minor portion of a song's lyrics, this would be likely to be considered a change in the fundamental character of the work and would not be permitted since the result would be a derivative work which cannot be made without the copyright owner's permission.

G. COPYRIGHTING THE UNCOPYRIGHTABLE

A copyrightable derivative work can be made based on a work that is in the public domain. A practice that is sometimes used by publishers that own valuable songs about to enter the public domain is to make a new copyrightable arrangement of the song. A publisher can then continue to commercially exploit the derivative arrangement after the copyright in the original song expires.

Example 6.10:

Chappell Music, which owned the copyrights to some extremely valuable Gilbert and Sullivan works, had new arrangements of the works made shortly before the expiration of their copyrights in the 1970s. This did not prevent the original works from entering the public domain, but Warner-Chappell (which purchased Chappell) still earns money from licensing the copyrighted derivative arrangements.

II. The Distribution Right

Another of the exclusive rights of a copyright owner is the right to distribute the work to the public. Section 106(3) of the Copyright Act provides that the copyright owner has the exclusive right to distribute, and to authorize others to distribute, "copies or phonorecords of the copyrighted work to the public by sale or other transfer of ownership, or by rental, lease, or lending." Section 106(3) covers not only the sale of a work, but all forms of transfer.

It is important to understand that the distribution right applies to the copyrighted work and not to any copies or phonorecords containing the copyrighted work. For instance, a record store that sells a compact disc containing a copyrighted sound recording does not infringe the distribution right.

A. RECORD PIRACY

In 1972, the United States finally amended its copyright law to include sound recordings as a category of copyrightable works. The main reason for this amendment was to provide legal protection against record piracy. Record piracy involves re-recording copyrighted sound recordings and distributing the unauthorized reproductions. Record piracy therefore always involves a violation of the copyright owner's reproduction and distribution rights. According to estimates by the Recording Industry Association of America, record piracy costs the music industry $300 million a year in the United States and $5 billion a year worldwide.

It is important to realize that not only record companies are harmed by piracy, but all participants in the music industry. Piracy involves a violation not only the rights of the sound recording copyright owner, but the copyright owner of any musical works contained on the sound recording as well. Consequently, recording artists, producers, songwriters, and music publishers, all of whom rely on royalties from the sale of legitimate recordings, are also harmed. Finally, consumers are harmed because some of the income lost due to piracy is passed on to consumers in the form of increased prices for legitimate recordings.

(1) Penalties for Record Piracy

In addition to civil awards for actual damages, lost profits, or statutory damages of up to $150,000 per infringement, record pirates can also be subject to penalties for criminal copyright infringement. The criminal penalties vary, depending on whether the infringing activity is for commercial advantage or private financial gain. Copyright law provides that financial gain includes bartering or trading anything of value, including sound recordings. If the infringing

activity is for commercial advantage or private financial gain, infringers are subject to up to five years in prison and $250,000 in fines. Repeat offenders are subject to imprisonment for up to 10 years.

In addition to copyright law, other federal and state laws also prohibit record piracy. On the federal level, the Federal Anti-Bootleg Statute[9] prohibits unauthorized recording, manufacture, distribution, or trafficking in sound recording or videos of artists' live musical performances. Violators are subject to up to $250,000 in fines and five years imprisonment.

Additionally, the No Electronic Theft Act provides for criminal prosecutions even if no monetary profit or commercial gain is derived from the infringing activity. The No Electronic Theft Act has been applied to copyright infringement involving the trading of MP3 files over the Internet.

Most states have enacted statutes prohibiting the reproduction and distribution of sound recordings without authorization. Importantly, most of these state statutes apply to sound recordings created prior to 1972, when sound recordings were made a class of works subject to the Copyright Act. Some states also have anti-bootleg statutes similar to the Federal Anti-Bootleg Statute and some states also address record piracy as part of their laws against unfair competition.

(2) Fighting Record Piracy

The Recording Industry Association of America (RIAA) wages a continuous war against record piracy. The RIAA works with law enforcement agencies to locate pirates and shut down their manufacturing and distribution facilities. The RIAA generally directs its enforcement efforts at manufacturers and distributors of pirated recordings. Recently, there has been growing concern over piracy of recordings using compact-disc recorders (CD-Rs). Consumers are buying blank CD-Rs and, in many cases, using them to copy music files downloaded using Napster and other file-sharing software. In addition to individuals copying music files from the Internet to CD-Rs, there has been an increase in the use of CD-R technology by large-scale record pirating operations.

Example 6.11:

On March 8, 2001, the U.S. Secret Service, assisted by the RIAA, conducted a raid of a large-scale New York-based record pirating operation. As a result, approximately 20,000 recorded CD-Rs and 1,200 master recordings were seized containing recordings by artists such as Santana, Jay-Z, Jennifer Lopez and the Beatles. Additionally, 102 CD-R burners, nine computer monitors, four computers, three thermal printers, two paper-cutting machines, two laptops, two industrial color copiers, and two industrial shrink-wrap machines were also seized.

The RIAA has also taken a very active role in enforcing the law against online piracy. The RIAA employs a team of Internet Specialists and uses a 24-hour automated webcrawler to track down web sites offering illegal recordings. The Digital Millennium Copyright Act allows the RIAA to send information subpoenas to Internet Service Providers (ISPs) which host web sites that allow unauthorized use of copyrighted music. These subpoenas require the ISP to provide contact information for the web site operator. The RIAA then sends warnings to web site operators and, in some instances, resorts to suing web site operators who fail to respond to these warnings.

The RIAA also attempts to deter piracy by educating the public about copyright law. The RIAA initiated a program called "Soundbyting" to educate college students and universities about copyright infringement on the Internet. The RIAA has also published anti-piracy guidelines providing suggestions for CD manufacturing plants to use in order to recognize pirated recordings. In addition, the RIAA's "CD-Reward" program provides monetary awards of up to $10,000 to people who provide information regarding CD manufacturers that are illegally producing RIAA member company sound recordings.

Example 6.12:

In 1999, the RIAA settled a lawsuit it had brought against Americ Disc, a CD manufacturing plant. Americ Disc had been manufacturing pirated copies of CDs including albums by virtually all of the world's most popular recording artists (Mariah Carey, Celine Dion, Madonna, etc.). The suit resulted in the largest copyright infringement settlement ever with Americ Disc agreeing to pay $10 million plus an additional $500,000 for reimbursement of the RIAA's legal fees and to help establish an anti-piracy program. Americ Disc also agreed to require its customers to supply copies of licenses for all copyrighted material to be reproduced.

Since piracy is by no means restricted to the United States, it is crucial that copyright laws and other laws prohibiting piracy are enforced on an international basis. In 1999, the International Federation of the Phonographic Industry initiated a plan under which record companies and music industry organizations will cooperate to fight piracy on a worldwide basis. Another weapon in the fight against piracy on an international level is the International Standard Recording Code (ISRC). The ISRC is a numerical identifying code for sound recordings which makes it easier to track and prevent the unauthorized reproduction and distribution of sound recordings. The RIAA administers the IRSC in the United States.

B. IMPORTATION OF COPIES OR PHONORECORDS INTO THE UNITED STATES

Although § 106(3) only applies to distribution in the United States, § 602(a) provides that the unauthorized importation into the United States of copies or phonorecords of a work that have been acquired outside the United States is an infringement of the exclusive right to distribute copies or phonorecords under § 106(3).

Section 602 distinguishes between piratical goods and gray market goods. Piratical goods are copies or phonorecords made without permission from the copyright owner while gray market goods are copies or phonorecords lawfully manufactured and marketed abroad but whose importation into the United States violates the terms of a territorial licensing agreement with the copyright owner. The United States Customs Service is authorized, under § 602(b), to bar the importation of piratical goods thus providing copyright owners with a way to stop pirated goods from entering domestic commerce.

Section 602 is not applicable to the following activities:

- Importation by or for use of a governmental body excluding use in schools or copies of audiovisual work for non-archival purpose.

- Importation of one copy or phonorecord for private use.

- Importation by or for nonprofit organizations operated for scholarly, educational or religious purposes; 1 copy of audiovisual work for archival purposes; up to

5 copies or phonorecords for library lending or archival purposes.

C. LIMITATIONS ON THE DISTRIBUTION RIGHT

(1) The First Sale Doctrine
Section 109(a) provides an important exemption from the distribution right by providing that:

the owner of a particular copy or phonorecord lawfully made under this title, or any person authorized by such owner, is entitled, without the authority of the copyright owner, to sell or otherwise dispose of the possession of that copy or phonorecord.

This provision, commonly known as the first sale doctrine, means that once the copyright owner sells or gives away a copy or phonorecord, he has no further rights with respect to that particular copy or phonorecord. In other words, the copyright owner controls only the first public distribution of a copy or phonorecord of the work. People make use of the first sale doctrine on a daily basis when they rent videocassettes or sell used CDs.

Under the first sale doctrine, the copyright owner gets to determine whether, when and in what format copies or phonorecords of a work are to be published for the first time, but once that first distribution has been authorized, the copyright owner cannot control any future distribution. The first sale doctrine is based on the idea that ownership of a material object is distinct from ownership of copyright.

Example 6.13:

If you bought (or otherwise lawfully acquire) the copy of *Music Copyright for the New Millennium* that you are reading, you own that particular copy of the book. As the owner of that copy, under the first sale doctrine, you can keep it (which I hope you will do), sell it (which I hope you won't want to do) or even destroy it (which I really hope you won't do unless you're going to buy another one to replace it). However, the first sale doctrine does not give you the right to make copies or adapt the copyrighted work embodied in the copy you own.

The first sale doctrine is not applicable if a copy or phonorecord is unlawfully made or if the first sale occurs outside of the United States. It also applies only to the owner of the particular copy or phonorecord, not to someone who possesses the copy or phonorecord, but does not own it.

Example 6.14:

If you stole the copy of *Music Copyright for the New Millennium* that you are reading, you are a bad person and God will punish you. In addition to incurring God's wrath, you have no rights under the first sale doctrine since you possess an illegally acquired copy.

a. Used CDs
The first sale doctrine is responsible for the used CD business, which grew dramatically in the 1990s.[10] When a record company, which is the copyright owner of the sound recordings contained on a compact disc, sells compact discs to retailers, it loses all control over the further distribution of those phonorecords. The retailer is obviously free to sell the compact discs it has purchased to consumers. The consumers then become the owners of the compact discs and are consequently free to re-distribute them such as by selling them to used CD stores. The used CD stores can sell the discs to other consumers who can then distribute them as they see fit, including reselling them to used CD stores, starting the process all over again. The record company has no control over any of these actions except for the first sale to the retailer.

The resale of recordings affects copyright owners in two ways. First, the record company does not receive any additional compensation for any distributions beyond the initial sale. Second, every resale potentially displaces a sale of a new CD from a retailer to a consumer.

Several potential solutions to the problems posed by used CD sales have been considered, but none have been adopted. One solution is to require a resale royalty on sales of copyrighted works. The rationale for this resale royalty is that music creators require a portion of the income generated by used CD sales since CDs retain their high sound quality and value well beyond their initial sale. The resale royalty also recognizes the assumption that, given the choice between buying new and used compact discs, many consumer will buy used, denying the first sale of originals in a way that does not parallel other markets since most products depreciate over time. In order for a resale royalty to exist, Congress would have to enact legislation requiring used CD retailers to keep records of sales and pay royalties to record companies which would be split with recording artists. The odds of this happening are remote since any such legislation would likely be met with strong resistance from retailers and consumers.

b. Record Rental

Under the first sale doctrine, a compact disc purchaser is free to sell or rent the CD without the permission of the copyright owner and without paying any royalty. However, the Record Rental Amendment Act of 1984 imposes a limitation on the first sale doctrine. This Amendment, found in §109(b) of the Copyright Act, states that:

Unless authorized by the owners of the copyright in the sound recording and musical works embodied therein, the owner of a particular phonorecord may not, for purposes of direct or indirect commercial advantage, dispose of, or authorize the disposal of, possession of that phonorecord by rental, lease or lending.

In other words, although people are free to sell or give away recordings that they own, they cannot rent them unless they have the permission of the copyright owners of the sound recording and songs contained on the recording. This provision was passed in response to the development of record rental outlets. Congress feared that record rentals would displace sales and record companies would be forced to spread their costs over the smaller number of records sold. Record companies would become more conservative and less likely to release records by unknown artists. An exception to the prohibition against record rental exists for rentals by nonprofit libraries or nonprofit educational institutions.

c. Imported Copies and Phonorecords

Several cases have held that the first sale doctrine is not applicable to unauthorized importation into the United States of copies or phonorecords acquired outside the United States. In the first such case, *Columbia Broadcasting System, Inc. v. Scorpio Music Distributors, Inc.*, Scorpio had purchased phonorecords from a corporation that manufactured them legally in the Philippines.

Scorpio then imported the records into the United States without authorization from CBS, the copyright owner of the recordings. CBS sued under § 602(a). The court rejected Scorpio's assertion that since the records had already been the subject of a lawful first sale, the action was barred under the first sale doctrine holding that the first sale doctrine is not available to a seller who acquired ownership in the United States of phonorecords that, although lawfully made abroad, were unlawfully imported. The court based its decision on the belief that § 109(a)'s phrase "lawfully made under this title" means legally manufactured and sold within the United States and stated that "construing § 109(a) as superseding the prohibition on importation would render § 602 virtually meaningless."[11]

(2) Other Limitations on the Distribution Right

Many of the limitations on the reproduction right are also applicable to the distribution right. For example, § 108's reproduction privileges for libraries and archives also allow for the distribution of copies made. Section 114(b)'s exemption for sound recordings included in educational television and radio programs applies to the reproduction, distribution, and derivative rights.

1. 17 U.S.C. § 101.
2. *D'Almaine v. Boosey,* 160 Eng. Rep. at 123.
3. *Carte v. Duff,* 25 F. 183 (S.D.N.Y. 1885).
4. 841 F. Supp. 118 (1993).
5. 73 F. Supp. 165, 167 (S.D.N.Y. 1947).
6. 166 F. Supp. 681 (S.D. Cal. 1958).
7. 3 L.R.-Q.B. 223, 229-30 (1868).
8. *Supreme Records, Inc. v. Decca Records, Inc.,* 90 F. Supp. 904, 908 (S.D. Cal. 1950).
9. 18 U.S.C. § 2319A.
10. In 1993 several major record retailers (Wherehouse, Hastings, etc.) announced their intention to sell used CDs. The major record companies threatened to withdraw promotional allowances and refused to supply new releases of several well known artists who objected to the practice. The record companies reversed their position on promotional allowances after being faced with a federal antitrust lawsuit. See *Wherehouse Entertainment, Inc. v. CEMA,* No. 93-4253 (C.D. Cal. filed Jul. 19, 1993).
11. Although the Scorpio decision has been followed by other courts such as the Ninth Circuit in *BMG Music v. Perez,* many authorities believe that the reasoning of Scorpio is incorrect.

CHAPTER 7

Public Performance and Display Rights

▼

*"For all songs I whistle while at work, I will be
sure to get a license before I whistle."
Michael Robertson, chairman and chief
executive officer of MP3.com*

I. The Public Performance Right

Section 106(4) of the Copyright Act gives copyright owners the exclusive right to perform, and to authorize others to perform, their works publicly. Consequently, anyone who wants to publicly perform or make available a public performance of a copyrighted musical composition must obtain the copyright owner's permission. Like all of the other exclusive rights, the public performance right is not unlimited and is subject to many exemptions, the most important of which are discussed later in this chapter. However, one very important limitation to be aware of is that the public performance right of § 106(4) does not apply to copyrighted sound recordings (see section E below). Consequently, the discussion of the § 106(4) performance right is limited to musical compositions.

A. WHAT IS A PERFORMANCE?

The term "perform" is defined very broadly by the Copyright Act and includes not only the initial rendition of a work, but also any further act by which the rendition is transmitted or communicated. Section 101 provides that to perform a work means:

to recite, render, play, dance, or act it, either directly or by means of any device or process or, in the case of a

motion picture or other audiovisual work, to show its images in any sequence or to make the sounds accompanying it audible.

The performance right includes not only live performances, but also recorded performances and transmitted performances. For instance, a band playing a song in a nightclub constitutes a live performance while the nightclub's playing a compact disc or jukebox is a recorded performance. Finally, a radio station's broadcast of either a live or recorded performance is a transmitted performance. In order to understand how the public performance right works (especially in connection with performance rights licensing), it is crucial to realize that performances occur not only with the initial rendition of a work, but also all further acts by which that rendition is transmitted or communicated to the public.

Example 7.1:

If I sing a song, I have performed the song. If a radio or television station broadcasts my performance, that transmission by the radio station constitutes a second performance. If a person sitting at home with their radio tunes in to the radio station, that constitutes a third performance. Although all three performances are based on the same initial rendition (i.e., my performance), the radio or television station's action and the home listener's action are further acts by which the initial rendition is transmitted or communicated to the public.

B. WHAT IS A PUBLIC PERFORMANCE?

Not every performance requires the permission of the copyright owner of a work. This is because the copyright owner's exclusive right is limited to "public" performances. Anyone is free to perform copyrighted works in private.

Example 7.2:

If I sing a copyrighted song at home, I have not infringed the performance right since this would be a private performance (unless I invite the public to join me). Similarly, when an individual plays a CD or turns on their television at home, any performances of copyrighted music are private rather than public and do not require the copyright owner's permission. However, a television station's broadcast is a public performance which requires permission since the broadcast is available to the public.

Sometimes, it is not easy to determine whether a performance is public or private. In between the performances that are clearly public or private, there are many performances that occupy a middle ground, combining some characteristics of public performances and some characteristics of private performances. Under copyright law, there are four categories of performances that are classified as public performances:

(1) A public performance occurs anytime a work is performed at a place open to the public. A place that is open to the public is a place where the general public is free to go regardless of how many people are actually present and regardless of whether an admission fee is charged. Some examples include concert venues, theaters, nightclubs, bars, restaurants and retail stores.

(2) A public performance occurs when a work is performed at a place where a substantial number of people other than family and friends are gathered. This includes what are commonly known as semi-public places such as private clubs, work places and schools. Exactly how many people constitutes a substantial number is not specified by the Copyright Act.

(3) A public performance occurs when a work is transmitted to a place open to the public or where a substantial number of people other than family and friends are gathered. To transmit a work means to communicate it by any device that enables images or sounds to be received beyond the place where they originated. An example would be a radio broadcast of a copyrighted song that is received by a bar. Although the performance originates at the radio station, it is transmitted over the airwaves to a place open to the public.

(4) A public performance occurs when a work is transmitted by a device, regardless of whether the public receives it in the same or separate places or at the same or different times. It is not necessary that anyone actually tune in as long as members of the public could have done so.

As technology continues to bring about new ways to make recorded music available, the distinction between public and private places has become increasingly blurred. Modern technology such as the Internet has begun a trend toward distributing copyrighted works to private places such as people's homes rather than public places. For instance, are performances that originate from a web site allowing visitors to listen to music files of copyrighted musical works (commonly known as webcasting) public or private performances? On one hand, this might seem to be a private performance since the copyrighted work is being transmitted to one person at a time and generally to a private place such as a home. However, Congress has stated that a transmission may be considered to be made "to the public" when "the transmission is capable of reaching different recipients at different times, as in the case of sounds or images stored in an information system and capable of being performed or displayed at the initiative of individual members of the public."[1] In a way, the webcaster is like a radio station in that it allows people to listen to music without having to purchase the recordings. The main difference is that webcasting, to some degree, allows for the public to make their own programming choices rather than being totally subject to the programming choices made by a radio station.

C. PERFORMING RIGHTS ORGANIZATIONS

(1) History of Performing Rights Organizations

The public performance right was first made applicable to musical works under the 1909 Copyright Act. Even after 1909, although the performance right existed, there was no practical way to license and collect payments for public performances. Consider the amount of work that would be involved if a copyright owner had to negotiate individual licenses for performances of its music in every restaurant, bar, nightclub, concert venue, radio station, television station and so forth throughout the world. The costs of tracking all of the performances of your music, not to mention licensing and collecting payments would be much greater than the amount of money you would be able to collect.

This was the problem that existed for songwriters and publishers until 1914 when a group of popular composers including Irving Berlin, Victor Herbert and John Philip Sousa decided that the only practical way they could get paid for public performances of their music was to form an organization to enforce the performance rights of many composers and publishers. As a result, they formed the American Society of Composers, Authors and Publishers (ASCAP) in order to act as a clearinghouse for licensing performances and collecting license fees.

Initially, venues that allowed performances to take place were very resistant to paying for licenses and ASCAP had to file lawsuits to enforce its members' rights. The 1909 Copyright Act provided that only for-profit performances had to be licensed and some early court decisions held that there had to be a direct charge for music in order to constitute a for-profit performance. However, the Supreme Court set a crucial precedent regarding what constitutes a for-profit performance in the case of *Herbert v. Shanley*.[2] Composer Victor Herbert sued Shanley's Restaurant for allowing the performance of one of his compositions without a license. Shanley contended that the performances that occurred in its establishment were not for profit since they didn't charge customers to listen to the music. The Supreme Court ruled that a direct charge to the customer for listening to music was not required. Instead, it is sufficient to show that music was used in the process of making a profit. The Court believed that music was a part of the total service for which the public pays, stating that:

If the rights under copyright law are only infringed by a performance where money is taken at the door, they are very imperfectly protected. Music is part of the total for which the public pays and the fact that the price of the whole is attributable to a particular item which those present are expected to order is not important. It is true that music is not the sole object, but neither is the food, which probably could be got cheaper elsewhere.

The Supreme Court's view makes perfect logical sense since businesses would not be likely to use music if they did not believe that music contributes to the atmosphere of the business, thereby increasing profitability. Music can be used to increase profitability in several ways (e.g., to enhance the atmosphere, to relax or stimulate customers, or to promote a theme). Although a bar or restaurant might not charge customers directly for the music it plays, it charges them indirectly in the price of food or drinks that it sells. In actuality, there are many things reflected in the price that a restaurant sells food for. For instance, most restaurants are decorated in some way, whether it be with high class art or the movie memorabilia of Planet Hollywood. Restaurants would have a difficult time convincing whomever they obtain such decorations from that they shouldn't have to pay for them since they don't directly charge their customers to look at them. Obviously, if a restaurant believes that music does not contribute to its profitability, it is free to let is customers eat in silence.

Although music certainly plays a role in the profitability of many types of businesses, businesses have always been very reluctant to pay for it and there is a common perception among businesses that having to pay for music is not justified. This is illustrated by the fact that the public performance right has been challenged in virtually every business context over the years since its establishment (live performance venues such as restaurants and nightclubs, radio broadcasters, television broadcasters, Internet-based music companies, etc.).

After the important precedent established by the *Shanley* decision, ASCAP began licensing restaurants, nightclubs, concert halls and other venues where public performances took place. In the early 1920's, radio stations resisted obtaining licenses contending that since they did not charge the public for their broadcasts, they did not have to obtain licenses. However, the Supreme Court once again sided with copyright owners, holding that radio broadcasts were for profit and had to be licensed.[3] In 1931, the Supreme Court decided a case involving a hotel that broadcast a radio signal over loudspeakers to both private and public rooms.[4] The hotel argued that merely receiving a radio broadcast should not be considered a performance since both the radio station and the hotel could not be simultaneously performing the same work. The Court disagreed, holding that the hotel's action constituted a public performance and that the radio station's broadcast and the hotel's receiving that broadcast were two distinct performances.

In 1931, a second performing rights organization began operating in the United States. The Society of European Stage Authors and Composers (SESAC) originally represented European composers and publishers. SESAC began to establish itself in the fields of country and gospel music and, although much smaller than ASCAP and BMI, is currently active in representing songwriters and publishers of all styles of music.

In the 1930s, ASCAP increased the license fees it charged to radio stations. Broadcasters claimed that ASCAP's practices constituted monopolistic price fixing and that radio airplay was a source of free advertising for sheet music and records. With ASCAP's licenses about to expire the next year, broadcasters formed their own society, Broadcast Music Incorporated (BMI) in 1939. Broadcasters refused to agree to increased license fees and BMI began acquiring songs, sometimes luring songwriters by paying them advances on future royalty income. On January 1, 1941, the majority of radio stations stopped playing ASCAP music, instead, playing mostly songs in the public domain. As a result, ASCAP eventually agreed to reduce its license fees. Since then, the three performing rights organizations (ASCAP, BMI and SESAC) have co-existed in the United States, each licensing the music of different songwriters and publishers. Although having more than one performing rights organization benefits songwriters and publishers by providing a degree of competition, licensees are less than thrilled at having to obtain licenses from three organizations to play music that they would much rather not pay for at all.

(2) Operation of Performing Rights Organizations

The three American performing rights organizations as well as the over 40 foreign performing rights organizations all operate in a similar manner. In order to get paid for performances of music, songwriters and publishers must join a performing rights organization. A songwriter or publisher who meets standards specified by the organization can join the organization.

Although the exact requirements differ slightly among the different organizations, if you have songs that are being publicly performed on the radio or television, you are eligible to join. Upon joining, the songwriter or publisher transfers the nonexclusive right to license non-dramatic public performances of its songs to the organization.

The performing rights organizations have three main responsibilities: (1) issuing licenses and collecting license fees; (2) monitoring public performances of music; and (3) paying songwriters and publishers based on the number of performances of their music.

The performing rights organizations issue licenses to businesses that allow public performances of music to occur such as radio stations, television stations and live performance venues. Most of the licenses issued by the performing rights organizations are blanket licenses giving the licensee the right to publicly perform any music in the performing rights organization's repertory an unlimited number of times for a set fee. The amount of a blanket license fee depends on several factors, but is essentially based upon the licensee's potential audience size, gross revenues and the amount of music used. Each of the performing rights organizations has a fee schedule that specifies the fees for different types of licensees. The highest blanket license fees are paid by network television stations since performances broadcast over network television reach the largest audience.

> **Tip:** Performance licenses are obtained by the performance venue rather than the performer. In other words, if a band plays copyrighted music at a bar, it is the bar's responsibility to obtain a performance license rather than the band. Not only does the band not have to worry about obtaining a performance license, it doesn't even have to be concerned with what music it performs since the performing rights organizations are responsible for this (even though they don't monitor performances of live music in the vast majority of live performance venues). In contrast, some foreign countries impose obligations on performers to keep track of the music they perform. In England, performers are required to file a report specifying the music to be performed.

Although blanket licenses are by far the most common type of performance license, copyright owners may issue other types of performance licenses. Direct licenses and source licenses are sometimes obtained for the performance of music on television. Direct licenses are obtained by the television broadcaster, while source licenses are obtained by the producer of the television program. Both direct and source licenses are usually issued for a one-time fee rather than a royalty based on the number of performances.

> **Tip:** If a publisher or songwriter issues a direct or source license, they should inform their performing rights organization of the song, the songwriters, the publishers, the licensee and the term of the license in order to receive performance royalties for performances authorized by a direct or source license.

Another type of performance license is the per-program license, which covers the music performed during a particular television program. Fees for per-program licenses are negotiated between the performing rights organizations and television industry associations and are paid on a monthly basis. A per-program licensee is required to submit a cue sheet listing the specific music performed on the program, the times the program is broadcast and other relevant information.

> **Tip:** Performance rights organizations only license non-dramatic public performances of music. A license to use music in a dramatic performance such as a play must be obtained directly from the copyright owner.

Since there are millions of public performances of music taking place, it would be impractical to attempt to keep track of all performances. The costs of doing so would greatly exceed the license fees collected. Instead, the performing rights organizations use sampling procedures to estimate the number of times songs are performed. The majority of performances sampled are radio and television broadcasts. Live performances, other than at major concert venues, are not sampled. Instead, the performing rights organizations assume that live performances are generally the same as broadcast performances. Obviously, this assumption is a bit flawed since there are many live performances of music that is not performed on radio or television. This unfortunately results in some songwriters who perform their music in bars and other small venues not being paid royalties for these performances. However, the costs involved in sampling the huge number of live performances that take place in such venues would be disproportionate to the amount of income generated.

The performing rights organizations use formulas to assign a value or weight to different performances. Some of the factors taken into consideration by these formulas include the size of the potential audience (e.g., a network television performance would receive a greater weight than a local radio performance), the time of the performance (e.g., a performance at 5 p.m. would receive a greater weight than a performance at 2 a.m.), and the type of performance (e.g., a featured performance would receive a greater weight than a background performance). Based on these weights, different types of performances are assigned different values. For example, a radio broadcast which takes place at 5 p.m. might be worth five times the value of a broadcast which takes place at 2 a.m. (reflecting the size of the listening audience at the different times). The estimated number of performances of a song is then multiplied by the value of different types of performances to reach a dollar amount.

ASCAP and BMI are non-profit organizations. From the total license fees collected, ASCAP and BMI first deduct their operating expenses and then distribute the remaining money among their songwriters and publishers. Operating expenses are generally between 15-20% of the total income collected, so songwriters and publishers receive 80-85% of the total income collected. SESAC, which is a for-profit organization, distributes over 50% of the income it collects to its songwriters and publishers, keeping the remaining income to cover its operating expenses and make a profit. Some songwriters assume that since SESAC pays only 50% of its collections to the publishers and songwriters, they will receive less money than from ASCAP or BMI. This is not necessarily true since SESAC is a for-profit organization and is not subject to many of the restrictions ASCAP and BMI are such as government approval of their license fees.

The performing rights organizations pay 50% of the amount due for performances of a song to the publisher or publishers who own the copyright to the song and 50% to the songwriter or songwriters who wrote the song.[5] The 50% of performance royalties paid to the publisher(s) is commonly known as the "publishers' share" and the 50% paid to the writer(s) is known as the "writers' share."

Example 7.3:

If a song composed by two authors, each of which has a publishing contract with a separate music publisher, earns $10,000 in royalties, the performing rights organization will pay $2500 to each of the publishers and songwriters. The publishers' share of income (i.e., $5000) is split among the two publishers and the writers' share of income (i.e., $5000) is split among the two writers.

(3) Foreign Performing Rights Organizations

Although ASCAP was the first performing rights organization in the United States, the idea to form a collection organization was not an original one. SACEM, the Societe des Auteurs, Compositeurs et Editeurs de Musique had been in existence since 1851 in France. The formation of SACEM resulted from similar circumstances that led to the formation of ASCAP in the United States. In 1847, a French composer named Bourget got upset after hearing one of his songs played at a restaurant. While drinking a glass of wine he had ordered, Bourget complained to the restaurant owner about the unauthorized performance and offered to accept the glass of wine free in return for the performance. The restaurant owner refused and Bourget sued him for copyright infringement and won.

Today, virtually every country in the world has a performing rights organization. Foreign performing rights organizations license performances and collect license fees for performances that take place in their country. The three American performing rights organizations have reciprocal agreements with these foreign organizations that provide a way for American songwriters and publishers to get paid for foreign performances of their music.

D. LIMITATIONS ON THE PUBLIC PERFORMANCE RIGHT

Although a copyright owner has the right to publicly perform copyrighted works that it owns, this right is not absolute. Under the 1909 Copyright Act, copyright owners only had the right to control for-profit performances. This provision proved to be very problematic since distinguishing for-profit performances from non-profit performances was not always easy. Instead of retaining this distinction, the 1976 Copyright Act provided for a broad performance right which applies regardless of whether a performance is for-profit or not. However, § 110 of the 1976 Copyright Act provides several exemptions from the performance right for certain types of uses. Most of these exemptions apply to certain non-profit, educational or charitable uses, which Congress believed to be in the public interest or which would cause only minor loss of income to copyright owners.

(1) Face-to-Face Teaching Activities

Section 110(1) exempts the performance of copyrighted works:

by instructors or pupils in the course of face-to-face teaching activities of a nonprofit educational institution, in a classroom or similar place devoted to instruction.

This exemption allows teachers and students to read aloud from copyrighted books, to play or sing musical works, and to perform motion pictures.

In order to fit within the § 110(1) exemption, four conditions must be met. First, the performance can only be by students or teachers. If a band plays a concert in a school, the exemption will not apply. However, if a musician is brought into a class as a guest lecturer and performs copyrighted music as part of the lecture, the exemption will apply.

Second, the performance must be made in the course of face-to-face teaching activities and must be for teaching purposes rather than merely for entertainment. This means that the teacher and students must be in the same place. If a performance is broadcast (e.g., on radio or television) or transmitted (e.g., via the Internet) to a classroom, the exemption will not apply. Additionally, even if a teacher performs copyrighted music in a classroom, the purpose of the performance must be somehow related to what is being taught.

Third, the place where the teaching activities occur must be a nonprofit educational institution. A performance that takes place in a for-profit institution will not qualify for this exemption. For instance, a performance of copyrighted music in a dance studio or an aerobics class would not be exempt under § 110(1).

Lastly, the performance must take place in a classroom or similar place devoted to instruction. This does not necessarily mean that the place where the performance occurs must be a full-time classroom. For instance, a performance that takes place in an auditorium would be exempt as long as there is an instructional purpose. In contrast, a performance in an auditorium during a school play or a performance in a school gym during a sporting event would not be exempt.

If, in my copyright law classes, I sing a copyrighted song in order to illustrate that a performance that occurs in face-to-face teaching activities is covered by the § 110(1) exemption and therefore not an infringement of copyright, my performance would fit within the § 110(1) exemption. However, if I performed a copyrighted song just to entertain my students (though the entertainment value of such a performance other than for comedic purposes would be dubious at best), the § 110(1) exemption would not be applicable.

(2) Instructional Broadcasts

Under § 110(2), performances made in connection with transmissions for certain instructional purposes and to specified instructional settings are exempt. This exemption is similar to the 110(1) exemption except that it applies to transmissions of a performance. It applies only to nondramatic literary or musical works and therefore would not be applicable to a television broadcast of a dramatic work such as an opera.

Three requirements must be met to fit within the § 110(2) exemption. First, the performance transmitted must be "a regular part of the systematic instructional activities of a governmental body or a nonprofit educational institution." Second, the performance must be "directly related and of material assistance to the teaching content of the transmission." As in the face-to-face teaching exemption, this means that the performance must be used for teaching purposes rather than simply for entertainment. Third, the transmission must be made primarily for reception in "classrooms or similar places normally devoted to instruction."

In one of my copyright classes, I sing a song in order to illustrate how the song could be infringed. If, in addition to being heard by students in the classroom, my performance is transmitted to copyright law classes in other locations, the transmissions would be exempt under §110(2). As distance education and web-based classes become commonplace, this exemption will take on increased importance.

(3) Religious Services

Section 110(3) provides an exemption for performances of nondramatic literary or musical works and dramatic musical works of a religious nature "in the course of services at a place of worship or other religious assembly." Since this exemption includes dramatic as well as non-dramatic works, performances of religious works such as masses and choral services may be exempt. In contrast, performances of secular dramatic works are not exempt even though they contain some religious subject matter.

Example 7.6:

A performance of the musical *Jesus Christ Superstar* (a dramatic work) would not be exempt under § 110(3) since, even though it is about Jesus, it is a secular work.

To fit within the religious services exemption, a performance must be made during the course of religious services. Performances that take place at a place of worship, but are for social, educational, fund raising or entertainment purposes would not be exempt. Additionally, a performance must take place "at a place of worship or other religious assembly." For instance, a performance at a person's home would not be exempt even if a religious service took place in the home.

Example 7.7:

If a group of Satan worshippers play Beatles songs backwards during their religious services held at their church, the religious services exemption would be applicable. If, however, the Satan worshippers played Beatles songs backwards in order to raise money to help promote Satan worship, the performance would not be exempt since it would be for fund raising rather than a religious purpose.

(4) Nonprofit Performances of Nondramatic Literary or Musical Works

Section 110(4) provides an exemption for certain nonprofit performances of nondramatic literary or musical works. There are four requirements that must be satisfied in order to fit within this exemption. First, the exemption does not include transmissions of performances and is therefore limited to performances made directly in the presence of an audience whether by live performers or the playing of recorded music. It would not include radio or television broadcast performances since such performances constitute transmissions.

Second, the performance must be for non-profit purposes. There cannot be any direct or indirect commercial purpose for the performance. The exemption is not applicable to any profit-making performances even if the public is not charged a fee to see or hear the performance.

Third, the performers, promoters and organizers of the performance cannot receive any compensation. This requirement is intended to prevent the free use of copyrighted works under the guise of charity.

Fourth, there cannot be any direct or indirect admission charge unless the proceeds go solely to educational, religious or charitable purposes. Section 110(4) gives copyright owners the right to prevent performances where there is an admission charge even if the proceeds are for educational, religious or charitable purposes in order to allow copyright owners to prevent performances of their works in connection with charities which they do not support. A copyright owner can give written objection stating the reasons for the objection at least seven days before the performance. The usefulness of this objection right is limited since a copyright owner will often not be aware that a charitable organization intends to perform its song in a fundraising event. However, it is also possible for performing rights organizations to give blanket objection notices to all potential users covering all performances of works within their repertories.

Example 7.8:

Benefit concerts such as Farm Aid where admission fees are used to cover the costs of the event and any excess goes to charity will generally fit the requirements of the § 110(4) exemption. However, if a benefit concert was intended to raise money for abortion rights and a copyright owner of a song to be performed was a pro-life advocate, the copyright owner could prevent the use of its work by sending written notice stating its objection to the use.

(5) The Homestyle Receiving Apparatus Exemption

One of the most problematic situations involving performance rights has involved performances that take place in business establishments. Many businesses cause public performances of music to take place, but few want to pay for those performances.

Section § 110(5) of the Copyright Act provides an exemption (sometimes referred to as the "small business exemption") for businesses who play radio or television broadcasts on standard radio or television equipment. There are three requirements necessary to fit within this exemption. First, the reception of the transmission containing the performance must be on a single receiving apparatus of a kind commonly used in private homes. Second, no direct charge can be made to see or hear the transmission. Finally, the transmission cannot be further transmitted to the public.

Many problems in applying the homestyle exemption resulted from the difficulty in determining what type of equipment constituted "a single receiving apparatus of a kind commonly used in private homes." The intention of this requirement was to apply to situations where a business plays music or television broadcasts over an ordinary receiving system commonly sold for in-home use. Factors that could be considered in order to determine whether a sound system was a home-style or commercial sound system include size, physical arrangement, areas within the establishment where the transmissions take place, and the extent to which the receiving apparatus is altered or augmented to improve transmission quality for the audience. Many court cases have construed the extent of the homestyle exemption, with the results being inconsistent from one case to another.

Example 7.9:

In *Cass County Music Co. v. Muedini*,[6] a restaurant in Wisconsin used a Radio Shack receiver connected by concealed speaker wire to nine speakers that were recessed into a dropped acoustic tile ceiling to provide background music for its customers. Between 1985 and 1991, ASCAP sent letters and visited the restaurant in order to get the restaurant owner to obtain a performance license for $327. The owner repeatedly refused and ASCAP sued. The court held that the restaurant did not qualify for the § 110(5) exemption since the nine speaker system used was not the type of sound system commonly used in a home.

Example 7.10:

In *Sailor Music v. The Gap Stores, Inc.*,[7] a radio broadcast in two Gap stores (each of which occupied about 3500 square feet) was held not exempt. The court noted that the stores were "of sufficient size to justify, as a practical matter, a subscription to a commercial background music service."

Example 7.11:

In *Springsteen v. Plaza Roller Dome, Inc.*,[8] the defendant operated a putt-putt golf course which received radio broadcasts of copyrighted songs. The receiving apparatus used by the golf course consisted of a radio receiver wired to six separate speakers mounted on light poles interspersed over the 7,500 square foot area of the course. The defendant argued that since its speakers were fairly poor quality, did not project well, and were inferior to many home systems, and the golf course was not of sufficient size to justify a subscription to a commercial background music system, it should be exempt. The court agreed and found that the golf course qualified for the § 110(5) exemption. The court's decision seems to be based more on its belief that the golf course was too small to bother with rather than an interpretation of § 110(5) since few people are likely to have six speakers mounted to light poles spread over 7500 square feet in their homes. The court also mistakenly emphasized that the golf course generated very limited revenue. However, the § 110(5) exemption is not conditioned on whether a business is profitable or not. It would be extremely unfair if businesses could avoid all of their financial obligations if they are unprofitable or only modestly profitable.

Example 7.12:

In *Broadcast Music, Inc. v. Claire's Boutiques, Inc.*,[9] a court held that § 110(5) exempted a retail chain store, despite the store's relatively large size and revenues. Claire's provided most of its stores with a Radio Shack 5-watt stereo receiver and two Realistic speakers. The receivers were connected to hidden speakers by wire running above dropped ceilings. The court identified four factors referred to in the statute: (1) the number of receiving apparatuses; (2) whether the sound system is of a type commonly used in private homes; (3) whether music is further transmitted; and (4) whether the establishment charges admission. The court believed that infringement occurs only when the user either uses any non-home type components or arranges the components in a non-home type configuration. According to the court, the store used only home-type equipment arranged in a typical configuration.

Due partly to the inconsistencies in interpreting the homestyle exemption and mostly to very strong lobbying by the National Restaurant Association, an amendment (The Fairness in Music Licensing Act) was passed to the Copyright Act in 1998 which provides an additional exemption to many small businesses.

(6) The Fairness in Music Licensing Act

In 1993, the National Restaurant Association and other groups began lobbying Congress to change the law arguing that the homestyle exemption was too difficult to interpret. From 1993 to 1998, music industry organizations resisted the National Restaurant Association's efforts. However, in a clever political move, the National Restaurant Association persuaded Congress to combine the Fairness in Music Licensing Act with another bill designed to add 20 years to the term of copyright. Due to the desire to pass the term extension bill, Congress passed the Fairness in Music Licensing Act in 1998.

The Fairness in Music Licensing Act provides a much broader exemption than the homestyle exemption. Under the Fairness in Music Licensing Act, certain businesses which perform music received from licensed radio, television, cable and satellite broadcasts are exempt. The exemption does not apply to live performances.

There are three requirements that must be satisfied to fit within the exemption. First, the business cannot re-transmit a performance beyond its establishment. Second, no admission fee can be charged. Third, the business must meet certain size requirements. Specifically, restaurants and bars must be smaller than 3,750 square feet while any other retail businesses must be smaller than 2000 square feet. However, if a business exceeds the size limitations, it can still qualify for the exemption if it uses six or fewer speakers with no more than four speakers in any one room or uses audiovisual equipment consisting of no more than four television sets with no more than one in each room and none having a diagonal screen size greater than 55 inches.

A business which claims to be subject to the exemption, but which does not satisfy the requirements can be subject to damages (beyond those available for copyright infringement) of up to 2 times the amount of the license fee that should have been paid during the preceding 3-year period when the business did not have reasonable grounds to believe it was exempt.

It is possible that The Fairness in Music Licensing Act as well as the § 110(5) homestyle receiver exemption are violations of two treaties, the Berne Convention and the TRIPS Agreement. The European Commission filed a complaint to the World Trade Organization objecting to these exemptions in American copyright law. In order for the U.S. to be in compliance with these treaties, the Fairness in Music Licensing Act may have to be repealed although it appears that the U.S. prefers to ignore its treaty obligations.

(7) Retail Record Sales

Section 110(7) provides an exemption for performances of nondramatic musical works in connection with the sale of phonorecords or sheet music that embody the works. This exemption is intended to allow stores that sell recordings to play them in order to promote sales. In order to qualify for this exemption, the store must: (1) be open to the public at large; (2) not receive any direct or indirect admission charge; (3) perform the records for the sole purpose of promoting record sales; and (4) not transmit the performance beyond the store.

Example 7.13:

A record store such as Tower Records which plays recordings in-store would fit within the § 110(7) exemption. Even though such performances serve as entertainment for customers, their primary purpose is at least arguably to interest customers in buying a copy of the record being performed. Years ago, when I managed a record store, an employee who happened to be in a rock band often played loud rock records in the morning while the only customers in the store were a few senior citizens. Arguably, this performance would not fit the exemption since its primary purpose was to entertain the employee rather than to promote record sales.

A 1998 amendment to the Copyright Act (part of the Fairness in Music Licensing Act) expanded the retail exemption to include retailers whose sole purpose in performing recorded music is to promote the sale of recording equipment such as radios, stereo systems and televisions used for the playback of music. Accordingly, a store such as Circuit City, which sells stereo playback equipment, would be covered by the exemption even if it didn't also sell recordings.

(8) Jukebox Performances

Under the 1909 Copyright Act, jukebox performances were exempt from performance licensing as long as the business where the jukebox was located did not charge an admission fee. The 1976 Copyright Act eliminated this exemption and instead imposed a compulsory license on jukebox operators, which required an annual fee for each jukebox. When the United States joined the Berne Convention in 1988, it was forced to eliminate the compulsory license provision since the Berne Convention does not permit compulsory licensing of non-broadcast performances. The Copyright Act's compulsory license provision was replaced with a provision that encourages the music publishing and jukebox industries to negotiate licenses. If the parties cannot agree, they can submit the fee dispute to arbitration.

In 1990, a ten-year agreement called the Jukebox License Agreement was reached between the Amusement and Music Operators Association and the three American performing rights organizations. The agreement was renewed in 1999 and provides for annual rates starting at $323 for the first jukebox, $61 for the next nine jukeboxes and $50 each for all subsequent jukeboxes.

(9) Noncommercial Broadcasting

Although public broadcasters are not exempt from performance licensing, § 118 of the Copyright Act provides for a compulsory license permitting the performance of published, non-dramatic musical works. The rationale for this compulsory license is that public broadcasters should have easy access to copyrighted works. In order to obtain a compulsory license, the performance must be by public broadcasting entities by or in the course of transmissions made by noncommercial, educational broadcast stations. Royalty rates under the compulsory license are significantly lower than those paid by commercial broadcasters and are determined by copyright arbitration royalty panels. Section 118 also provides that the compulsory license provisions may be altered by voluntary licenses between the parties that must be filed with the Copyright Office.

E. SOUND RECORDINGS AND THE PERFORMANCE RIGHT

Although the public performance right applies to musical compositions, with one exception (the Digital Performance Right in Sound Recordings Act discussed below), it does not apply to sound recordings. Section 114(a) specifically provides that:

The exclusive rights of the owner of copyright in a sound recording do not include any right of performance under section 106(4).

Since sound recordings were added to the Copyright Act as a type of copyrightable work in 1972, the record industry has wanted to extend the public performance right to sound recordings, but its attempts to do so have been unsuccessful due to resistance from the broadcasting industry. Broadcasters do not want to have to pay more than what they are already obligated to pay to copyright owners of musical works. Broadcasters also argue that free radio airplay of sound recordings benefits artists and record companies by promoting record sales and live performances. The practical result is that if a recording of a copyrighted song is broadcast over the radio, on television, or performed in a live setting, the copyright owner of the song (typically a music publisher) and the songwriter will receive a royalty for the performance while the copyright owner of the sound recording (typically a record company) and the recording artist will not.

Example 7.14:

The song "I Don't Wanna Miss a Thing" was written by Diane Warren and is owned by her publishing company, Realsongs. Aerosmith's recording of the song became their first number one single. Another recording of the song became a number one country single for Mark Chestnutt. Although both the Aerosmith and Mark Chestnutt recordings received substantial radio airplay, neither Aerosmith, Chestnutt nor the record companies that released their records received any performance royalties from that airplay. However, Diane Warren and Realsongs earned a fortune in performance royalties as the songwriter and copyright owner of the song.

The lack of a performance right in sound recordings creates several inequities. First, many foreign countries recognize a performance right in sound recordings. However, copyright owners of sound recordings in the United States do not receive royalties for performances of their recordings in these countries since most international copyright treaties provide for reciprocal treatment. In other words, since U.S. copyright law doesn't provide for royalties to be paid for the performance of foreign copyrighted sound recordings in the U.S., foreign countries do not pay for performances of U.S. copyrighted sound recordings. This has a serious adverse impact on the U.S. recording industry since American recordings are performed on an international scale to a much greater degree than recordings from any other country.

Another problem is that since performance royalties earned by songwriters and copyright owners of songs contained on sound recordings can be a substantial source of income, many artists and producers are eager to record songs that they write even if their songs are not as good as many other songs available. An even more unfortunate result is that some artists and producers who are not songwriters insist on songwriting credit or partial song ownership as a condition to recording someone else's song so that they can receive part of the income earned by the song. This practice is commonly referred to as a "cut-in" which, despite being unethical, occurs fairly commonly.

F. THE DIGITAL PERFORMANCE RIGHT IN SOUND RECORDINGS ACT

For several decades, the recording industry had unsuccessfully tried to convince Congress to amend the Copyright Act to recognize a right of public performance for sound recordings. By 1990, Congress began to be concerned with the impact that digital technology would have on the record industry.[10] Over the next several years, Congress conducted hearings, examined reports, supervised negotiations, and considered several bills to amend the Copyright Act. Finally, in 1995, Congress amended the Copyright Act by enacting the Digital Performance Rights in Sound Recordings Act (DPRSRA), which granted a limited public performance right for sound recordings.

The DPRSRA is a very detailed and complicated piece of legislation.[11] Its complexity is primarily due to the competing interests of protecting sound recording copyright owners from losses caused by digital audio technology while allowing digital technology to advance and flourish. The DPRSRA made two basic changes to copyright law affecting the use of musical works, both of which have turned out to be very important in the context of music distribution over the Internet. First, the DPRSRA added a new exclusive right of public performance for sound recordings. Second, the DPRSRA expanded the compulsory mechanical license provision to include the reproduction and distribution of musical compositions in digital format *(discussed in chapter 5)*.

Although the DPRSRA was intended to provide sound recording copyright owners with protection in the digital environment, it failed to anticipate some of the developments that took place in connection with the digital transmission of music. For example, disagreements had developed between record companies and online music services over whether they were required to pay public performance royalties to record companies and recording artists under the DPRSRA. Consequently, the Digital Millennium Copyright Act (DMCA), which was passed in 1998, contains some provisions amending the DPRSRA, the most important of which extended the digital performance right to the practice of webcasting.[12] The following discussion of the DPRSRA consequently includes the relevant amendments made by the DMCA.

The DPRSRA amended the list of exclusive rights specified in § 106(6) of the Copyright Act by giving copyright owners of sound recordings the exclusive right "to perform the copyrighted work publicly by means of a digital audio transmission" subject to certain conditions and limitations. A digital audio transmission is defined as a digital transmission "that embodies the transmission of a sound recording."

At the time of the DPRSRA's passage, the Internet was not in common usage and the main types of digital audio transmissions contemplated were transmissions made by cable and satellite. However, the definition of digital audio transmission is also broad enough to include transmissions made over the Internet such as webcasting *(discussed in more detail in chapter 14)*.

One digital audio cable service, DMX, offers more than 100 channels of music of various genres available twenty-four hours a day, seven days a week. DMX's programming is played on CD players, whose signals are uplinked to satellite and downlinked to local cable systems, regional telephone companies and direct satellite dish subscribers. The programming is commercial-free and customers pay a subscription fee.

There are several basic limitations on the § 106(6) performance right in sound recordings. First, the sound recording performance right applies only to performances made by "digital" audio transmission. This means that radio and television performances of sound recordings are not subject to § 106(6) since these broadcasts are analog rather than digital. Second, the right only applies to transmissions involving the communication of a performance where the recorded sounds are received beyond the place from which they are sent. It does not apply to performances that are not transmitted, such as live performances or playing recorded music in business establishments. Third, the right only applies to digital transmissions of sound recordings. It does not apply to digital transmissions of audiovisual works since audiovisual works are subject to the performance right of § 106(4). Fourth, the right only applies to digital audio transmissions that are "publicly" performed. For instance, it does not apply to audio files transmitted to a friend.

Referring back to example 7.14, the performance of the Aerosmith or Mark Chestnut recordings of "I Don't Wanna Miss a Thing" are not subject to the § 106(6) performance right since the radio broadcasts are analog rather than digital. However, public performances of the same recordings over the Internet are subject to the § 106(6) performance right.

In addition to the basic limitations discussed above, there are some additional limitations that are dependent upon the specific type of performance being made. These limitations are very technical in nature, but are all motivated by a concern for protecting copyright owners of sound recordings from public performances of sound recordings that could be easily used by people to make high quality, digital

copies of the recorded music without having to pay for them.

The DPRSRA classifies digital audio transmissions into three categories, which determine whether a license is required, and if so, what type of license is required for the performance. The rationale for this classification is that certain types of transmissions are more likely than others to displace record sales. If there is very little likelihood of displacing record sales, the transmission is exempt from the digital public performance right and a license is not required. If there is a high likelihood of displacing record sales, the transmitter must negotiate a license with the sound recording copyright owner. Finally, if there is a only a moderate likelihood of displacing record sales, a compulsory license is available.

(1) Exempt Performances

Some digital audio transmissions of sound recordings are exempt from the digital public performance right and licenses are not required for these types of transmissions. The reason these transmissions are exempt is that they are not likely to displace record sales since they do not give listeners advance notice of the recordings to be played and do not contain all of the songs from an artist's album.

The main type of exempt transmission is the "non-subscription transmission." Non-subscription transmissions are like traditional radio broadcasts except that they transmit performances of sound recordings in digital rather than analog form. Services making these transmissions do not charge any subscription fee to listeners. Additionally, they are non-interactive which means that the transmitter rather than the listeners decide what music is transmitted. Interactive services, on the other hand, transmit digital performances of music chosen by listeners.

Initially, under the DPRSRA, retransmissions of radio broadcasts (e.g., digitally transmitting an AM or FM radio broadcast over the Internet) were exempt. However, the Copyright Office recently issued a regulation stating that transmissions of an AM/FM broadcast signal over a digital communications network, such as the Internet, are subject to the sound recording copyright owner's digital public performance right. At the time of the writing of this book, the radio industry is challenging the Copyright Office regulation in court although they are not likely to be successful. Consequently, radio stations that simulcast their broadcasts over the Internet must obtain compulsory licenses for the sound recordings to be transmitted.[13]

WXYZ broadcasts its signal over-the-air and webcasts or simulcasts that broadcast over the Internet. WXYZ must either obtain compulsory licenses and pay royalties for the right to publicly perform sound recordings over the Internet since these performances involve digital audio transmissions. However, WXYZ is not required to obtain any licenses for the right to broadcast its FM signal over-the-air since these performances are analog rather than digital in nature. Additionally, WXYZ must obtain licenses from the performing rights organizations allowing it to broadcast the various musical compositions contained on the sound recordings it broadcasts and webcasts.

(2) Performances Subject to Compulsory Licenses

Some subscription transmissions (i.e., where customers pay subscription fees to hear the transmissions), although not exempt, are subject to a compulsory license since they are not too likely to displace record sales. The types of services that make subscription transmissions available include satellite and cable companies which offer digital performances to subscribers, webcasters which transmit recordings over the Internet, and companies which transmit music to specially equipped automobiles, cell phones, and other devices. To be subject to the compulsory license, a subscription transmission must satisfy the following detailed requirements that exist primarily to prevent home taping of sound recordings:

Non-Interactivity: The transmission must be non-interactive, meaning that it cannot allow listeners to choose what recordings they will hear.

Sound Recording Performance Complement: The transmission cannot, during any three-hour period, contain: (1) more than two consecutive songs or more than three songs in total from any individual sound recording; (2) more than three consecutive songs or more than four songs in total by the same recording artist.

No Advance Notice: The transmitter cannot publish advance notice of the recordings to be transmitted. It is permissible to specify what artists will be played in order to illustrate the types of music that will be available and to identify titles of songs immediately before they are performed.

No Automatic Switching: The transmitter cannot automatically switch listeners from one channel to another.

Archived Programs: Archived programs are programs posted on a web site for listeners to hear repeatedly on demand. Archived programs cannot be less than five hours duration. Additionally, archived programs cannot be posted for more than two weeks. The DMCA also prohibits merely changing a few songs in an archived program to avoid this condition.

Looped Programs: Programs performed continuously (i.e., repeated over and over) cannot be less than three hours in duration.

Identifiable Programs: Programs of less than one hour which contain performances of recordings in a predetermined order for which the transmission times have been announced in advance (identifiable programs) cannot be transmitted more than three times in a two-week period. Identifiable programs of more than one hour cannot be transmitted more than four times in a two-week period.

Scanning Prevention: The transmitter must cooperate with copyright owners to prevent listeners from using devices that scan transmissions for particular artists or recordings.

Advertising Prohibition: Transmitters are prohibited from falsely suggesting any connection between a song's copyright owner or recording artist with any products or services.

Copy Prevention: The transmitter cannot cause or aid listeners in making copies of transmitted recordings and must, when possible, use technology to prevent copying by listeners.

No Bootlegs: Bootleg recordings cannot be transmitted.

Identifying Information: The transmitter must identify, during but not before the time of the transmission, the title of songs performed, the recording artist and the album title.

Encoded Information: The transmitter cannot interfere with any identifying information (i.e., title, name of artist, name of copyright owner, etc.) encoded in recordings. This differs from identifying information since encoded information is embedded in sound recordings to track use rather than to provide identifying information to listeners.

a. How Are Compulsory Licenses Obtained?

If you qualify for the compulsory license, you must file a notice of intent to obtain a compulsory license with the Copyright Office. The notice should specify your full legal name, address, phone number, fax number and the date of first transmission. It must also be accompanied by a $20 filing fee. You can then make ephemeral copies of sound recordings (i.e., copying selections from different sound recordings) that can only be used for Internet transmissions by means of streaming technology and must be destroyed within six months unless preserved solely for archival purposes.

b. What Will the Compulsory Royalty Rate Be?

At the time of this book's writing, the royalty rate for the compulsory license had not been determined. The Digital Millennium Copyright Act gave webcasters and record companies one year to agree on a rate, but their efforts were unsuccessful. The recording industry requested the rate be 0.4 cents per recording; webcasters have asked for a rate 30 times lower than that. Consequently, the rate is to be determined by a Copyright Arbitration Royalty Panel and will probably be decided by early 2002.

c. Who Gets the Money?

The DPRSRA specifies how royalties earned under statutory licenses are to be distributed. After the licensing agent deducts its collection fee, royalties are paid to the record company, which keeps fifty percent and distributes the remaining fifty percent to the creative contributors to the sound recording as follows:[14]

45 percent to the featured artist

2.5 percent to any non-featured musicians (backup musicians that are not part of the recording artist)

2.5 percent to any non-featured vocalists

A controversy has arisen over who will license and collect royalties for non-interactive webcasting. The Recording Industry Association of America (RIAA) has formed an organization called Sound Exchange that will collect royalties for more than 300 record labels, including all of the major labels, which distribute close to 90 percent of the records sold worldwide. In return for its services, Sound Exchange is entitled to keep a percentage of the royalties it collects to cover its administrative costs. Under copyright law, this percentage must be a reasonable amount. Reportedly, Sound Exchange plans on keeping 16-20 percent of the royalties it collects.

Several organizations have expressed concern about an RIAA-affiliated organization being in charge of the licensing and royalty distribution process. Their concern is that the RIAA will favor the major record companies or will find some way not to pay artists the share they are legally entitled to. Although the DMCA provides that 45 percent of webcast royalties be paid to featured performers, many contracts between artists and record labels contain provisions allowing for recoupment of various expenses which could prevent artists from actually receiving any of these royalties.

The DMCA does not require that there be just one licensing organization and several other organizations have expressed interest in operating as a licensing agent for sound recordings. However, in practical terms, the RIAA's Sound Exchange is one of only a few organizations that is likely to be capable of acting as such a licensing agent. Due to the volume of recordings and the even greater volume of webcasted performances of those recordings, operating as a licensing agent is not a simple task. It will require maintaining an enormous computerized database designed to keep track of sound recordings, webcast performances of those recordings, and the parties entitled to royalties from those performances.

(3) Performances Subject to Negotiated Licenses

Some digital transmissions of sound recordings have a high likelihood of displacing record sales. Consequently, the only way such transmissions can be made is by negotiating licenses with the copyright owners. The types of transmissions for which licenses must be negotiated include interactive transmissions and subscription transmissions, which do not qualify for the compulsory license described above.

Interactive transmissions allow listeners to choose the recordings they will hear and therefore have a relatively high potential to displace record sales. For instance, a consumer could choose all of the recordings by a particular artist rather than buying any of that artist's recordings. An artist or the artist's record company might choose not to negotiate licenses for all of the artist's recordings in order to avoid this potential scenario.

For webcasters, obtaining negotiated licenses is not a very practical option since they would have to negotiate with many different record companies for many different sound recordings. However, if a record company agreed to issue a license to a webcaster, the webcaster would pay the record company the agreed upon fee or royalty directly. The record company would then be responsible for paying the recording artist according to the royalty provisions of their recording contact.

Example 7.18:

On May 24, 2001, the Recording Industry Association of America (RIAA) filed a lawsuit against webcasting company, Launch Media Inc. The RIAA claims that record companies sound recording copyrights are being infringed by the Launch service, which allows users to influence what recordings they hear in streamed webcasts. The RIAA therefore claims that since Launch's service is interactive, it cannot obtain compulsory licenses and would have to negotiate with each record company to use their recordings. This suit was subsequently settled when the parties reached a license agreement.

II. The Public Display Right

Section 106(5) gives copyright owners the exclusive right to display and to authorize others to display the copyrighted work publicly. This right is limited to the display of copyrighted works in copies and not phonorecords. The public display right is therefore not applicable to sound recordings. Although the public display right is applicable to musical works, it is the least important of the copyright owner's exclusive

rights since musical works are generally performed rather than displayed. To display a work means:

to show a copy of it, either directly or by means of a film, slide, television image, or any other device or process or, in the case of a motion picture or other audiovisual work, to show individual images nonsequentially.

The right to display a work includes showing the original work, either directly, as by exhibition in a museum, or indirectly, as by a showing on television, as well as showings of reproductions of the work, such as by transmitting stored text from a data base to a computer screen or by projecting individual images on a screen. The display right does not include the showing of images in sequence, which is instead covered by the performance right.

In order to infringe the display right, a display must be made in public. The display must therefore be made at a public place or must be transmitted or otherwise communicated to a public place.

Example 7.19:

In *ABKCO Music, Inc. v. Stellar Records, Inc.,* the defendant made a product which it called Compact Disc +Graphics (CD+G's). CD+G's were compact discs containing recordings of instrumental versions of popular songs for use in karaoke bars where amateur singers sing along to the recording. In addition to the audio recording, the CD+G's also allowed a song's lyrics to be shown on a television screen for the singer to read. The defendant had obtained compulsory mechanical licenses to record several songs by the Rolling Stones (e.g., Satisfaction, Jumping Jack Flash, etc.) on a CD+G.

ABKCO, the publishing company that owns the copyrights to the Rolling Stones songs, sued for copyright infringement claiming that the compulsory licenses did not include the right to display the song lyrics. The court agreed with ABKCO, holding that showing the lyrics implicated the display right in addition to the reproduction and distribution rights. Although the compulsory licenses covered the reproduction and distribution of the CD+G's, it did not authorize the display of song lyrics.

A. LIMITATIONS ON THE PUBLIC DISPLAY RIGHT

(1) Display of a Single Image at a Single Site

Section 109(c) allows the owner of a copy to display the copy publicly. However, the copy must have been lawfully made and the display must be either a direct display or a display by the projection of no more than one image at a time, to viewers present at the place where the copy is located.

Example 7.20:

If you buy a compact disc, you are free to display the album cover artwork publicly. Similarly, if you buy a copy of a painting by Ringo Starr, you would be able to display it in a museum. However, you would not be able to display the painting on a web site over the Internet since the display made pursuant to § 109 (c) can only be made to viewers present at the place where the copy is located.

---

(2) Display in Situations Where Performance Is Exempted

Several of the exemptions discussed in connection with the public performance right also apply to the display right. Section 110 exempts displays for purposes of face-to-face teaching activities, instructional transmission, religious services and reception by a home receiving apparatus. Additionally, section 118's provisions for compulsory licensing of transmissions by noncommercial educational broadcasting stations apply to displays as well as performances.

1. 1967 House Report.
2. 242 U.S. 591 (1917).
3. *M. Witmark & Sons v. L. Bamberger & Co.*, 291 F. 776 (D.N.J. 1923).
4. *Buck v. Jewell-LaSalle Realty Co.*, 283 U.S. 191 (1931).
5. In contrast to the American system, some foreign performing rights organizations do not follow the equal split of performance royalties between songwriters and publishers. For example, the split for Dutch songs is 2/3 to the writers and 1/3 to the publishers.
1. 55 F.3d 265 (7th Cir. 1995).
6. 516 F. Supp. 923 (S.D.N.Y. 1981).
7. 602 F. Supp. 1113 (M.D.N.C. 1985).

8. 754 F. Supp. 1324 (N.D. Ill. 1990), aff'd, 949 F.2d 1482 (7th Cir. 1991).
9. In 1990, the Senate Subcommittee on Patents, Copyrights, and Trademarks requested a report on the implications of digital audio broadcasts on copyright from the Copyright Office in response to the advent of digital technology. The Copyright Office issued a report in 1991 which primarily addressed the issue of digital home taping of copyrighted works.
10. Senator Orrin Hatch, who co-sponsored the DPRSRA, remarked that it was a "complex" piece of legislation. An article reviewing the DPRSRA referred to Hatch's comment as an understatement stating that "The Internal Revenue Code is 'complex'; the Digital Performance Right in Sound Recordings Act of 1995 is something else. 'Incomprehensible' perhaps, though 'You had to be there to appreciate it' may be fairer, because the convoluted language of the new Act appears to have been required by a number of very specific problems which the Act attempts to address with precision." Lionel S. Sobel, "A New Music Law for the Age of Digital Technology," Vol. 17, No. 6 "Entertainment Law Reporter" p.3 (November, 1995).
11. The webcasting regulations of the DMCA are contained in 17 U.S.C. §§ 112 and 114.
12. Alternatively, a radio station could negotiate individual licenses with the copyright owners of the sound recordings to be transmitted since the law allows for negotiated licenses in place of compulsory licenses. However, it is unlikely that radio stations will want to negotiate licenses due to the great number of sound recordings they will be simulcasting.
13. 17 U.S.C. 114(g)(2).
14. 96 F.3d 60, 40 U.S.P.Q.2d (BNA) 1052 (2d Cir. 1996).

CHAPTER 8

Duration of Copyright

▼

"It is good that authors should be renumerated; and the least exceptionable way of remunerating them is by a monopoly. Yet monopoly is evil. For the sake of good we must submit to evil; but the evil ought not to last a day longer than is necessary for the purpose of securing the good."
Lord Macaulay in a speech delivered to the British House of Commons in 1866

The length of time that copyright protection should last for has been debated since the early 1700s and continues to be a controversial issue. Under the United States Constitution, copyright protection must be limited in duration. In other words, if Congress were to pass a law that provided that copyright would last forever, that law would be unconstitutional. When the term of protection for a copyright ends or expires, the work enters what is referred to as "the public domain." A work that is in the public domain cannot be owned by anyone and anyone is free to use it.

The rules governing the duration or term of copyright can be quite complex, primarily due to the fact that there are different terms of protection for different works. In order to determine which rules are applicable to a particular work, you must first know when the work was created. Works created before 1978 are governed by the provisions of the 1909 Copyright Act, while works created from 1978 to the present are governed by the provisions of the 1976 Copyright Act. However, the duration provisions of both the 1909 and 1976 Acts have been amended on several occasions, which makes things even more complicated.

I. Evolution of Copyright Term

In order to understand the rules governing the duration of copyright, it is helpful to understand how these rules have evolved in the United States. After discussing this evolution, the current rules for copyright duration will be explained.

A. THE 1909 COPYRIGHT ACT

Until 1978, a dual system of copyright existed in the United States. Under the 1909 Copyright Act, federal copyright protection began upon publication of a work with proper copyright notice or on the date of copyright registration for certain unpublished works such as songs. Unpublished works were not protected under the 1909 Act and instead were protected by common law copyright until published. Common law copyright lasted until the work was published or registered as an unpublished work. If a work was never published or registered, it could be protected indefinitely under common law copyright.

Once a work was published or registered, it became subject to the 1909 Copyright Act. The 1909 Act provided for an initial term of 28 years of protection and a renewal term of an additional 28 years. Consequently, the maximum term of protection under the 1909 Copyright Act was 56 years. However, in order to receive protection during the renewal term, a renewal registration had to be made for the work. If a copyright was not renewed properly during the last year of the initial term, the copyright expired and the work entered the public domain.

> **Tip:** The turning point between common law copyright and federal copyright under the 1909 Act revolved around the concept of publication. Publication is defined as the distribution of copies or phonorecords to the public by sale or other transfer of ownership, by rental, lease or lending; or the offer to distribute for purposes of further distribution. For example, if a record company distributes records to retailers, who offer them for sale to the public, publication has occurred. On the other hand, if the distribution is restricted as to who receives the work and the use to be made of it, publication would not have occurred. Also, the performance of a work does not constitute a publication.

The main reason for dividing the term of copyright into two periods (i.e., initial and renewal) was to protect authors. Often, authors of a work transfer rights to their work upon or shortly after creation of a work, before the value of the work is known. The renewal term was intended to protect authors from this situation. According to one court:

These provisions were introduced in response to the problem of unremunerative grants of copyright by authors. Because of the impossibility of predicting the commercial value of a work upon its creation and because of the weak bargaining position of authors, they sometimes assigned their copyrights in return for very little remuneration, such as small lump sum payments or inadequate royalty rates, and were thus prevented from sharing fairly, if at all, in the rewards from works that later became commercial successes. The termination provisions give authors an opportunity to renegotiate in the light of more knowledge as to the value of their works, and thereby obtain a fair share of the rewards from their works.[1]

The renewal right belonged to the author of the work even if the author had previously transferred copyright ownership to someone else. Since the 1976 Copyright Act provides that the renewal requirement continues for works protected by federal copyright prior to 1978,[2] it is still important to have an understanding of the renewal provisions.

(1) Who Can Renew?

The renewal right belongs to the author of the work. If the author dies before the 28th year of the initial term, the renewal right will belong to the author's surviving spouse or children if they are alive upon the 28th year of the initial term. If there is no surviving spouse or children, the renewal right belongs to the author's executor. An executor is a person named in the author's will who acts on behalf of the people named in the author's will. If the author dies without a will, the author's next of kin would be entitled to the renewal right.

If an author dies before the 28th year of the initial term, the author has no right to the renewal term since the right passes to the author's successors as described above. Consequently, if an author had transferred his renewal rights during the initial term, but died before the 28th year of the initial term, his transferee would not have any rights to the renewal term. If the author lived to the 28th year of the initial term, the transferee would have the right to the renewal term even if the author died before the renewal term actually began.

If a work is created by two or more authors (i.e., a joint work), each author has the right to renew the copyright to the work. Any coauthor can file the renewal registration and it is not necessary for all coauthors to join in the renewal.

(2) When to Renew?

Under the 1909 Copyright Act, a copyright owner could file the renewal application at any time during the last (i.e., the 28th) calendar year of the initial term. It was crucial that the renewal registration be made during the 28th year of the initial term since the failure to do so ejected the work into the public domain. Many copyrights expired at the end of the initial term due to the failure to renew. In fact, only about twenty percent of works published before 1978 were renewed.

The Copyright Renewal Act of 1992 amended the 1976 Copyright Act making renewal automatic for works created from 1964 to 1977. However, instead of totally eliminating the renewal system, the Copyright Renewal Act made it optional. Under § 304(a), copyrights in works created from 1964 through 1977 automatically receive a 67-year renewal term. However, works published before 1964 still had to be renewed.

A work published in 1963 had to be renewed in 1991 to receive the renewal term while a work published in 1964 is automatically renewed.

Even though renewal is optional for works created beginning in 1964, there is an important benefit afforded to copyrights for which a renewal registration is filed. If a renewal registration is filed within one year of the expiration of the initial term, the registration certificate constitutes evidence of validity of the copyright and the facts stated in the renewal certificate during the renewal term.[3] This means that a copyright owner who has renewed won't need to call witnesses to prove all of the facts stated in the renewal registration if there is ever a dispute over ownership.

> **Tip:** In the music publishing field, when a publisher has an arrangement or translation of a song made, the resulting work will normally be a work made for hire and the publisher rather than the arranger or translator would be the proper party to file a renewal registration.

(3) Assignment of Renewal Rights

The renewal provision was largely ineffective at achieving its purpose since the Supreme Court held that authors could transfer their rights to the renewal term during the initial term. In *Fred Fisher Music Co. v. M. Witmark & Sons*,[4] the songwriters of "When Irish Eyes Are Smiling" transferred the copyright in the song as well as their renewal rights to a publisher. The Court held that the songwriters' assignment of their renewal rights was valid and that the publisher therefore had the right to renew. After this decision, it became a common practice in publishing contracts for publishers to require that authors assign their right to the renewal term to them.

In order for an assignment of an author's renewal right to be valid, the assignment must explicitly convey the renewal right. For example, an assignment by an author which grants "all of my rights" in a song to a publisher would not be effective at transferring the author's renewal rights since renewal rights are not specifically mentioned.

An author can make a promise to transfer his renewal rights at any time. However, transfers of renewal rights made before the time for renewal (i.e., in the 28th year of the initial term) will be conditioned upon the author's surviving until the time for renewal. Similarly, an author's successors may also promise to transfer their renewal rights, but their promises are also conditioned upon their surviving until the time for renewal. If an author or an author's successors promise to transfer their renewal rights, but die before the 28th year of the initial term, the transferee does not have the right to renew. Instead, the renewal right will belong to the next succeeding successor specified by § 304(a).

A songwriter wrote a song in 1950 and transferred all of his rights to the song, including the renewal right, to a publisher. If the songwriter dies before 1978, leaving a wife and children, the wife and children rather than the publisher will own the renewal right. The rationale for this result is that the songwriter's transfer of the renewal right was conditioned upon his living until 1978.

(4) Termination of Transfer of Renewal Term

An author or the author's heirs have the right to get back copyright ownership for the last thirty nine years of the copyright term by terminating any pre-1978 transfers of the renewal term. This termination right can be exercised during a five-year period beginning 56 years after first publication of the work or January 1, 1978, whichever comes later. The provisions for termination are otherwise essentially the same as the provisions for termination of transfer under section 203 of the 1976 Copyright Act.

> **Tip:** Since the provisions for termination are somewhat complex, it is a good idea to consult with a copyright attorney no later than 54 years after the work's publication (earlier if possible) in order to insure that the termination of pre-1978 works is carried out properly.

B. THE 1976 COPYRIGHT ACT

Duration of copyright under the 1976 Copyright Act differs substantially from duration under the 1909 Act. Under the 1976 Act, copyright protection begins upon creation of the work and is not dependent upon publication. Creation occurs when an original work is fixed in tangible form.

Congress did away with the renewal term and instead decided to base copyright duration on the author's lifetime. The 1976 Act provides that copyright lasts for the life of the author plus an additional 50 years[5] (this period has since been increased to the life of the author plus 70 years). There were several reasons behind Congress' decision to make this change. First, due to increased life expectancies, the 1909 Act's maximum term of 56 years was not sufficient to compensate authors throughout their lives. Second, the renewal requirement often resulted in the inadvertent loss of copyright for many works due to the failure to file a renewal registration. Third, most foreign countries based their term of copyright on the author's lifetime plus a period after death. Finally, with a term based on the author's life, all works of an author enter the public domain at the same time.

> **Tip:** It is important to note that a copyrighted work's duration never changes regardless of any transfers of ownership in the work. The term is based on the original author's life regardless of who owns the copyright.

II. Determining Copyright Duration

In order to determine how long copyright lasts for a particular work, it is helpful to divide works into three categories: (1) works created in 1978 and after; (2) works created but not published before 1978; and (3) works published before 1978. Table 8.1 summarizes the copyright duration rules for works created and published during different time periods.

A. WORKS CREATED FROM 1978 TO PRESENT

For most works created on or after January 1, 1978 (i.e., other than anonymous works, pseudonymous works and works made for hire), the term of copyright begins with the work's creation and ends 70 years after the death of the work's author.

Example 8.3:

If a songwriter wrote a song in 1990 and died in 2000, the song's copyright will last through 2070 (i.e., 2000 + 70 years).

If a work is created by two or more authors (i.e., joint authorship), the term of copyright will last for the life of the last surviving author plus 70 years after the last surviving author's death.[6]

Example 8.4:

If two songwriters write a song in 1990 and one of the songwriters dies in 2000 while the other dies in 2010, the song's copyright will last through 2080.

(1) Anonymous Works, Pseudonymous Works and Works Made for Hire

There are three types of works (i.e., anonymous works, pseudonymous works and works made for hire) that involve authors who are either unknown or not an individual. An anonymous work is a work whose author is not identified in the copyright registration for the work. A pseudonymous work is a work whose author is identified by a fictitious name in the copyright registration. Works made for hire are created by an individual on behalf of an employer. For these types of works, the term of copyright cannot be based upon the life of the author. Instead, the 1976 Copyright Act provides that copyright protection will last for 95 years from the work's first publication or 120 years from the work's creation, whichever expires first.[7] The rationale for having a dual period based on either creation or publication is to have a specific time period for all works, even if unpublished.

Example 8.5:

A song written as a work made for hire is composed in 1995 and released on records (i.e., published) in 2000. The song's copyright will expire in 2095 (95 years from 1st publication). If, on the other hand, the song was not published until 2025, the copyright would expire in 2145 (120 years from creation).

Table 8-1: Copyright Duration

Date of Work	Protection Begins	Duration
Created 1/1/78 & after	On date of fixation in tangible form	General Rule: Life of author + 70 years Joint Works: Life of last surviving author + 70 years Works For Hire, Anonymous & Pseudonymous Works: 95 years from publication or 120 years from creation, whichever is shorter
Created before 1978, but published between 1/1/78 & 12/31/2002	Upon creation under common law; 1/1/78 under 1976 Copyright Act	Life of author + 70 years or 12/31/2047, whichever is longer
Created before 1978, but not published	Upon creation under common law; 1/1/78 under 1976 Copyright Act	Life of author + 70 years or 12/31/2002, whichever is longer
Published from 1964 to 1977	Upon publication with copyright notice (if published without notice, may be in public domain)	28 year initial term + 67 year automatic renewal term
Published from 1923 to 1963	Upon publication with copyright notice (if published without notice, may be in public domain)	28 year initial term + 67 year renewal term (if renewal registration filed during 28th year of initial term)
Published before 1923	In public domain	Expired

In the case of anonymous works and pseudonymous works, the term of copyright can be converted to the life of the author plus 70 years by making the author's identity known to the Copyright Office before the expiration of the 95 or 120 year term.[8] Any person having an interest in a copyright may notify the Copyright Office of the actual author's identity in one of three ways: (1) Registering under the author's true name; (2) Filing a supplementary registration if the work has already been registered; or (3) Recording a statement which specifies the name of the person filing the statement, the nature of that person's interest in the copyright, the title of the work, and the registration number if known.

Tip: If an author believes that he or she is not likely to live longer than 25 years, the author could register works under a pseudonym, thereby potentially receiving a longer term of copyright protection. For instance, if a chain-smoking, heavy-drinking, highly overweight 65-year-old author who does not expect to live to age 90 writes a song in 2000, he might choose to register the song under a pseudonym and the copyright would quite possibly last longer than if the song were registered under the author's actual name. The same result could also be accomplished if the author formed a corporation and wrote songs under work made for hire agreements with the corporation.

(2) How Do You Know If a Copyright Owner Is Dead?

Since, under the 1976 Copyright Act, copyright duration is based upon the author's life, it is helpful to know whether an author is still living and if not, the author's date of death. The Copyright Act provides for recordation in the Copyright Office of information concerning the lives and deaths of authors. Section 302(d) provides that:

Any person having an interest in a copyright may at any time record in the Copyright Office a statement of the date of death of the author of the copyrighted work, or a statement that the author is still living on a particular date.

The Register of Copyrights is required to maintain current records on the deaths of authors of copyrighted works derived from statements recorded by copyright interest holders. There is also an incentive for copyright owners to provide the Copyright Office with statements allowed under section 302(d). Under section 302(e), if after 95 years from a work' first publication or 120 years from its creation, whichever expires first, a prospective user obtains a certified report from the Copyright Office that the Office' records disclose nothing to indicate that the work's author is still living or died less than 70 years before, the prospective user is entitled to the benefit of a presumption that the author has been dead for at least 70 years. This creates a presumption that a work is in the public domain if the Copyright Office records show nothing indicating that the author is alive or has been alive during the past 95 years. A certified report can be obtained from the Copyright Office and if a person relies on such a report in good faith, that reliance constitutes a complete defense to an action for copyright infringement. This defense will not be applicable if the copyright owner can prove that the user had notice that less than 70 years had elapsed from the year of the author's death.

> **Tip:** It is advisable for copyright owners to file statements regarding the author's status with the Copyright Office from time to time. For example, a copyright owner can file a statement saying that the author is still alive as of a certain date or giving the date of the author's death, thereby preventing people from relying on the presumption that a work is in the public domain.

(3) Copyright Actually Lasts Longer Than Life + 70 Years

Section 305 of the 1976 Copyright Act provides that all terms of copyright run to the end of the calendar year in which they expire. In other words, all copyrighted works will expire on December 31st, 70 years after the author's death.

Example 8.6:

A song written on January 1 of any year would receive an actual copyright term of the author's life plus 70 years, 11 months and 30 days since it would expire on December 31st of the year occurring 70 years after the author's death.

B. WORKS CREATED BUT NOT PUBLISHED BEFORE 1978

Works that were created but had not been published prior to 1978 were protected by state common law copyright, which lasted indefinitely. The 1976 Copyright Act abolished common law copyright for works fixed in a tangible medium. Section 303 of the Copyright Act provides that works which were protected by common law copyright on the effective date of the 1976 Act (i.e., January 1, 1978) became subject to the term of protection specified by the 1976 Act (i.e., life + 70 years) or until December 31, 2002, whichever expires later. The second potential expiration date (i.e., 12/31/02) protects works created by authors who have been deceased for more than 70 years by 1978 (which otherwise would not receive any federal copyright protection). Additionally, if such works are published before December 31, 2002, the copyright will not expire before December 31, 2047, thereby encouraging publication.

Example 8.7:

Sally Songwriter wrote a song in 1950 that is not published. If Sally died in 1980, when does the copyright expire? The song was protected by common law copyright until 1978, at which time it became subject to federal copyright protection for the life of Sally plus 70 years, or until 2050.

Sammy Songwriter wrote a song in 1872 that was not published. If Sammy died in 1898, when does the copyright expire? The song was protected by common law copyright until 1978, at which time it became subject to federal copyright protection lasting until 12/31/2002 since that period is longer than Sammy's life plus 70 years or 1948. However, if Sammy's song is published before December 31, 2002, the copyright term would be extended to December 31, 2047.

As a result of the 1976 Copyright Act, the concept of common law copyright has lost most of its importance. There are however, two categories of works that may still be protected under common law copyright. These are: (1) works that have not been fixed in any tangible form such as unrecorded improvisations; and (2) sound recordings fixed before February 15, 1972, which are protected until February 15, 2047.

C. WORKS PUBLISHED BEFORE 1978

The most confusing rules governing duration of copyright are for works that were published or registered prior to 1978. These works are governed by the 1909 Copyright Act which provided for an initial term of 28 years from first publication with proper copyright notice. The 1909 Act also provided for a renewal term of an additional 28 years, resulting in a maximum term (i.e., initial + renewal) of 56 years. In order to get the renewal term, a renewal registration had to be filed during the last year of the initial 28-year term.

A song published in 1951 would have an initial term that expired in 1979. If the copyright to the song was renewed during 1979, it would have received an additional 28 years under the 1909 Act. The copyright therefore would have expired in 2007 (1951 + 56 years).

(1) First Extension of Renewal Term

The 1976 Copyright Act extended the duration of the renewal term for an additional 19 years, making the total renewal term 47 years. With this extended renewal period, works published before 1978 received a maximum of 75 years of copyright protection. The rationale for this extension was to give copyrights existing under the 1909 Act protection of approximately the same length as copyrights under the 1976 Act.

The copyright to the song from Example 8.9 would now expire in 2026 rather than 2007 (1951 + 75 years).

(2) Second Extension of Renewal Term

The Sonny Bono Term Extension Act of 1998 (which became effective in 1999) amended § 302(a) and (b) of the 1976 Copyright Act, extending the previous 47 year renewal term by an additional 20 years. Consequently, the renewal term now lasts for 67 years and the maximum term for works in the initial or renewal term as of 1999 is 95 years (i.e., 28 + 67 years) of copyright protection.

The copyright to the song from Example 8.9 would now expire in 2046 rather than 2026 (1951 + 95 years).

The Term Extension Act was passed despite considerable controversy over whether it was necessary. It was passed at the instigation of copyright owners of some extremely valuable works that would have entered the public domain if the term had not been extended. Both the Disney Corporation and the Gershwin family estate lobbied vigorously for passage of the Term Extension Act. Its passage assured that copyrighted works such as the Mickey Mouse character and "Rhapsody in Blue" by George Gershwin will continue to earn millions of dollars over the additional 20 years of protection.

D. DETERMINING WHETHER A WORK IS IN THE PUBLIC DOMAIN

Since public domain works are free for all to use anyone can freely copy them. However, it is often difficult to know whether a particular work is in the public domain. In order to determine whether a work is in the public domain, it is helpful to know when the work was first published. The date of first publication is usually specified in the copyright notice for copies or phonorecords of the work that have been distributed to the public. For works published prior to 1964, you will also need to know whether a renewal registration for the work was filed. To find out whether a renewal registration was filed, it is normally necessary to have a search of the Copyright Office records conducted in one of the following ways:

(1) Perform your own search by looking up the title of the work in the Catalog of Copyright Entries ("CCE"). The CCE is a series of annual catalogs listing and cross-referencing all registrations and renewals filed with the Copyright Office. The CCE is available at the Copyright Office as well as at certain libraries. Registrations and renewals made beginning with 1978 are also available online at the Copyright Office web site at **http://www.loc.gov/copyright/rb.html.** Although there is no charge to perform your own search, it may be advisable to use one of the following methods instead if you are not sure of what you are doing.

(2) Have the Copyright Office search its records for you. The Copyright Office charges a $65 per hour fee and most simple searches will not take longer than one hour. Fill out a search request form and send it (along with a $65 check) to Reference & Bibliography Section, LM-451, Copyright Office, Library of Congress, Washington, DC 20559. The only disadvantage to having the Copyright Office perform a search is that it can take a fairly long time to receive the search results (i.e., 1-3 months).

(3) There are professional search firms that will conduct a search for you. Using these firms is more expensive than having the Copyright Office perform a search, but you will obtain a much quicker result (i.e. 1-5 days).

Many works that one might believe to be in the public domain are still protected by copyright. For instance, the song "Happy Birthday To You" was written in the 1890s. The copyright in a version with new lyrics was registered in 1935 by Warner-Chappell, a music publishing company. This copyright will not expire until 2030. Although it can be difficult to determine when a particular work will enter the public domain, the following are some general rules:

• Any work published in 1922 or earlier is in the public domain.

• The Copyright Term Extension Act of 1998 delayed works published in 1923 or after from

being injected into the public domain. For instance, a work published in 1923 will now be protected through 2018 rather than 1999.

• No work created from 1978 on will enter the public domain until at least 2069.

E. RESTORATION OF COPYRIGHT IN FOREIGN WORKS

In general, once a work has entered the public domain, it remains in the public domain forever. This rule is always true for works copyrighted in the United States. However, there is an exception for certain foreign works. The copyrights in some foreign works published in the United States before 1964 entered the public domain in the United States due to the copyright owner's failure to file a renewal registration. Since most foreign copyright laws did not follow a renewal system, many foreign works lost protection in the United States although they were still protected in their country of origin.

The General Agreement on Trade and Tariffs ("GATT") remedied this situation by restoring the copyright in certain of these foreign works effective as of January 1, 1996. In order for copyright in a foreign work to be restored, the following three conditions must be satisfied:

(1) The work must have been created by an author who is a citizen or resident of a member country of the Berne Convention, World Trade Organization or a copyright treaty with the United States.

(2) The work must have been first published in the foreign country and not published in the United States within thirty days after foreign publication.

(3) The work's copyright must not have expired under the foreign country's copyright law.

Restoration only applies to foreign works and is intended to compensate for the inadvertent loss of copyright due to failure to renew which was not required under foreign copyright laws. Restored works receive the same term they would have received if a renewal registration had been filed.

A song was published in Germany in 1949 and in the U.S. in 1950. If the copyright owner failed to file a renewal registration in 1978, the work entered the public domain in the United States in 1979 although it was still protected under German copyright law. Under GATT, the copyright is automatically restored as of January 1, 1996 and lasts through 2045.

The copyright owner of a restored work cannot recover for infringements that occurred before 1996 when the work was in the public domain. Additionally, the copyright owner must give notice to people who continued to use the work after 1996 before filing an infringement suit against them.

If a record company released a recording of the song from Example 8.12 in 1980, the copyright owner could not recover damages from the record company for any records sold from 1980 to 1996, because the song was in the public domain during that time period. The copyright owner could however, provide notice to the record company that the copyright has been restored in the United States and then recover for any infringements that occur after the record company's receipt of the notice.

F. DURATION OF ASSIGNMENTS

It is important to understand the difference between the term of copyright as specified by law and the term of copyright ownership under a contract. A contract may limit a person's ownership of a copyrighted work to a period less than the full term of copyright protection. If an assignment of copyright does not clearly indicate the term of its duration, it will be deemed effective for the remainder of the copyright term, subject to the author's termination rights.

A contract between a songwriter and a music publisher provides that the songwriter assigns the copyright in a song to the publisher for 10 years. At the end of the 10-year period, the ownership of the song reverts to the songwriter. The songwriter would then own the song for the remaining period of copyright protection or could assign it to someone else.

1. *Harry Fox Agency, Inc. v. Mills Music, Inc.*, 543 F. Supp. 844 (1982).
2. Under the 1976 Copyright Act, renewal is mandatory for works subject to renewal prior to 1964 and optional for works subject to renewal between 1964 through 1977.
3. 17 U.S.C. § 304(a)(4)(b).
4. 318 U.S. 643 (1943).
5. 17 U.S.C. § 302(a).
6. 17 U.S.C. § 302(b), as amended by the Copyright Term Extension Act of 1998.
7. 17 U.S.C. § 302(c).
8. 17 U.S.C. § 302(c).

CHAPTER 9

Copyright Formalities

▼

*"I didn't know anything about copyright
laws or anything like that. I didn't have
$2 a lot of times to have a copyright paper
on a song sent into Congress."*
Willie Dixon, I Am the Blues 99-100 (1989)

Throughout most of the 20th century, copyright protection in the United States had been conditioned upon compliance with certain formal requirements: copyright registration, deposit, and notice. Since the 1976 Copyright Act's amendment by the Berne Convention Implementation Act of 1988, these formalities are no longer required as a condition to copyright protection, and registration and notice are both optional although strongly recommended. However, these formalities still serve practical functions and continue to provide important benefits to copyright owners.

I. The Copyright Office

Until 1870, copyright ownership claims were recorded by clerks of the United States District Courts. In 1870, the Library of Congress was given the responsibility of handling copyright registrations, and in 1897, the Copyright Office was formed as a department of the Library of Congress to handle this responsibility.

The Copyright Office processes registration applications and maintains records of copyright registrations and other recorded documents dealing with copyright ownership such as assignments, wills, mortgages, and security interests.[1]

In addition to handling copyright registrations, the Copyright Office also performs some other important functions. Some of these functions are:

• Advising Congress on anticipated changes in United States copyright law as well as compliance with international treaties.

• Analyzing and assisting in drafting copyright legislation.

• Conducting studies for Congress on copyright matters. In recent years, such studies have included Project Looking Forward—Sketching the Future of Copyright in a Networked World (July, 1998) and Copyright and Distance Education (May, 1999), both of which are available on the Copyright Office web site at **www.loc.gov/copyright/reports.**

• Providing assistance to foreign countries in developing their copyright laws.

• Overseeing the administration of Copyright Arbitration Royalty Panels, which meet periodically to set rates for compulsory licenses and to decide other matters.

• Issuing regulations dealing with copyright in order to implement the provisions of the Copyright Act. These regulations must comply with the provisions of the Copyright Act and are subject to the Librarian of Congress' approval. Regulations are also subject to a public review and comment procedure.

After adoption, all regulations are listed in volume 37 of the Code of Federal Regulations. Finally, all regulations are subject to court challenge if they are not consistent with the Copyright Act.

• Conducting searches of the Copyright Office indexes and records and assisting members of the public making their own searches.[2]

• Providing the public with information about copyright law and about the Copyright Office's policies and practices. However, Copyright Office employees are not allowed to give specific legal advice regarding copyright issues such as infringement.[3] The Copyright Office is also not authorized to refer members of the public to lawyers, publishers or agents.

> **Tip:** The Copyright Office is an excellent source of information on copyright law in general and copyright registration specifically. It provides easy to understand summaries on different subjects dealing with copyright (known as Information Circulars), registration forms and instructions for submitting registration applications, and summaries of recent and pending changes to copyright law. Much of this information is available from the Copyright Office website at **www.loc.gov/ copyright/**. The Copyright Office is also open to the public from 8:30 a.m. to 5: p.m. on weekdays and is located at 101 Independence Avenue, S.E., Washington, D.C.

A. STRUCTURE OF THE COPYRIGHT OFFICE

Chapter 7 of the 1976 Copyright Act sets forth the rules governing the Copyright Office. Under § 701(a), the person responsible for the overall direction of the Copyright Office is the Register of Copyrights who is appointed by the Librarian of Congress. The Librarian of Congress oversees the activities of the Register of Copyrights and the other officers and employees of the Copyright Office. The Copyright Office employs about 500 people and its responsibilities are divided among the following six divisions:

(1) Receiving and Processing Division

The Receiving and Processing Division is responsible for receiving materials such as registration applications and transfer documents for recordation. It records and deposits payments for copyright fees.

It also establishes and maintains deposit accounts, routes applications for registration and handles incomplete claims. Finally, this division maintains files on all office correspondence cases, assigns copyright registration numbers, and creates and mails certificates of registration.

(2) Examining Division

The Examining Division examines registration and renewal applications, transfer recordation documents and any accompanying materials such as deposit copies. It processes about 620,000 registration applications a year. The examination process consists of making sure that the application has been filled out correctly and that the material deposited constitutes copyrightable subject matter. It is important to understand that the Copyright Office makes no decision as to the validity of a registration applicant's ownership claim. In reality, the Copyright Office registers claims of copyright ownership rather than granting or issuing copyrights. If the materials submitted are in order, the Copyright Office will issue a certificate of registration. If any necessary information is missing, the examiner will contact the applicant by letter or phone to try to resolve any problems.

(3) Cataloging Division

The Cataloging Division prepares a bibliographic description of registered works as part of a database used to create the Copyright Office's catalog of entries. This allows for public access to all information of record relating to copyright registrations, deposits, recorded assignments, and other documents.

(4) Information and Reference Division

The Information and Reference Division is responsible for educating the Copyright Office staff as well as the public. It prepares and distributes informational materials and responds to reference requests. Additionally, the Information and Reference Division prepares search reports upon request for a fee of $65 per hour. This service can be extremely helpful if you want to find out information about a specific copyrighted work such as who is claiming ownership of the work and how that ownership has been obtained. The Information and Reference Division also prepares certifications and other legal documents. The Records Management Section stores the official records and catalogs of the Copyright Office such as registrations, recordations, etc.

(5) Licensing Division

The Licensing Division is responsible for carrying out compulsory license provisions of the Copyright Act such as the compulsory license for making and distributing phonorecords *(discussed in chapter 5)* and for the distribution of digital audio recording devices or media *(discussed in chapter 14)*.

(6) Copyright Acquisitions Division

The Copyright Acquisitions Division administers the mandatory deposit provisions and issues demands for published works which have not been deposited.

> **Tip:** The Copyright Office distributes a free electronic newsletter called NewsNet over the Internet. NewsNet alerts subscribers of proposed regulations, hearings, deadlines for public comments, new publications and other information. You can subscribe to NewsNet at the Copyright Office website.

B. COPYRIGHT OFFICE RECORDS

The Copyright Card Catalog consists of over 40 million individual cards and comprises an index for copyright registrations in the United States from 1870 to 1977. The Copyright Card Catalog combined with post-1977 automated files provide an index to copyright registrations in the United States from 1870 to the present.

The Catalog of Copyright Entries consists of the Copyright Card Catalog in book form from July 1, 1891 to 1978 and in microfiche form from 1979 through 1982. From the Copyright Office website, you can access the Library of Congress Information System ("LOCIS") which contains records of copyright registrations from 1978 to present.

The Assignment and Related Documents Index and the Copyright Office History Documents, an online file, can also be searched to investigate the ownership of a copyright.

II. Copyright Registration

A. WHAT IS COPYRIGHT REGISTRATION?

Many people have the mistaken belief that in order to own a copyright to a work, you have to register the work. In fact, copyright ownership arises automatically upon creation of a copyrightable work *(see chapter 3 for the requirements for copyrightable works)* and is not dependent upon registration. However, § 408 of the Copyright Act provides for a permissive or optional registration system. Copyright registration essentially means that someone has made a claim of ownership to a work as of a certain date. However, the fact that someone has registered a work claiming to be the copyright owner does not absolutely guarantee that they are really the owner since a registration can be contested in court. In other words, if you wrote a song and someone else registered the copyright claiming to be the owner, you can sue them alleging that their ownership claim and registration is invalid. Of course, you would have to offer proof that you really are the owner, but assuming you could do so, the court would invalidate the other party's fraudulent registration.

B. WHY SHOULD YOU REGISTER?

Although registration is not required, there are important benefits that are gained by registering a work. In general, copyright registration can be thought of as a relatively cheap form of insurance. Although it doesn't guarantee that your work will never be infringed, it makes it easier to prove that you own the work and to legally pursue infringements if they occur. The specific benefits afforded by registration are:

- Registration creates a public record of your claim of copyright ownership. Once a work has been registered, it is indexed in the Copyright Office records under the work's title and the author's name. Since the Copyright Office records are public records, anyone can search these records to determine who owns a work. This helps people find out who they need to obtain licenses from to use the work and helps to prevent fraudulent transfers of copyright ownership.

- Registration provides what is legally known as prima facie evidence of ownership. This means that if an ownership dispute ever arises, a court will presume that the registered claimant is the copyright owner unless the other party can disprove the registrant's ownership claim. Additionally, if you register within five years of a work's initial publication, a court will also assume that all of the information contained in the registration is valid. If a registration is made after five years of the work's publication, the amount of evidentiary weight given to the copyright certificate is up to the court.

• Under § 411(a), you <u>must</u> register a work before you can file a copyright infringement suit. This requirement applies to works first published in the United States or simultaneously in the United States and another country. It does not apply if the copyright owner is not a U.S. citizen or resident and the work is first published in a foreign country which is a Berne Convention member. Although you could register a work immediately prior to filing an infringement suit, it is better to register earlier since you would either have to wait until your registration application is processed which usually takes at least six months or pay $500 extra for an expedited registration (discussed in section G, below).

• If a work is registered prior to its infringement or within three months after its first publication, the owner has the right to elect to receive statutory damages and attorneys' fees in a successful infringement claim *(see chapter 13 for an explanation of the various remedies for copyright infringement)*. This can be extremely important since it is sometimes difficult to prove the actual monetary amount by which you are damaged due to an infringement. Further, the actual amount of damages may be comparatively small while the cost of litigating an infringement claim can be quite high. Finally, an infringer who knows you have registered may be more willing to settle due to the possibility of being held liable for statutory damages and legal fees.

• Copyright owners of musical compositions must register in order to be able to collect compulsory mechanical license royalties *(discussed in chapter 5)*.

• Registration allows the copyright owner to record its ownership claim with the United States Customs Service in order to prevent the importation of infringing copies.

C. WHO CAN REGISTER?

Anyone who owns all or part of the exclusive rights to a copyrighted work (or their authorized agent) can register a work. This would normally include the following parties:

• Any of the work's authors.

• Any party acquiring ownership of any of the exclusive rights. If only partial rights in a work are transferred, several parties may be entitled to register although only one registration is needed to protect all owners and normally only one registration should be made.

Example 9.1:

If a songwriter transfers copyright ownership to a publisher, the publisher would have the right to register the song. The songwriter should make sure that the publisher does so since, even though the writer is no longer the song's owner, it will normally still have a royalty interest (beneficial ownership) under its contract with the publisher in the song.

Example 9.2:

If four members of a band co-write a song, any of them may register the copyright. However, it is not necessary for more than one of them to register since only one registration is required to protect all co-owners.

D. WHEN SHOULD YOU REGISTER?

A work can be registered at any time during its term of copyright. Ideally, however, you should register a work as soon as possible after its creation. It is also highly advantageous to register within three months after a work's initial publication in order to have the right to receive statutory damages and legal fees in an infringement action.

Many copyright owners do not register their works immediately after they are created since they do not want to pay the $30 registration fee. For instance, a publisher that acquires ownership of many songs might not want to incur the $30 expense for each song until it knows whether specific songs will generate any income.

Tip: As a practical rule, I recommend that you register copyrights as soon as you know the work is going to be published (e.g., when it is recorded by an artist or licensed for use in a movie, etc.) and at the latest, within 3 months after publication. Additionally, authors can register multiple unpublished works as a collection as discussed below.

E. How to Register?

Generally, the registration process is very simple. The Copyright Office supplies application forms for different types of works (e.g., musical works, sound recordings, literary works, etc.). After filling out the proper form, send it to the Copyright Office along with the filing fee and deposit copy or copies.

> **Tip:** If you have questions about registration, you can call the Copyright Office at 202-707-3000 and an information specialist should be able to help you.

(1) Registration Forms

Copyright registration forms require the applicant to fill in information about the copyright claimant and the author of the work, information potentially required to determine the copyright's duration (i.e., creation date and author's death) and the basis of ownership for any parties other than the work's author. The forms most commonly used in the music industry are Form PA and SR, but Form TX and VA are sometimes used as well.

• **Form PA: Works of the Performing Arts**—This form should be used to register all works prepared to be performed directly before an audience. Form PA is used to register musical works (including accompanying words), dramatic works (including accompanying music), choreographic works, motion pictures and other audiovisual works, and multimedia works (works combining text with graphics, videos and sounds).

• **Form SR: Sound Recordings**—This form should be used to register sound recordings fixed on or after February 15, 1972 (sound recordings created before February 15, 1972 are not protected by federal copyright). Generally, form SR covers only the series of sounds that make up the recording and not any musical, literary or dramatic works contained on the recording. However, it is possible to use form SR to register the underlying musical composition or album cover artwork as well as the sound recording in certain circumstances. In order to do so, the owner must be the same party and you must specify that the application covers both works in the authorship statement in space 2 of the form.

• **Form TX: Nondramatic Literary Works**—This form is used to register written works such as books, poetry, magazine articles, etc. It can also be used to register song lyrics apart from music accompanying them.

• **Form VA: Works of the Visual Arts**—This form is used to register pictorial, graphic and sculptural works. Form VA can also be used for album cover art when the copyright owner is different than the copyright owner of the sound recording (when the copyright owner is the same, Form SR can be used for both).

The Copyright Office also has short forms available for the registration of certain works by their authors. The short forms are simplified versions of the full forms, consisting of one page rather than two and are available for forms PA, TX and VA. They can only be used if: there is only one author and owner of the work; the work is not a work made for hire; the work is completely new; and the form is signed by the work's author.

Registration forms can be easily obtained from the Copyright Office in the following three ways:

• **By Phone:** Call the Forms Hotline at 202-707-9100. This is an automated system that is open 24 hours a day. Leave your name, mailing address and specify the type of form and number of forms needed. The Copyright Office will send up to 10 copies of each form.

• **By Mail:** Write the Copyright Office at Information & Publication Section LM-455, Copyright Office, Library of Congress, Washington, DC 20559.

• **Online:** Forms can be downloaded from the Copyright Office's web site at **http://lcweb.loc.gov/copyright/forms**. The forms are available in Adobe Acrobat PDF format. You will need the Adobe Acrobat Reader, which can be downloaded for free, to read the forms.

(2) Filling Out Registration Forms

It is very important that you fill out registration forms clearly and accurately since it is possible that the form could be needed in court to prove your ownership claim. A person who intentionally lies on an application form is subject to a fine of up to $2500. Registration forms must be either typed or written in black ink. For purposes of illustration, the following describes in a step-by-step manner, how to fill out Form PA although most of the information would be applicable to other registration forms as well.

Space 1: Title Information

In this space, the applicant must supply information about the work's title. The title supplied is used by the Copyright Office to index the work once it is registered. You should also supply any previous or alternative titles that identify the work. Finally, you must give a brief description of the nature of the work. This description is important since it is used by the examiner to determine whether the work contains copyrightable subject matter. If the examiner finds the description to be insufficient or if it describes material not contained in your deposit, the examiner will usually send you a letter requesting that you correct and resubmit the application. Do not use the work's title as a description or merely specify the idea or concept that the work is based on. Usually, a simple description of the work will suffice. For example, if the work is a song, you should specify "music and lyrics." If you are registering a sound recording, the description should generally be "performance and sound recording."

Space 2: Author Information

In space 2, you must give information about the author or authors of the work. If a work has more than three authors, use a Continuation Sheet (Form PA/CON) for the additional authors and clip it to your PA form (do not staple or tape it to form PA).

A work's author is the person who created the work unless the work is a work made for hire, in which case the employer or commissioning party is the author. If the work is a work made for hire, you can include the name of the creator as well as the employer or commissioning party to make it part of the public record. You should specify the full legal name of the author, whether an individual or a business.

In addition to the authors' names, you must also fill in the authors' dates of birth and death (leave blank if the author is still living), the country of the authors' nationality, whether the work was made anonymously or under a pseudonym and the nature of authorship.

If the author is anonymous, you can either: leave the author line blank or mark it "N/A"; write "anonymous" in the space; or state the author's name. However, if you specify the author's name, it will be part of the public record and can be discovered by anyone who searches the registration files.

If the author is using a pseudonym, you can either: leave the space blank; specify the pseudonym and identify it as such; or specify the author's actual name and the pseudonym.

An author's date of birth is not required to be filled in, but the date of death is required unless the author is anonymous or pseudonymous since it determines the work's expiration date. If the author is a corporation or other business entity, leave these spaces blank. The author's nationality or domicile is also mandatory. An author's domicile is the author's country of principle residence.

The nature of authorship description should be the same as that provided in space 1 if there is only one author. If the work is a derivative work, you should specify only the new, original material added to the preexisting work. If there are more than one authors, specify the nature of each individual author's contributions.

Example 9.3:

If two authors co-wrote a song with one writing the music and the other writing the lyrics, the nature of authorship descriptions would be "music" for the composer and "lyrics" for the lyricist. If both authors contributed music and lyrics, the description for each would be "music and lyrics."

Space 3: Creation and Publication Dates

In space 3(a), specify the year in which the work was created. The creation date is the year in which the work was first fixed in tangible form. If the work has not been published, leave space 3(b) blank. If the work has been published, fill in the day, month, year and country of publication. If you are not sure of the exact publication date, specify an approximate date as accurately as you can.

Space 4: Copyright Claimant Information

Specify the name and address of the copyright claimants. The claimants will be either the authors of the work or any parties that have acquired ownership. If any copyright claimant is not an author of the work, you must also describe how that party acquired its ownership interest in space 4(b). There are several ways in which ownership can be acquired such as under a contract of transfer (commonly referred to as an "assignment of copyright"), by inheritance under a will or intestate succession or by gift. If you don't have enough space to list all of the work's claimants, you can use a Continuation Sheet (Form PA /CON).

Example 9.4:

If a music publisher is registering the copyright to a song it has acquired from a songwriter under contract, the publisher should state "by written contract" in space 4(b). Please note that it is not necessary to include a copy of the contract with the registration application and you should not do so since there may be confidential information in the contract and copyright registrations are public records.

Space 5: Previous Registration

If the work you are registering has never been registered before, mark the "No" box and skip the rest of the questions in space 5.

If any part of the work has been registered, mark the "Yes" box and check one of the three choices in spaces 5(a)-(c). Choice (a) applies to a work that was previously registered as an unpublished work. Choice (b) applies if an author is registering a work previously registered with someone other than the author listed as claimant. For example, if the work had previously been registered under a pseudonym and the author now wants to register in its legal name. Choice (c) applies to a

previously registered work that has been changed in some manner (i.e., a derivative work).

You must also provide the previous registration number and year of registration. The registration number is found stamped on the work's certificate of registration and consists of a two-letter prefix (three letters if the works was unpublished) followed by a number (e.g., PA 098765).

Space 6: Derivative Work or Compilation

If the work you are registering is a derivative work or a compilation, you must fill out space 6. If the pre-existing material used in your work has not been published or registered and is not in the public domain, simply mark "N/A" in space 6. Otherwise, you must identify the preexisting material used in your work in space 6(a) and distinguish it from any new material added in space 6(b). Your description of new material added in space 6(b) can usually be the same as the description of the nature of authorship stated in space 2.

When registering a derivative work, you must use the form that is applicable to the derivative work itself rather than the preexisting work.

Example 9.5:

If you are registering a song which is based on a pre-existing poem, the song would be registered using Form PA although the poem would have been registered using Form TX. You would identify the poem in space 6(a) and describe the new material (i.e., music) in space 6(b).

Space 7: Deposit Account

If you have a deposit account with the Copyright Office, you can charge the registration application fee to it by specifying the account name and number in space 7(a). You should also specify the name and phone and fax numbers of a contact person that the Copyright Office can contact if it has any questions in space 7(b). To open an account, you must have at least twelve transactions with the Copyright Office a year and deposit at least $250.

Space 8: Certification

In this space, the person signing the application must check the box that indicates the capacity in which they are signing. The application may be signed by any of the following people:

- Author: Only one author is required to sign even if there are more than one.

- Copyright claimant other than an author: Anyone who is not an author of the work, but has acquired ownership of all of the author's rights (such as a publisher) should mark this box.

- Owner of exclusive right(s): Anyone who has acquired some, but not all of the exclusive rights in the work (such as an exclusive licensee) should mark this box.

- Authorized agent: Mark this box if you are not signing on your own behalf, but as an authorized representative of the author, claimant or owner of exclusive rights (such as an officer or employee of a corporation or an attorney). You must also specify the name of the individual or organization on whose behalf you are signing.

> **Tip:** If you are registering a published work, make sure that the date specified in the certification space is not earlier than the date of publication specified in space 3.

Space 9: Return Address

Fill in your name and your return mailing address in this space; this is where your copyright registration certificate will be sent.

(4) Mailing the Registration Application

Once you have filled out the application form, you should mail the application and deposit copy or copies along with a check or money order covering the registration fee (currently $30 per application) in a single package. Your check or money order must be made payable to the "Register of Copyrights." Mail your package to Register of Copyrights, Copyright Office, Library of Congress, Washington, DC 20559.

> **Tip:** Before mailing your application to the Copyright Office, you should photocopy it and retain the copy for your records along with an exact copy of your deposit.

> **Tip:** Send registration applications by registered or certified mail, return receipt requested in order to make sure that the Copyright Office receives your application package. Approximately three weeks after mailing your package, you should receive a receipt card which specifies the date the package was received by the Copyright Office.

The Copyright Office has been working on implementing an online electronic system called CORDS for registration and deposit of works. In 2000, the Harry Fox Agency, on behalf of music publishers it represents, began working with the Copyright Office on online registration and deposit of musical works. There is also a system currently in development called Mixed CORDS which allows for the online registration applications along with physical deposits which could be used for sound recordings.

F. REGISTERING A COLLECTION OF WORKS

In certain circumstances, it is possible to register more than one work on one application form and pay only one fee.[4] This can be very beneficial, especially to prolific songwriters who would otherwise have to spend $30 for each song they register.

- You can register a group of songs using Form PA and paying a single application fee, provided that the following five requirements are satisfied:

- The works to be registered are unpublished.

- The same party must own all rights in the works and in the collection as a whole.

- The works must be by the same author or at least one author must be common to each work.

The collection of songs must be assembled in an orderly form. For example, if you are using a cassette tape for your deposit, clearly specify the number of songs and the title of each song in the order that they are contained on the tape.

The collection of songs must be identified by a single title. For example, I could name a collection of my song *Dave's Greatest Hits of 1999*.

In *Sylvestre v. Oswald*, two amateur musicians sued Jani Lane of the glam rock band Warrant alleging that his song *Heaven* was an infringement of their song of the same title. The musicians had obtained a registration for a collection of songs entitled *Cherry Bomb*. Although *Heaven* was included in the collection, it was not identified on the registration certificate. The issue decided by the court involved whether the registration for the *Cherry Bomb* collection extended to the individual song *Heaven* contained on the deposit tape. The court held that it did since *Heaven* was contained on the deposit tape submitted with the application. The court's ruling followed an earlier decision holding that the copyright in a collection of songs extends to the individual songs in the collection even if the individual songs are not listed in the copyright registration.[5]

The court denied Lane's motion to dismiss the suit, finding that the musicians had produced evidence of ownership and had offered sufficient evidence of access and substantial similarity for a jury decision to be required. The evidence of access was that tapes of the song were distributed to musicians in the Los Angeles and San Francisco rock scene in 1985, that the song was performed at parties in LA from 1984 to 1987 (where Lane was present) and that the song was played at an LA studio where Lane worked. As far as substantial similarity, the court concluded that the melody, lyrics and phrasing of the two songs was virtually identical, including the lyrics "heaven isn't too far away" being sung to eight identical notes. Since a jury trial never took place, it appears that the parties must have reached a settlement.

Even though the copyright in a collection of songs covers the individual songs contained in the collection, there is a practical problem that can arise from registering works as a collection. When you register a group of works as a collection, only the title of the collection will be indexed in the Copyright Office records. Since the individual songs contained in the collection are not indexed in the Copyright Office catalog of entries, someone who searches the Copyright Office records to find out whether one of the songs has been registered will not find the song title. There is, however, a way to prevent this problem from occurring. After you receive a registration certificate for a collection, you can file a Form CA listing the individual titles of songs contained in the collection. Although filing Form CA involves an additional fee (currently $65), it will cause the Copyright Office to index each song title. If you have four or more songs, registering them as a collection and filing a Form CA listing the individual song titles will be less costly than registering each song individually.

G. EXPEDITED REGISTRATION

The registration process usually takes six to eight months. However, it is possible to request that the Copyright Office expedite your application in certain circumstances. An expedited registration application will be usually be processed within five days. Expedited registration is only available if the registration is needed for litigation, to meet a contractual or publishing deadline, or for some other urgent need.

In order to obtain an expedited registration, you should send a letter stating why special handling is needed, if needed for litigation state whether a case has already been filed, who the parties are or will be and the court hearing the case. You must also include a certification that all of the statements you have made in connection with the application are true to the best of your knowledge.

In addition to the normal application fee, an additional fee of $500 is required for an expedited registration. If expedited registration is needed for litigation, you will also need to request a certified copy of the registration certificate that costs an additional $25.

Mail your letter, application form, deposit and check or money order to Library of Congress, Department 100, Washington, DC 20540 and mark "Special Handling" on the outside of the mailing envelope.

H. THE EXAMINATION PROCESS

After the Copyright Office receives your registration application, it will examine the registration form and deposit material and will usually issue a registration certificate if everything is filled out correctly and the material deposited contains copyrightable subject matter. It is important to note that the Copyright Office does not make any judgment as to the merit of your copyright claim. Its review of applications is limited to whether the work is copyrightable and whether the applicant has satisfied the registration requirements.[6]

You should receive some type of response from the Copyright Office within six months after your application is received, although sometimes the process takes longer due to the Copyright Office's workload. If you haven't received any response within 6-8 months, send a letter to the Copyright Office identifying yourself, the copyright owners, authors, date of application, form used and briefly describe the work. If you have a canceled check for the application fee, include a copy of it as well.

If your application is approved, you should receive a registration certificate (a copy of your application with the Copyright Office's official seal and a registration number and date). The effective date of registration is the date on which the Copyright Office receives all of the required materials rather than the date the registration is actually issued.

If your application contains any errors or omissions, the Copyright Office will return the application with a letter explaining what needs to be corrected. You must respond to a request for correction within 120 days or you will have to submit a new application and pay another fee. Some common errors to avoid include the following:

• Failure to sign the application form.

• Failure to enclose the proper application fee.

• Failure to provide the required deposit.

• Failure to adequately describe the nature of authorship of the work.

• Checking the work for hire box, but failing to list the employer as the work's author or claimant.

• Failure to specify how ownership was transferred to a claimant.

• Failure to describe new material in a derivative work.

If the Copyright Office determines that a work can't be registered, it will deny the application. In practice, the Copyright Office rarely denies registration. Under what is known as the rule of doubt, the Copyright Office will usually grant registration even if it has a reasonable doubt about the copyrightability of a work. When the Copyright Office is not sure about the copyrightability of a work, it will usually send a letter informing the applicant that its ownership claim may not be valid even though a registration is issued. If a dispute ever arose over the work's copyrightability, a court would have to make the ultimate determination.

If your application is denied, you can make a written objection and request that the Copyright Office reconsider the application. You must do so within 120 days of receiving the denial notice. When sending such an objection letter, the mailing envelope should be marked "FIRST APPEAL/EXAMINING DIVISION" and a fee of $200.00 must be included. If your first appeal is refused, you can make a second request for reconsideration within 120 days after receiving notice of denial of your first appeal. Your second request should be sent to Board of Appeals, Copyright GC/I&R, PO Box 70400, Southwest Station, Washington DC 20024 along with a fee of $500.00. This request will be reviewed by the Copyright Office Board of Appeals, which consists of the Register of Copyrights, the general counsel and the chief of the examining division. If your second appeal is refused, you can bring a legal action for a court to review the Copyright Office's decision.

I. CORRECTING AND SUPPLEMENTING REGISTRATIONS

Once a registration has been made for a work, it is generally not possible to make additional registrations for the same work. However, you can correct or supplement information supplied in a previous registration using Form CA. The main reason for correcting or supplementing a registration is that if you are ever involved in a legal dispute over the copyright, the registration certificate will be used as evidence in court. If your certificate contains errors or omissions, it could be detrimental to your case. Additionally, keeping your registration information accurate and current will make it easier for people searching the Copyright Office records to contact you for permission to use your work. The filing fee for Form CA is $65 (through at least June, 2002).

(1) Correcting a Registration
Form CA can be used to correct significant errors made in a registration application. Some examples would include incorrectly identifying an author or copyright claimant, registering an unpublished work as published or inaccurately stating the extent of a

claim. It is not necessary to use Form CA to correct obvious errors that the Copyright Office should have caught and immaterial, inadvertent errors will not affect the status of your registration. Instead, simply send the Copyright Office a letter notifying them of the error and requesting that it be corrected. Although it is permissible to file a supplemental registration to correct or amplify information contained in the original registration, this does not mean that the type of corrections or amplifications that can be made are unlimited.

The U.S. Court of Appeals for the 3rd Circuit ruled that songwriters who had initially registered a musical composition as an "audiovisual work" (with a copy of a music video for deposit) could not file a supplemental registration to change the nature of the work registered to the "performance" of the song.[7] The Court believed that the songwriters were trying to change the nature of the work rather than merely correct or amplify information contained in the original registration. The reason for the requested change was that the district court had dismissed the songwriters' copyright infringement suit against an advertising agency holding that the advertising agency owned the copyright to the video.

(2) Supplementing a Registration

You can also use Form CA to supplement the information contained in an existing registration. You can supplement a registration by providing additional information or by clarifying information provided in the registration. This would usually be done when there has been a change in some of the information which occurred after the registration was made. The supplementary registration must clearly identify the registration it refers to (include the registration number, title of the work and date issued). Some examples of supplementary information include the following:

• Change of address—It is not required that you supplement your registration when you change addresses, but it is a good idea to do so in order for potential licensees to contact you.

• Change in the claimant's name other than due to ownership transfer.

• Change in the title of a work.

• An author or claimant was omitted from the original registration.

John, Paul, George and Ringo co-write a song together. Paul's publisher registers the copyright, but inadvertently fails to list Ringo as an author of the song. A Form CA could be filed with the Copyright Office to supplement the previous registration by specifying that Ringo is also an author of the song.

A supplementary registration should not be made to reflect a change in ownership that occurred after the registration. Instead, the transfer of ownership can be recorded *(see Chapter 4—recordation of transfers)*. Further, if changes are made in the content of a work, you should register the new work separately as a derivative work rather than supplementing the original work's registration.

(3) Effect of Supplemental Registration

After the Copyright Office examines your supplemental registration, it will assign a new registration number and issue a certificate of supplementary registration. The supplementary registration augments the original registration rather than replacing it. The Copyright Office will place a note on the records of the original registration referencing the supplementary registration.

K. ALTERNATIVES TO REGISTRATION

(1) Poor Man's Copyright

In order to save money on copyright registrations, some people utilize a procedure known as poor man's copyright although the name is misleading since it is not part of copyright law. Poor man's copyright involves putting a copy or phonorecord of a song in an envelope, sealing it, and sending it to yourself by certified mail. When you receive the envelope in the mail, leave it sealed. The idea is that if you are ever involved in a dispute, the envelope can be opened in court, proving that you created the work no later than the date of the postmark stamped on the envelope.

Poor man's copyright, although it may be used as proof of creation of a work as of a certain date, is not a substitute for registration. First of all, the court must be convinced that the envelope has not been tampered with (i.e., opened and resealed). Additionally, poor man's copyright does not entitle you to any of the benefits provided by registration, such as the right to seek statutory damages and legal fees in an infringement action. Consequently, poor man's copyright is of very limited value and is not recommended.

(2) Songwriter Association Registration Services

Some organizations, such as the Songwriters Guild of America, allow authors to register their claims to copyright ownership. The only benefit of such registration is as a means of providing proof that a work was in existence as of a certain date. As with poor man's copyright, these services do not entitle you to any of the benefits provided by registration.

> **Tip:** If you do not want to spend $30 to register each song you write, you could wait until a song is about to be recorded or published in some other manner and register at that time. Since unpublished songs are of no financial value, spending $30 to register them may not be worthwhile. As long as you register a work within three months after publication, you will not lose any of the benefits associated with registration. Many music publishers follow this procedure, registering songs only when they have secured a recording by an artist. You can also register a group of unpublished songs as a collective work as explained in section F above.

II. Copyright Deposit

A. MANDATORY DEPOSIT

Of the three copyright formalities, deposit is the only one that is still mandatory in the United States, even though it is arguably the least important. Section 407 of the 1976 Copyright Act provides for a mandatory deposit system for published works. The purpose of the deposit requirement is to enrich the resources of the Library of Congress. The law requires that two copies of the best edition of every copyrightable work published in the United States be deposited with the Copyright Office within three months of publication. Deposit should be made by the copyright

owner or the owner of the exclusive right of publication and should be sent to:

Library of Congress
Register of Copyrights
Attn: 407 Deposits,
101 Independence Avenue, S.E.
Washington, D.C. 20559-6000

The mandatory deposit requirement is not applicable to unpublished works. Although unpublished works may be deposited by sending only one copy of the work, the Copyright Office does not encourage the deposit of unpublished works due to the additional workload that would result.

Although the deposit requirement is separate from the registration process, § 408(b) provides for deposit in connection with registration. The copies or phonorecords deposited under § 407 can be used to satisfy the deposit provisions of § 408(b) if they are accompanied by the registration application form and filing fee.

B. PENALTIES FOR FAILURE TO DEPOSIT

Although the deposit requirement is mandatory, many copyright owners do not make the required deposit unless they are also registering a work. There are no adverse consequences for failing to satisfy the deposit requirement. However, the Register of Copyrights may make a written demand for the deposit at any time after a work's publication, although generally only published works wanted for the Library of Congress' collections are demanded. If the deposit is not made within three months of this demand, the copyright owner can be fined up to $250 plus the retail price of the copies required for deposit. If a refusal to comply is willful or repeated, an additional fine of $2,500 may also be incurred.

C. WHAT MUST BE DEPOSITED

A deposit must contain two complete copies or phonorecords of the best edition of the work (if the work is unpublished, only one copy or phonorecord is required). The "best edition" is defined as the edition published in the United States at any time before the date of deposit that the Library of Congress determines to be most suitable. Generally, this means that if there is more than one edition of a work, the one of the highest quality should be used. For sound recordings, the deposit should include, in addition to two complete phonorecords (e.g., compact discs, cassettes, etc.) of the best edition, any text or pictorial matter published with the phonorecord. Textual material includes all packaging, record sleeves, and separate leaflets or booklets.

III. Copyright Notice

Copyright notice is a way of informing people that a work is protected by copyright and who owns it. Prior to March 1, 1989, placing notice of copyright on published copies of a work was required in order to have copyright protection in the United States.

Under the 1909 Copyright Act, the failure to use copyright notice had very harsh consequences. If notice was omitted or improperly placed on a work, the work automatically entered the public domain. Section 19 of the 1909 Act specified the required form and location of notice for different types of works. For example, the notice for a musical work was to be placed on the title page or the first page of the music. However, some courts interpreted the precise notice requirements liberally as long as they were substantially complied with.

The 1976 Copyright Act maintained the notice requirement, but liberalized it by allowing for the correction of innocent errors or omissions of notice. However, if someone used a work that did not contain notice without knowledge that the work was protected by copyright, they could not be held liable for copies of the work sold prior to the copyright owner's correction and notification from the copyright owner.

Unlike the United States, the vast majority of foreign countries did not require copyright notice as a condition to copyright protection. In fact, the Berne Convention specifically states that copyright protection cannot be subject to any formality such as notice. Consequently, when the United States decided to join the Berne Convention, it had to eliminate the mandatory notice requirement. Under the Berne Convention Implementation Act of 1988, which became effective on March 1, 1989, notice is no longer required in order to have copyright protection. This did not change the law with respect to works created before March 1, 1989, which still require notice.

Although copyright notice is no longer required, it is still recommended and there are some advantages to using it. One practical advantage is that placing notice on copies of a work that are distributed makes it clear that the work is protected by copyright. It also makes it easier for people to identify the copyright owner in order to request a license to use the work. Another advantage is that someone who infringes a work that contains notice cannot claim innocent infringement (reducing the amount of damages they are liable for) even if they actually believed the work was in the public domain.

A. WHAT SHOULD A COPYRIGHT NOTICE CONTAIN?

There are three required elements for a valid copyright notice. They are as follows:

- The word "Copyright," the abbreviation "Copr." or the copyright symbol "©." For sound recordings, the symbol "℗" should be used instead of the © symbol.

- The year of initial publication of the work, or, if the work is unpublished, the year of creation.

- The copyright owner's name. This refers to the current owner rather than the author of the work. For example, the song credits on an album will specify the name of the music publisher that owns the copyright to the song rather than the songwriter although songwriters may also be listed in the liner notes to give credit. If there is more than one copyright owner, specify all of their names in the copyright notice.

> **Tip:** Since some countries do not recognize the word "copyright" or the abbreviation "Copr." as valid for copyright notice, it is best to use the symbol—"©."

In addition to the three required elements, some copyright notices contain additional information. For instance, some notices will contain the phrase "all rights reserved" which is required in some Latin American countries under the Buenos Aires Convention. Sometimes notices will also contain some type of warning statement such as "unauthorized reproduction is prohibited by law—Violators are subject to civil and criminal penalties." Such warnings are not required, but are used to deter potential infringers. Finally, when someone else's copyrighted material has been used, the notice might contain "used by permission" to indicate that a license has been obtained.

B. WHERE SHOULD COPYRIGHT NOTICE BE PLACED?

A copyright notice should be placed on every reproduction of a copyrighted work. According to the Copyright Act, notice should be placed "in such manner and location as to give reasonable notice of the claim of copyright."[8] For sound recordings, notice should be placed on the actual phonorecord (or its label) and on its container since the phonorecord can easily be separated from the container. Notice is usually placed on the back side of the album jacket and on the disc label.

In many situations, there is more than one copyrighted work embodied on a phonorecord (i.e., the sound recording itself, any underlying musical compositions, album cover artwork and liner notes, etc.). In such situations, separate copyright notices can help distinguish between the owners of the various copyrighted works. At the least, there should be a notice on a phonorecord covering the sound recording and identifying its owner which is normally a record company. If the copyright owner's name is not contained in the notice and the record producer's name is listed elsewhere on the label or container, the producer's name will be deemed part of notice. In many instances, the record company will also be the copyright owner of any artwork and textual material contained on phonorecords. In such situations, the sound recording notice covers both although many record companies use both the ℗ and © symbols. If the record company is not the owner of the artwork or textual material, a separate notice should be placed near the artwork or textual material.

Example 9.9:

Kramerica Records is the copyright owner of a sound recording entitled *Serenity Now* (consisting of performances by Jerry Seinfeld and George Costanza) as well as the accompanying artwork and liner notes. The copyright notice found on a phonorecord such as a compact disc or cassette of *Serenity Now* would appear as follows: "℗ & © 2000 Kramerica Records." Alternatively, if the artwork and liner notes had been created by Elaine Benes as an employee of Pendant Publishing, the copyright notice for the sound recording would appear as ℗ 2000 Kramerica Records" while a separate copyright notice would appear near the artwork as "© 2000 Pendant Publishing."

1. 37 C.F.R. 201.4(c) (1991).

2. 37 C.F.R. 201.2(a)(1) (1991).

3. 37 C.F.R. 201.2(a)(3) (1991).

4. See 17 U.S.C. §408(c) and Copyright Office Regulation 37 C.F.R. § 202.3(b)(3)(i)(B).

5. *Szabo v. Errisson*

6. § 410(a) of the Copyright Act directs the Register of Copyrights to register any claim to copyright that constitutes copyrightable subject matter and meets the other legal and formal requirements of the Copyright Act.

7. *Racquel v. Education Management Corp.,* 98-3321 (Nov. 9, 1999).

8. 17 U.S.C. § 401(c).

Infringement of Copyright

▼

*"We were the biggest nickers in town;
plagiarists extraordinaire."*
Paul McCartney

I. What Is Copyright Infringement?

In the intangible property realm of copyright, infringement is the equivalent of stealing physical property. In general, infringement occurs whenever someone exercises any of the copyright owner's exclusive rights without permission to do so. As stated in section 501(a) of the Copyright Act:

Anyone who violates any of the exclusive rights of the copyright owner as provided by sections 106 through 118, or who imports copies or phonorecords into the United States in violation of section 602, is an infringer of the copyright.

A single act of infringement may violate one or more of the copyright owner's exclusive rights. For instance, someone who makes a recording of a copyrighted song without obtaining a license from the copyright owner of the song has infringed the reproduction right. If that person gives away or sells his recording, he has also violated the distribution right.

The key to winning an infringement claim is proving that the defendant copied the plaintiff's work. However, there are some circumstances where, even though the defendant has copied from the plaintiff's work, infringement will not result. This is because the copying must amount to an improper appropriation of the copyrighted work. In order to constitute improper appropriation, at least some of the elements copied must be copyrighted subject matter rather than public domain elements.

It is important to understand that just because another person's work is similar to yours does not necessarily mean that it is an infringement of your work. Many similarities can exist due simply to coincidence rather than by one person copying another person's work. In the field of music where the creative vocabulary is quite limited, there will be many similarities among different works. Songs will routinely share notes, common chord progressions, common rhythmic patterns and so forth.

Copyright infringement claims have become a commonplace occurrence, especially against highly popular recording artists. There are few highly successful artists that have escaped being sued by someone claiming to have written one of the artist's biggest hit songs. This trend in bringing copyright infringement claims began in the 1970s and has resulted in record companies and music publishers being much less receptive to listening to material submitted by new artists and songwriters. All of the major record companies have strict policies of not accepting any unsolicited material partially due to the fear that accepting such materials will be used against them in a copyright infringement claim.

II. What Should You Do When You Believe Your Work Has Been Infringed?

Before initiating legal action against an infringer, a copyright owner will usually notify the alleged infringer and request that the infringer stop infringing. This is usually done by having a lawyer send the alleged infringer a cease and desist letter. The copyright owner may also request payment for the unauthorized use that has been made. In some instances, the infringer may be willing to settle the claim by agreeing to pay the copyright owner some amount of money. Settlement agreements usually do not contain any admission of liability and are usually confidential so the amount paid by the infringer is not known to the public.

Example 10.1:

Billy Joel reportedly settled an infringement claim brought against him in 1980 in connection with his song "My Life" for about $50,000. Joel denied copying the song, but may have decided that paying $50,000 was cheaper than defending an infringement lawsuit.

If you cannot reach a settlement with an alleged infringer, your remaining option is to file a copyright infringement lawsuit. However, this is not always a practical option because infringement lawsuits can be very expensive and time consuming. Additionally, even if you win an infringement suit, the amount of money you can actually recover may not be enough to make it worthwhile. If you are considering filing an infringement suit, you should consult with an attorney who can advise you as to the validity of your claim, your chances of success and the likely amount of money you may recover. Since copyright is a very specialized area of the law, most attorneys are not competent to give advice on infringement claims so it is crucial that you find an experienced entertainment attorney.

III. How to Bring an Infringement Lawsuit

A. WHO CAN SUE FOR INFRINGEMENT?

Generally, the author or copyright owner of a work can sue anyone who infringes upon one or more of the copyright owner's exclusive rights. For instance, if a songwriter transfers copyright ownership of a song to a publisher, either the publisher or the songwriter could sue for infringement of the song. Prior to the enactment of the 1976 Copyright Act, only the copyright owner of a work could sue for infringement since copyright ownership was indivisible. This meant that an exclusive licensee could not sue for infringement unless the copyright owner was also a party to the lawsuit. The 1976 Copyright Act changed this result by providing that any "legal or beneficial owner of an exclusive right" can sue for infringement of that right.[1] This rule reflects the concept of divisibility of copyright, which means that a copyright can be split up and any of the exclusive rights can be owned separately.

Example 10.2:

Most music publishers do not print sheet music of their songs. Instead, they license print rights to one of a few companies specializing in this area such. If a publisher licensed a print company the exclusive right to print sheet music of a song and someone else began selling sheet music, the print company could sue the infringer as the song's exclusive print licensee without having to get the publisher to join as a party to the lawsuit.

B. WHERE TO BRING A COPYRIGHT INFRINGEMENT LAWSUIT

Copyright infringement lawsuits must be filed in one of the federal district courts in the United States. This is because copyright law in the United States is derived from a federal statute, the 1976 Copyright Act, and only federal courts have jurisdiction over federal statutes.

Although any claims that deal with a copyright owner's rights under the Copyright Act such as infringement claims must be brought in federal courts, there are many types of disputes involving copyrights that do not actually involve any interpretation of the Copyright Act. For instance, disputes over copyright ownership or the right to receive royalties do not usually involve interpretation of the Copyright Act and would have to be filed in state rather than federal court.

A songwriter signs a contract with a publishing company which provides that the publisher will pay the songwriter royalties based on sales of records containing songs written by the songwriter. If the songwriter believes that the publisher has not paid the proper amount of royalties, his claim is for breach of contract and should be brought in state court. Although the claim involves copyrighted works (i.e., songs), the dispute does not involve any interpretation of the Copyright Act. It merely requires that the court examine the situation in order to determine whether the provisions of the contract have been complied with.

Sometimes a dispute will involve several different legal claims, some of which might involve an interpretation of copyright law and some of which do not. In such situations, the lawsuit will usually be filed in federal court in order to address the copyright claim. The district court will often decide any related claims such as those involving a contractual dispute as well.

On January 1, 1999, a record company obtains a mechanical license from a publisher to record and distribute a song on records. Initially, the record company complies with all of the provisions of the license. However, after a year, the record company stops making accountings and royalty payments to the publisher. If the publisher believes that the record company had been underpaying royalties, it would have a claim for breach of contract for any royalties that should have been paid from 1999 to 2000 under the license. It would also have a claim for copyright infringement for any records sold after January 1, 2000 since the record company terminated the license when it stopped accounting. Since the record company's continued use of the song after termination of the license is a copyright infringement claim, the lawsuit could be filed in federal court and the court could decide the breach of contract claim as well as the infringement claim.

If you want to sue someone for copyright infringement, suit may be brought in any federal district where the defendant can be found. For instance, if an infringer lives in New York, you could sue him in a federal district court located in New York.

Additionally, if the infringer has sufficient contacts with other jurisdictions, you could sue in one of these jurisdictions as well. For instance, if you want to sue a big corporation, such as one of the major record companies, for copyright infringement, you could probably bring suit in any state where the corporation does business. However, a court can transfer a suit to another district where the suit could have been filed if the court believes it will be more convenient for the parties and witnesses.

IV. How Do You Prove Infringement?

Since the essence of a copyright infringement claim involves copying, a copyright owner must prove that he owns a copyrighted work that has been copied without permission. In order to prove an infringement claim, a copyright owner must prove two elements:

(1) Ownership of a valid copyright;

(2) Copying of a copyrighted work. Copying is in turn established by proving two elements:

• Access to the copyrighted work by the alleged infringer; and

• Substantial similarity between the copyrighted work and the alleged infringer's work.

A. OWNERSHIP OF A VALID COPYRIGHT

Obviously, in order for someone to have committed an infringement, they must have taken part of a copyrighted work. As discussed in Chapter 3, in order for a work to be protected by copyright, it must be original, contain expression and be fixed in tangible form.

The best way to prove ownership of copyright is to present a copyright registration certificate in court. If the registration was made within five years of the work's first publication, the court will presume that the plaintiff owns a valid copyright and that all of the information contained in the registration application is true. The plaintiff will therefore not have to offer any other evidence that the work is original or that he is the author or owner. If the defendant believes that the copyright is not valid or that the plaintiff is not the owner, it is up to the defendant to offer evidence proving its beliefs, which will normally be very hard to do.

If the plaintiff's work was not registered within five years of its publication, the plaintiff will have to offer some other evidence of its ownership of copyright. For instance, the plaintiff could take the witness stand and testify as to when and how he acquired ownership. If the plaintiff is the author of the work, he would testify that he created the work and has not transferred it to anyone else. He could also have witnesses testify if they had direct knowledge of the plaintiff's ownership (e.g., someone who was present and witnessed a songwriter composing a song). If the plaintiff is someone other than the work's author, he would have to offer into evidence some written document under which ownership was acquired. The main disadvantage of using testimony rather than written documentation to prove ownership is that the judge or jury is allowed to decide whether or not to believe the testimony.

> **Tip:** A copyright registration is the best possible proof that you own a copyrighted work. If there is ever a dispute over copyright ownership, the $30 registration fee is money well spent.

B. COPYING OF A COPYRIGHTED WORK

After the plaintiff has established that it owns a copyrighted work, it must prove that the defendant copied protected parts of the work. It is important to understand that infringement cannot occur unless the defendant has copied the plaintiff's work. There are two common ways for copying to occur. First, an infringer may directly copy the copyrighted work by duplicating it in some form. For example, a record pirate who manufactures copyrighted sound recordings without authorization to do so directly copies the sound recordings as well as any underlying copyrighted musical compositions contained in the sound recordings. The other type of copying involves indirect copying of part of a copyrighted work. For example, if a songwriter composes a song by copying part of another copyrighted song, whether intentionally or not, indirect copying has occurred.

Direct evidence of copying is rarely available because a defendant will rarely admit copying a work. Additionally, finding witnesses who physically saw a defendant copy the works is not likely since most copying is done in private. Consequently, copying can be inferred from circumstantial evidence. A plaintiff may prove copying by offering evidence of two elements: (1) access by the defendant to the copyrighted work; and (2) substantial similarity between the plaintiff's and the defendant's works.

(1) Access

In order to copy a work, one must have access to the work copied. Without access, copying is not possible. In legal terms, access means that the defendant had a reasonable opportunity to view or hear the copyrighted work.

a. Direct Evidence of Access

In the best of circumstances, a plaintiff will be able to present direct evidence of access. For example, a defendant might admit that it had access to the plaintiff's work. However, the fact that a defendant admits access does not necessarily mean that the defendant also admits copying the plaintiff's work.

Example 10.5:

In *Bright Tunes Music Corp. v. Harrisongs Music, Ltd.,*[2] George Harrison's song "My Sweet Lord" was held to be an infringement of the Chiffons' hit song "He's So Fine." In this case, Harrison admitted hearing the Chiffon's song.

Additionally, if the plaintiff can find a witness who can testify that he saw the defendant copy the plaintiff's work, this would also constitute direct evidence of access. Alternatively, if a witness heard the defendant admit he had heard the plaintiff's song, this testimony would also be direct evidence of access.

b. Circumstantial Evidence of Access

In most situations, a plaintiff will not be able to offer direct evidence that a defendant had access to his work. In such situations, the plaintiff will have to rely on circumstantial evidence instead. One type of circumstantial evidence of access involves showing that the plaintiff's work was widely available to the public. For instance, if the plaintiff's song was a major hit which received widespread exposure to the public through radio airplay or television broadcasts, it is reasonable to assume that the defendant heard it at some point. Alternatively, if the plaintiff's song has been widely disseminated through sales of sheet music or records, this would be circumstantial evidence of access. The more widely available the work, the more likely access will be found.

In the George Harrison case referred to in the previous example, although Harrison admitted hearing the Chiffon's song, access could also have been proven circumstantially based on the fact that "He's So Fine" was a number one hit on the Billboard charts for five weeks and received substantial radio airplay. In contrast, in a case brought by an unknown composer named Ronald Selle, it was held that the Bee Gee's song "How Deep is Your Love" did not infringe Selle's song "Let It End."[3] The court's decision rested on the fact that Selle could not offer sufficient proof that the Bee Gees had access to his song. Selle offered evidence that "Let It End" was performed publicly two or three times in the Chicago area, but could not prove that the Bees Gees or anyone associated with them was in the area at the time of those performances.

Another type of circumstantial evidence of access involves showing that the plaintiff's work was available to the defendant. This usually results from the plaintiff proving that it distributed its work to the defendant or to some third party who is likely to have distributed it to the defendant such as the defendant's record company or publisher. In one case, where the plaintiff had sent copies of her song to four individuals and two companies all of which were returned, the court stated that:

To support a finding of access there must be a reasonable possibility of access—not a bare possibility as we have in this case."[4]

Sometimes the link between the plaintiff's work and the defendant will be quite tenuous. In a suit filed against Mariah Carey that was dropped before trial, a plaintiff alleged that Carey's song "Can't Let Go" infringed her song. As evidence of access, the plaintiff claimed that she gave a demo tape containing her song to Carey's hairstylist. It is unlikely that a court would consider this sufficient evidence of access unless the hairstylist testified that he gave the tape to Carey (which still would not conclusively prove that she listened to it).

In *Gaste v. Kaiserman,*[5] the composer of an obscure French song, "Pour Toi," claimed that Morris Alpert's 1970's hit song "Feelings" was an infringement. Seventeen years before "Feelings" was written, Gaste had sent a recording of his song to Alpert's publishing company. Somewhat surprisingly, the jury held that Gaste's evidence of access was sufficient even though the publisher claimed it had never actually listened to Gaste's song. The court stated "the lapse of time between the original publication of 'Pour Toi' and the alleged infringement and the distance between the locations of the two events may make copying less likely but not an unreasonable conclusion."

> **Tip**: In order to reduce the possibility of being found guilty of copyright infringement, many famous recording artists as well as record companies and publishers have adopted policies of not accepting any unsolicited material. In other words, they will not accept demo tapes from anyone they don't know and trust since to do so could be used against them as evidence of access.

(2) Substantial Similarity

Even if a plaintiff proves that the defendant had access to his work, this alone does not prove that the defendant copied his work. The plaintiff must also prove that there are substantial similarities between the plaintiff's and the defendant's works. The substantial similarity test is often a difficult one since there is no clear line that can be drawn between substantial and insubstantial similarities. If the similarities between the defendant's and the plaintiff's works are so great that it is more likely than not that the defendant copied the plaintiff's work, they will be deemed substantial. However, there is no set number of notes or words that must be taken from a work in order to constitute substantial similarity.

Substantial similarity is a somewhat imprecise concept and is normally determined by what is known as the ordinary observer test. This test asks whether the defendant took from the plaintiff's work so much of what is pleasing to the ears of lay listeners, comprising the audience of such music, that the defendant wrongfully took what belongs to the plaintiff. Even though substantial similarity is determined according to the ordinary observer, expert testimony will often be used to show the similarities between two works. Plaintiffs will normally use expert testimony to attempt to prove that the defendant could not have independently created its work and that similarities between highly unique elements indicate copying.

The substantial similarity test is often especially difficult to apply to cases involving music since the elements of musical composition are much more limited than the elements of literary or dramatic composition. First of all, musical composition is limited by the 12 notes of the musical scale. Further, even though these 12 notes can be arranged in many ways, only a few of these arrangements will be aesthetically pleasing. It is therefore quite possible that two songs may contain a great degree of similarity even though both songs are independently created. As stated by one court:

It must be remembered that, while there are an enormous number of possible permutations of the musical notes of the scale, only a few are pleasing; and much fewer still suit the infantile demands of the popular ear. Recurrence is not therefore an inevitable badge of plagiarism."[6]

Evidence of similarities between songs will usually focus primarily on similarities in the melodies of the songs since melody is usually the most memorable element of a song. However, rhythmic and harmonic similarities can also be examined. In many infringement cases, each side will hire an expert who will prepare exhibits comparing similarities between songs. Experts might also try to identify similarities in compositional irregularities or errors between two works.

It is also important to understand that not all of the similarities between two works will be applied in the substantial similarity analysis. In order to count, the similarities must be of copyrightable expression rather than merely uncopyrightable ideas. This is often referred to as "improper appropriation" which means that the defendant must appropriate elements of the work that are protected by copyright. If a defendant literally copied all of a plaintiff's song, this would clearly involve improper appropriation. However, many situations do not involve literal copying and it then becomes necessary to dissect the two works in order to determine what elements are copyrightable expression as opposed to non-copyrightable ideas.

It will often be permissible to copy a musical phrase from a copyrighted work. This would be true if the musical phrase copied is fairly simple and therefore not sufficiently original to merit copyright protection. If one could obtain copyright ownership over simple musical phrases or other compositional elements, this would have the effect of limiting musical composition since no one else could use such elements without permission. The most difficult question in analyzing issues of substantial similarity is how much copying is too much? Unfortunately, there are no bright-line rules and the determination must be made on a case-by-case basis.

> **Tip:** A common misconception among musicians is that it is permissible to use up to six measures or bars of music from a copyrighted song. This misconception has become known as the "six bar rule" which is really not a rule at all. In fact, there is no universally accepted minimum amount of music that may be freely copied. Courts have held that copying as few as two to four bars or even just six notes can constitute infringement.

(3) Striking Similarity

In rare circumstances, a court may conclude that a defendant copied a work even if the plaintiff cannot prove that the defendant had access to the work. A court would do so only when it believes that the similarities between the two works are so striking that there is no reasonable possibility that the defendant independently created its work and that the similarities are coincidental. In other words, the only reasonable explanation for the similarities between the two works is that the defendant copied the plaintiff's work.

(4) Presumption of Copying

If a copyright owner proves both access and substantial similarity, a court will presume that the defendant copied the plaintiff's work. The reason for this presumption is that there is no other reasonable explanation for the similarities other than copying. However, this presumption of copying can be countered or rebutted by the defendant.

A defendant can attempt to rebut the presumption that it copied the plaintiff's work in several ways. For instance, if the plaintiff offered evidence of access by proving that it submitted a demo tape to a record company, the record company could offer evidence that it had a policy of not listening to unsolicited demos or evidence proving that whoever the demo was submitted to at the record company had no contact with the artist.

To rebut evidence of similarities between two works, a defendant could offer evidence of the existence of other works containing the same similarities and showing that it was these other works rather than the plaintiff's which were copied. If the other works are in the public domain, they can be freely copied by anyone. Alternatively, a defendant could offer evidence that its work was created before the plaintiff's work. A defendant could also attempt to prove that regardless of any similarities, it created its work independently.

Example 10.8:

In *Selle v. Gibb*,[7] the Bee Gees presented several witnesses who were present when the Bee Gees composed the song "How Deep Is Your Love." They also submitted into evidence a work tape made during their song's creation that showed how ideas, notes and lyrics were combined in order to create the song. The court believed that this evidence proved that the Bee Gees had independently created the song even though an expert witness for the plaintiff testified, "the two songs had such striking similarities that they could not have been written independent of one another."

C. FAMOUS MUSIC INFRINGEMENT CASES

It is not uncommon for copyright infringement lawsuits to be brought by relatively unknown songwriters against the writers and owners of extremely successful hit songs. Although it is certainly possible that a hit song could be an infringement of a song by an amateur writer, when an infringement claim is made against a superstar artist over a hit song, it is possible that the amateur songwriter is merely attempting to extract a large cash settlement from the artist. In other situations, a songwriter will genuinely believe that his or her song has been infringed based on coincidental similarities rather than copying.

Michael Jackson may have the dubious distinction of being the person most often sued for copyright infringement. Jackson reportedly received over 25 letters threatening infringement lawsuits and demanding large settlement sums after the release of his *Dangerous* album. However, Jackson

has successfully defended every infringement suit brought against him.

The following, although only a small sample, are some of the more notable and interesting copyright infringement cases involving musical works. If you would like to read the actual court decisions, they (and many others) are compiled in the Case Supplement to this book which can be ordered from the author's website.

(1) The Song Is Mine—*Sanford v. Jackson*

In 1984, Fred Sanford, an amateur musician from Illinois, sued Michael Jackson for $5 million claiming that Jackson's song "The Girl Is Mine" infringed his song "Please Love Me Now." Sanford claimed that Jackson had access to his song because he gave a tape containing the song to an executive at CBS Records (Jackson's record label) on March 10, 1982. Sanford also alleged that at that time Jackson was behind schedule for his *Thriller* album and was looking for a duet to perform with Paul McCartney (Sanford's song was a duet).

Jackson claimed that he had never heard Sanford's song and that he composed "The Girl Is Mine" in November 1981 while in London by singing the melody and other parts into a tape recorder. At trial, Jackson spent four hours on the witness stand demonstrating how he composed his song by clapping his hands, snapping his fingers, playing a work tape and singing the melody over some of his other songs to show that it was part of his songwriting repertoire.

The jury reached a verdict in favor of Jackson after deliberating for over 21 hours. Sanford's attorney stated that he believed that his client would have won if it weren't for Jackson's fame. Although this is debatable, it is certainly possible that an artist of Jackson's stature could have a prejudicial affect on a judge or jury. In fact, it was reported that the judge had Jackson come to his chambers to meet his 15-year-old daughter. Interestingly, CBS Records instituted a strict policy of not accepting any unsolicited material after this lawsuit was filed.

(2) Being Famous Can Be Dangerous—*Cartier v. Jackson*[8]

In 1992, Crystal Cartier, an aspiring songwriter from Denver, sued Michael Jackson for $40 million claiming that Jackson's song *Dangerous* infringed upon her song of the same title. Cartier claimed to have written her song in 1985 and registered it in 1991 while Jackson registered his song in 1992.

There were many problems with Cartier's claim, reflected by the fact that she could not find any entertainment attorney willing to represent her (Cartier maintained that everyone connected with the music industry was afraid to take her case). Instead, she was represented by a small personal injury and real estate law firm that was frequently lectured by the judge during the trial on how to proceed with their case. It also became apparent that Cartier was obsessed with Jackson. She had written a novel featuring a vampire named Michael the Meek and wanted Jackson to co-star with her in a film based on the novel.

For proof of access, Cartier contended that she gave Jackson's road manager a copy of her demo tape backstage at a concert in 1988. She also claimed to have given a demo tape to an executive at Warner-Chappell Music, a publishing company that administered Jackson's publishing catalog. The executive claimed that he threw the tape away without listening to it. One of the many factors that hurt Cartier's claim was that she did not have a copy of the demo tape she allegedly distributed. She claimed that she had given all of her copies of the tape away and wasn't able to locate any of them. The court refused to allow her to submit a recording that allegedly recreated the original demo from Cartier's memory.

Jackson testified that he had never heard Cartier's song and that he had a strict policy of never accepting unsolicited tapes. He also stated that his "Dangerous" grew out of a song called "Streetwalker" that he had previously written in 1985. Supporting Jackson's explanation of how he composed "Dangerous," a co-writer of "Dangerous" testified that he had developed the song's musical structure by taking a bass line from "Streetwalker," after which Jackson wrote the melody and lyrics of the song.

Cartier used an expert witness to testify as to the similarities between the songs. He testified that both songs were in the key of D-minor, the rhythmic structures and melodies of the songs were identical, both recordings contained urban sound effects and rap passages, the bass and drum patterns were similar, and the word "dangerous" was repeated in the third measure of each song's chorus. The court gave little weight to the expert's opinion, partly due to the fact that he was employed as a construction worker (although he had formerly been an assistant to the Doors' producer) and held that Cartier failed to prove access or substantial similarity.

(3) Thieving Diva Or Publicity Hungry Plaintiff?—*Selletti v. Carey*[9]

Christopher Selletti brought a copyright infringement lawsuit against Mariah Carey and her co-writer in 1996, alleging that Carey appropriated a poem he had written in 1989 as the basis of her song "Hero," recorded in 1993 on her *Music Box* album.

Selletti's case was so weak that the judge stated that "I am firmly convinced that Selletti's allegation that defendants misappropriated the lyrics to 'Hero' from him is a complete fabrication." Selletti's only evidence of access was his testimony that he had worked for musician Sly Stone in 1989 as a personal assistant when he wrote his poem. He gave a copy of the poem to Stone shortly before being fired and never heard from Stone about the poem again.

In 1993, Selletti's fiancee brought home a CD of Carey's *Music Box* and he "freaked out." The judge found it patently unbelievable that "two successful songwriters, including one who is a superstar of pop music, misappropriated his lyrics and published them as their own essentially without changing a word."

The judge also stated that Selletti appeared to be more interested in "extorting potentially deep-pocket defendants" than in proving his claim. Selletti had repeatedly failed to comply with court orders to produce evidence while taking every opportunity to publicize his case in the media. For example, Selletti appeared on the NBC television show *Court TV: Inside America's Courts* in a segment that showed a photograph of Carey with the headline "Thieving Diva?" Selletti also contradicted himself repeatedly during the case, apparently changing his version of the facts as he thought up new ones.

On the other hand, Carey and co-writer Walter Afanasieff, who had previously written several hit songs together, presented extremely strong evidence of their independent creation of "Hero." They submitted tape recordings of two writing sessions during which they worked on the song with Afanasieff playing the piano, Carey singing and the two discussing different options.

Carey also submitted a notebook, which she used to write down song ideas. The notebook included various versions of the lyrics to "Hero" in Carey's handwriting, with some words crossed out or added in a different color. Many of the pages were dated from 1992 to 1993.

Additionally, Carey introduced evidence that the producers of the movie *Hero* (starring Dustin Hoffman) approached Afanasieff about writing a song for the movie and Afanasieff approached Carey about writing the song. Although the movie producers decided not to include the song in the movie, it appeared that it was written for the movie (i.e., the song and the movie plot revolve around the same theme, that there is a potential hero inside even the most unlikely individuals).

(4) Subconscious Songwriting—*Bright Tunes Music Corp. v. Harrisongs Music, Ltd.*[10]

Bright Tunes, a publishing company that owned the copyright to the song "He's So Fine," sued George Harrison claiming that his song "My Sweet Lord" was an infringement. "He's So Fine" was recorded by the Chiffons in 1962 and became a number one hit.

Proving access did not present a problem in this case because Harrison admitted having heard "He's So Fine" prior to writing "My Sweet Lord." Even without that admission, access could be inferred from the fact that "He's So Fine" was a highly successful song.

The court found Harrison guilty of infringement even though it believed that Harrison had not intentionally copied "He's So Fine." Instead, based on the fact that Harrison had access and that the songs were "virtually identical," the judge concluded that Harrison had subconsciously copied "He's So Fine," with the following explanation:

I conclude that the composer, in seeking musical materials to clothe his thoughts, was working with various possibilities. As he tried this possibility and that, there came to the surface of his mind a particular combination that pleased him as being one he felt would be appealing to a prospective listener; in other words, that this combination of sounds would work. Why? Because his subconscious knew it already had worked in a song his conscious mind did not remember ... Did Harrison deliberately use the music of He's So Fine? I do not believe he did so deliberately. Nevertheless, it is clear that "My Sweet Lord" is the very same song as "He's So Fine" with different words, and Harrison had access to "He's So Fine." This is, under the law, infringement of copyright, and is no less so even though subconsciously accomplished.

This case illustrates that you can be liable for infringement even if you are unaware that you are infringing. Harrison paid $587,000 in damages for his unintentional infringement. The idea of subconscious infringement has been criticized since it is based on knowledge of what is in a person's subconscious mind at the time a work is created. The next case presents an even more troubling example of subconscious infringement.

(5) Infringement Isn't a Wonderful Thing— *Three Boys Music Corporation v. Michael Bolton*

In a suit by the Isley Brothers against Michael Bolton for copyright infringement, a jury concluded that Bolton's song "Love Is a Wonderful Thing" was an infringement of a 1966 Isley Brothers song by the same title.

Bolton's defense relied on lack of access since he and his co-writer were only 15 years old when the Isley Brothers' song was released. Further, the Isley Brothers' song was not a hit and received only limited radio airplay. However, the song was played in 1966 and 1967 in suburban Connecticut where Bolton and his co-author grew up and has been played on oldies radio stations since that time as well as at Isley Brothers concerts.

The court found Bolton guilty of infringement, noting that it may have been subconscious infringement. The court's decision is somewhat troubling since it relies on the assumption that Bolton subconsciously copied a 20-year-old song that was not a hit. The appeals court admitted that this case presented a much more attenuated case of access and subconscious copying than the Harrison case, but did not believe that the evidence was so weak that it warranted a reversal of the jury verdict. The court stated that "it is entirely plausible that two Connecticut teenagers obsessed with rhythm and blues music could remember an Isley Brothers' song that was played on the radio and television for a few weeks, and subconsciously copy it twenty years later."

(6) Sell Your Song, Not Your Soul—*Tisi v. Patrick*

A songwriter named Michael Tisi sued Richard Patrick of the band Filter for copyright infringement claiming that Filter's song "Take a Picture" was copied from his song "Sell Your Soul." Tisi had recorded a demo of his song, which he then used to try to obtain a record deal. Between 1994 and 1995, the demo tape was sent to executives at virtually every major record company. However, none of these companies expressed any interest in Tisi or his song.

Richard Patrick claimed to have written "Take a Picture" between 1996 and 1998. He testified that he had never heard Tisi's song and that he does not accept or listen to unsolicited demos. "Take a Picture" was released in 1999 and peaked at number 12 on the Billboard Hot 100 singles chart and number 1 on the Billboard Dance chart.

The court held that Tisi failed to prove both access and substantial similarity. With regard to access, the court found that there was no evidence that Tisi's song was ever conveyed from any executives at any of the record companies (which Tisi had sent demos to) to Patrick or to anyone with creative input into "Take a Picture." The court also stated that although some "superficial" similarities existed between the two songs, they were "uniformly shared with most modern popular rock music." For instance, both songs contained an introduction, verse, chorus, and bridge, with harmonic and rhythmic similarities common to many musical genres. Additionally, both songs were in the key of A major and shared a "I–IV" chord progression.

The court also noted that "Take a Picture" shared many similarities with other songs recorded by Filter, which indicated independent creation. Further, there were many dissimilarities between the two songs (e.g., "Take a Picture" contained a lengthy distorted rock guitar intro, more complex harmonies, multiple layered guitar tracks, etc.)."

V. Liability for Infringement

Once it has been decided that an infringement has occurred, it is often necessary to determine who is legally liable or responsible for the infringement. A person who actually commits an infringement will always be liable. However, copyright law also recognizes that third parties who aid, contribute to, participate in, or benefit from infringement may be held liable as well.

There are three types of copyright infringement—direct infringement, contributory infringement, and vicarious infringement. Direct infringement applies to a person who actually commits the infringing act by violating one of the copyright owner's exclusive rights. However, in some cases, a direct infringer cannot easily be located or might be financially insolvent which makes suing the direct infringer impractical. In such cases, copyright owners will often attempt to hold third parties liable either in place of or in addition to any direct infringers under the doctrines of contributory and vicarious infringement.

A. CONTRIBUTORY INFRINGEMENT

Contributory copyright infringement occurs when a party has knowledge of the infringing activity and induces, causes or materially contributes to the infringing conduct of another. In other words, if a business has control over its business operations and knows that infringing activity occurs when these operations take place, continued tolerance of the infringing activity contributes to the infringement, and the business may be liable for the infringement as well as the direct infringer.

Example 10.9:

In *Gershwin Publishing Corp. v. Columbia Artists Management,*[11] the American Society of Composers, Authors and Publishers (ASCAP) sued Columbia Artists Management for copyright infringement. On January 9, 1965, concert artists managed by Columbia performed ASCAP songs for profit at a public concert. Although the performing artists rather than Columbia actually committed the infringing acts, Columbia knew that copyrighted music was being performed and that a license authorizing the performances had not been obtained. The court found Columbia liable for contributory infringement, holding that its participation in the formation, direction, and programming of the concert placed it in a position to police the conduct of the artists.

There are two requirements for contributory infringement. First, the defendant must have knowledge of the infringing activity. Second, the defendant must substantially participate in the infringing activity. Knowledge will often be proven by a copyright owner or its attorney sending a letter, known as a cease and desist letter, informing a business of infringing activity.

Substantial participation can include providing materials or facilities to commit the infringing activity. In one case,[12] an Internet bulletin board service was held liable for contributory infringement for downloading of copyrighted video games over its service. The court held that the bulletin board service had knowledge of and encouraged the unauthorized uploading and downloading of the video games, "including provision of facilities, direction, knowledge and encouragement" and that its participation in the infringement was therefore substantial. Another court ruled that a third party did not have to go so far as "expressly promoting or encouraging the sale of counterfeit products, or ... protecting the identity of the infringers" and that simply "providing the site and facilities for known infringing activity" constituted substantial participation.[13]

B. VICARIOUS INFRINGEMENT

Vicarious infringement occurs when a defendant has the right and ability to control an infringer's activity and receives a direct financial benefit from the infringement. While contributory infringement requires knowledge of the infringing activity, vicarious liability can be imposed regardless of the defendant's knowledge or intention. Although it may seem strange to impose liability on someone who is not even aware of the infringement, vicarious liability is based in part on the third party's ability to supervise infringing conduct.

In *Shapiro, Bernstein & Co. v. H.L. Green Co.*,[14] a department store that leased floor space to a concessionaire who sold records was held liable for the sale of bootleg records even though it was not aware that the records being sold were not legitimate. The court stated that:

When the right and ability to supervise coalesce with an obvious and direct financial interest in the exploitation of copyrighted materials, even in the absence of actual knowledge that the copyright monopoly is being impaired, the purposes of copyright law may be best effectuated by the imposition of liability upon the beneficiary of that exploitation.

Since the store received a percentage of the revenue from record sales, it directly benefited from the infringing activity. Another important rationale for the court's decision was to discourage large department stores from using dummy concessions that protect them from liability for copyright infringement while allowing them to benefit from infringement. This illustrates one of the underlying rationales for vicarious liability—businesses should not be able to escape liability by using others to actually commit infringing acts while either pretending to be ignorant of or intentionally remaining ignorant of the infringing conduct.

One area where vicarious liability has often been found involves the public performance right. Many court decisions have held that a business that actively operates or supervises a place where unauthorized performances of music occur and receives a direct or indirect benefit from the performances will be liable as a vicarious infringer. Owners of bars and nightclubs have been found vicariously liable for infringements committed by performers at their premises because of their ability to supervise the music which is performed and because they receive a direct financial benefit from performances which bring customers into the club.

Some club owners have attempted to escape liability by arguing that they do not directly profit from the infringing performances when the club does not receive any cover charge for the performances. However, most courts have found that clubs still receive an indirect financial benefit since the performances are meant to attracts customers who spend money on drinks and food. Alternatively, club owners have argued that they do not have any control over whether performers plays copyrighted music or not. However, courts have tended to view the control requirement fairly broadly, sometimes even holding clubs liable where they warned performers not to play any copyrighted works without a license.

Example 10.11:

In *Dreamland Ballroom v. Shapiro, Bernstein & Co.*,[15] a dance hall hired an orchestra that chose all of the music it performed, including copyrighted compositions owned by the plaintiff. The dance hall was found liable for the infringement committed by the orchestra since it hired the orchestra and stood to make a profit from its performance. The court's decision was based solely on the dance hall's financial benefit from the performance and did not even mention whether the dance hall had any control over the performance.

Example 10.12:

In *Fonovisa, Inc. v. Cherry Auction, Inc.*,[16] Cherry Auction ran a flea market where independent vendors set up booths to sell cassette tapes as well as other items. Fonovisa, a record company that specialized in Latin and Hispanic recordings, sued Cherry Auction alleging that many of the tapes sold were unauthorized copies of its copyrighted sound recordings. Fonovisa also alleged that Cherry Auction knew that most of the tapes being sold were counterfeit since they were being sold for prices well below normal sales prices (i.e., 3 tapes for $5). Although the vendors were direct infringers, Cherry Auction was found liable for both contributory and vicarious infringement. With respect to contributory infringement, the court found that Cherry Auction was clearly aware that massive quantities of counterfeited recordings were being sold and that Cherry Auction's provision of booth space, utilities, parking, advertising, plumbing and customers materially contributed to the infringement. With respect to vicarious liability, the court found that Cherry Auction controlled and patrolled the vendors during the flea market and received substantial financial benefits from the infringing sales, including rental fees from vendors, admission fees from customers, and payments for parking, food and other services.

One area where contributory infringement and vicarious liability are extremely important is for infringements that occur over the Internet. Since there are many direct infringers, it is not practical for copyright owners to sue them all individually for infringement. Instead, copyright owners usually prefer to sue the Internet Service Provider, which provides Internet access and other facilities that enable infringements to take place. See chapter 15 for further discussion of contributory infringement and vicarious liability in the context of the Internet.

C. JOINT AND SEVERAL LIABILITY

If a copyright owner wins an infringement suit, all infringing parties (whether direct, contributory or vicarious) will be jointly and severally liable for the infringement. In other words, the copyright owner can try to collect its judgment from any of the losing parties. This is an important reason why copyright infringement lawsuits often include more than one defendant.

Example 10.13:

If you believe that a song you own has been stolen by a famous recording artist, you would sue not only the artist, but also the artist's record company and the publishing company which claims to own the artist's song. If you sue and win, you would then be able to collect your award from whomever you can get it from quickest. If the artist claims he is broke and files for bankruptcy, you would still be entitled to collect the full amount from the record company and the publisher.

1. 17 U.S.C. § 501(b).
2. 420 F. Supp. 177 (SDNY 1976).
3. *Selle v. Gibb*, 567 F. Supp. 1173 (1983).
4. *Ferguson v. National Broadcasting Co.*, 584 F.2d 111, 113 (5th Cir. 1978).
5. 863 F.2d 1061 (1988).
6. *Darrell v. Joe Morris Music Co.*, 113 F.2d 80 (2d Cir. 1940).
7. 567 F. Supp. 1173 (1983).
8. 59 F.3d 1046 (1995).
9. 177 F.R.D. 189 (1998).
10. 420 F. Supp. 177 (1976).
11. 443 F.2d 1159 (2d Cir. 1971).
12. *Sega Enters. Ltd v. MAPHIA*, 857 F. Supp. 679 (N.D. Cal. 1994).
13. *Fonovisa, Inc., v. Cherry Auction, Inc.*, 76 F.3d 259 (9th Cir. 1996) (quoting *Fonovisa v. Cherry Auction, Inc.*, 847 F. Supp. 1492, 1496 (E.D. Cal. 1994)).
14. 316 F.2d 304 (2d Cir. 1963).
15. 36 F.2d 354 (7th Cir. 1929).
16. 76 F.3d 259 (9th Cir. 1996).

CHAPTER 11

Defenses to Infringement

▼

"If nature has made one thing less susceptible than all others of exclusive property, it is the action of the thinking power called an idea, which an individual may exclusively possess as long as he keeps it to himself; but the moment it is divulged, it forces itself into the possession of everyone, and the receiver cannot dispossess himself of it. Its peculiar character, too, is that no one possesses the less, because every other possesses the whole of it . . . That ideas should freely spread from one to another over the globe, for the moral and mutual instruction of man, and improvement of his condition, seems to have been peculiarly and benevolently designed by nature, when she made them, like fire, expansible over all space, without lessening their density at any point, and like the air in which we breathe, move, and have our physical being, incapable of confinement or exclusive appropriation." Thomas Jefferson

A copyright owner's exclusive rights are subject to various defenses. A defense is a defendant's assertion of a legal reason why the plaintiff's claim is not valid. In certain situations, even when someone has directly copied from a copyrighted work, the person may not be liable for copyright infringement if the otherwise infringing conduct is protected by a defense.

There are several general legal defenses that may apply to copyright infringement claims as well as certain specific defenses to copyright infringement claims. The most important of these defenses are discussed below.

I. Statute of Limitations

Like most types of legal claims, copyright infringement claims are subject to a statute of limitations. A statute of limitations is a law which specifies a maximum time period during which a claim can be made. Statutes of limitations are intended to encourage people to act promptly to enforce their rights. In general, the longer you wait to bring a legal claim, the more difficult it is to resolve a dispute fairly since witnesses' memories fade over time, relevant documents may be lost and witnesses may die or be unavailable to testify.

The 1976 Copyright Act provides that a claim for copyright infringement must be brought within three years from the date upon which the infringement should reasonably have been discovered.[1] When an infringement should have reasonably discovered is a question that must be resolved by a court as illustrated by the following examples.

Example 11.1:

In *Merchant v. Lymon*,[2] a court held that the three-year statute of limitations prevented the plaintiffs from recovering royalties from the hit song "Why Do Fools Fall in Love?" The plaintiffs (two members of the group Frankie Lymon and the Teenagers) claimed that the copyright registration for the song inaccurately attributed authorship credit and that they were co-authors of the song with Frankie Lymon. The song was recorded and released on Gee Records, which was owned by George Goldner. Goldner filed a registration application in 1956, listing himself and Lymon as co-authors. He later amended the registration to state that the actual authors were Lymon and Morris Levy, who had purchased Gee Records and Goldner's publishing company. Levy was reported to have ties to the mafia and although the plaintiffs alleged that the reason they had not brought their claim earlier was that Levy had threatened to have them killed, the court refused to accept this allegation. Since the plaintiffs took no formal legal action until bringing their lawsuit in 1987, the statute of limitations prohibited them from recovering royalties earned prior to three years before commencement of the lawsuit.

The three-year limitations period for copyright infringement claims begins to run from the moment the infringement begins. If the infringement is of a continuing nature, the limitations period begins to run from the date of the last act of infringement. Generally, if you win a suit for copyright infringement, you can only recover the damages or profits that were earned within three years before the suit.

In some circumstances, courts will decide to toll or delay the application of the statute of limitations. This is usually only done for equitable reasons that would make it unfair to apply the statute of limitations to the particular case. For instance, in cases where an infringer has concealed the infringing activity from the copyright owner, courts will almost always toll the statute of limitations. When deciding whether the statute of limitations should be tolled, courts will usually balance the degree to which the copyright owner was justifiably ignorant of the infringing conduct against the degree to which the infringer justifiably relied on the copyright owner's failure to sue within the limitations period. When the statute of limitations is tolled, it will not be applied until the copyright owner discovered or by reasonable diligence should have discovered the infringing activity.

Example 11.2:

A recording artist in Australia records a song copyrighted in the United States without obtaining a license and without the copyright owner's knowledge. The record containing the artist's song is released solely in Australia in 1990. If the copyright owner doesn't find out about the record until 1999, a court might toll the statute of limitations and allow the copyright owner to recover damages for all of the record sales that occurred since 1990. However, if the record received radio airplay in the United States, a court would be much less likely to toll the statute of limitations because the copyright owner should have known of its existence. In this situation, the copyright owner would still be able to recover damages for infringements that occurred during the three years before the copyright owner files suit for infringement (1996-1999).

> **Tip:** If you believe that a copyrighted work that you own is being infringed, contact a copyright attorney promptly to avoid potential statute of limitations problems. The longer you wait to enforce your rights, the greater the risk that you will lose your rights.

A related defense to the statute of limitations is known as laches. In rare circumstances, even though the statute of limitations has not expired, a defendant might claim that the plaintiff has unreasonably delayed bringing an infringement lawsuit. Normally, courts will only seriously consider the laches defense when the delay was very unreasonable and has somehow prejudiced the defendant, making it unfair for the plaintiff to proceed with an infringement claim.

II. Abandonment of Copyright

A copyright owner can abandon its copyright by committing some act that clearly indicates an intent to surrender rights in the copyrighted work and to allow the public to copy it. For instance, a copyright owner may declare its intent to abandon the copyright to a work by placing a statement on copies of the work that the work is free to be reproduced, performed or displayed. Prior to March 1, 1989 (the effective date of the Berne Implementation Amendment), abandonment could occur due to the copyright owner's distribution of a work without copyright notice. Abandonment will generally not be implied by actions such as the failure to prosecute copyright infringements or to promote the copyrighted work.

III. Independent Creation

If a defendant in a copyright infringement action can prove that it created its work independently, rather than having copied it from the plaintiff's work, the defendant will not be liable for infringement. This makes perfect sense because the essence of copyright infringement is copying, and if the defendant did not copy the plaintiff's work, there could not possibly be an infringement. Independent creation is technically not a defense to copyright infringement since if there is no copying there is nothing to defend against. However, independent creation is like a defense in that it is something that must be proved by a defendant.

In order to prove independent creation, the defendant would have to prove that any similarities between its work and the plaintiff's work are coincidental. If the defendant can prove that its work was created before the plaintiff's work, it will be clear that its work was independently created since it obviously could not have copied a work that didn't exist. In such a situation, if the defendant had registered its work shortly after its creation, the registration certificate would be proof of independent creation. If the work was not registered or registered after creation of the plaintiff's work, the defendant would have to offer some other form of proof of when it created the work such as witnesses who observed the defendant creating its work or dated notes.

Example 11.3:

In some copyright infringement trials, the artist being sued will actually play the song or portion of the song in order to show how they created it. In a suit over her song "9 to 5," Dolly Parton sang the Ray Charles song "I Can't Stop Loving You" in the same style as "9 to 5" in order to show how you can make one song sound like another. In another case, *Fantasy, Inc. v. Fogerty,* John Fogerty played guitar and sang portions of several of his including "Proud Mary," "Down on the Corner," "Born on the Bayou," "Run through the Jungle," and "Have You Ever Seen the Rain." In 1999, during an infringement trial in Canada, Sarah McLachlan spent a considerable amount of time performing portions of her songs to illustrate her songwriting process.

Tip: Songwriters should keep any written notes (e.g., lyric sheets, etc.) created during the songwriting process or record their songwriting sessions. Mark any notes or recordings with the titles of the songs worked on, the names of the writers and the date or dates during which the songwriting activity took place. This kind of documentation can be extremely useful if you are ever sued for copyright infringement because the notes or recordings can be used as evidence of independent creation.

IV. Fair Use

A. WHAT IS FAIR USE?

The defense of fair use is one of the broadest and most confusing doctrines in copyright law. Basically, fair use means that although certain uses of copyrighted works would otherwise be infringements of copyright, these uses should be allowed due to some public benefit derived from them. Fair use can be defined as a privilege that allows someone other than the copyright owner to use a copyrighted work in a reasonable manner without the owner's consent, notwithstanding the monopoly granted to the owner.[3] The purpose of the fair use defense is to help accomplish copyright law's primary goal of providing the widest possible access to creative works. It also allows for the right of free speech guaranteed by the 1st Amendment. The fair use doctrine is intended to allow certain uses of copyrighted works that encourage the advancement of learning and knowledge. As stated by the Supreme Court, fair use:

allows courts to avoid the rigid application of the copyright statute when, on occasion, it would stifle the very creativity which that law is designed to foster."[4]

Example 11.4:

A music reviewer's quotation of lyrics from a copyrighted song in a review of the song or the album it's contained on would be fair use.

It is important to understand that fair use is a defense rather than an affirmative right. Consequently, the only way to know for sure whether a particular use is fair or not is if the copyright owner sues for infringement and the court upholds the fair use defense. Although many people use copyrighted works on the assumption that their use is fair, this assumption can be risky since no use is technically a fair use until a court says so. There is no way to be absolutely certain in advance whether a use will be considered fair. You cannot prevent being sued for copyright infringement by claiming fair use.

> **Tip:** Some people have misconceptions about the fair use doctrine, often believing that it allows them to use copyrighted works as long as they think it is fair to do so. Fair use, however, depends on whether a court thinks your use is fair. Even if you believe that your use qualifies as fair use, it can be very costly to prove that in court. Consequently, it is often advisable to request permission for the use of copyrighted works and pay the customary fee or royalty even if you think the use may be fair. The amount you pay under a license to use a work will almost always be less than the amount you will spend in defending a copyright infringement claim (i.e., attorneys fees, deposition fees, etc).

> **Tip:** Some people mistakenly believe that it is fair use as long as you give credit to the author or copyright owner of the work used. There is no such rule and crediting the author is not likely to be helpful in proving fair use.

B. ORIGINS OF FAIR USE

Unfortunately, courts have applied the fair use defense inconsistently over the years. The fair use doctrine developed through court decisions in the United States and was made a part of the Copyright Act of 1976. The first case to apply the fair use doctrine, *Folsom v. Marsh*,[5] involved an infringement suit brought in 1841 by the copyright owner of a twelve-volume historical work on George Washington against a defendant who had made a condensed version of the plaintiff's work. In doing so, the defendant copied 353 pages of the plaintiff's work. The Court stated that to determine whether a particular use of a copyrighted work is fair, the court should examine:

[The] nature and objects of the selections made, the quantity and value of materials used, and the degree in which the use may prejudice the sale, or diminish the profits, or supersede the objects, of the original work.

Applying these criteria, the court found that the defendant's use was not fair since it would unduly reduce the economic incentive of authors to produce. The court also relied on the fact that the defendant did not really create a new work, but merely edited an existing work into a shorter version. The factors put forth in *Folsom* to evaluate fair use became the basis for every subsequent fair use case in the United States and for the fair use provision of the 1976 Copyright Act. In essence, fair use involves a balancing test between the social benefit that the public derives from the unauthorized use against the interest of the copyright owner.

C. FAIR USE UNDER THE 1976 COPYRIGHT ACT

The 1976 Copyright Act recognized the fair use doctrine, which had developed through case law. However, the Copyright Act does not actually define fair use. In fact, the legislative history to the Copyright Act stated that the fair use doctrine is "an equitable rule of reason," and, as such, is not susceptible of any "generally applicable definition."[6] Instead of providing a definition, the Copyright Act lists several illustrative examples of the types of use that are likely to be fair use and specifies a four factor test to be used to determine whether a use is fair. The fair use provision of the Copyright Act is contained in § 107 which provides that:

Notwithstanding the provisions of sections 106 and 106A, the fair use of a copyrighted work, including such use by reproduction in copies or phonorecords or by any other means specified by that section, for purposes such as criticism, comment, news reporting, teaching (including multiple copies for classroom use), scholarship, or research, is not an infringement of copyright. In determining whether the use made of a work in any particular case is a fair use the factors to be considered shall include -

(1) the purpose and character of the use, including whether such use is of a commercial nature or is for nonprofit educational purposes;

(2) the nature of the copyrighted work;

(3) the amount and substantiality of the portion used in relation to the copyrighted work as a whole; and

(4) the effect of the use upon the potential market for or value of the copyrighted work.

The first part of § 107 gives some examples of the types of uses that may be fair use (i.e., criticism, comment, news reporting, teaching, scholarship, and research). It is important to note that these examples are not exhaustive and there may be other types of uses that will be considered fair use as well. Further, the fact that a use fits one of these categories will not guarantee a finding of fair use.

The second part of § 107 lists the four factors that must be considered in evaluating a fair use question. To determine whether a particular use is fair, a court must evaluate each of the four factors and weigh them. Although § 107 does not specify what weight should be given to each of the four factors, courts usually give the greatest weight to the first and fourth factors. A court may also consider any additional factors that it believes are relevant.

(1) The Purpose and Character of the Use
The analysis of the first factor of the fair use test involves determining the purpose for which the use is being made. There are several considerations that are normally involved in analyzing the purpose of the use such as whether the use is for a commercial or noncommercial purpose and whether the use is for an educational or some other socially valuable purpose.

One important consideration under the first factor is whether the use is for a commercial or a nonprofit purpose. In general, commercial uses will weigh against fair use while nonprofit uses will weigh toward fair use. However, not all commercial uses will be unfair and not all nonprofit uses will be fair. In reality, most uses are commercial to some extent. According to the Supreme Court:

[T]he crux of the profit/nonprofit distinction is not whether the sole motive of the use is monetary gain but whether the user stands to profit from exploitation of the copyrighted material without paying the customary price."[7]

Even a commercial use can qualify as fair use if the public will receive some benefit from the defendant's use. In fact, the majority of cases finding fair use have involved commercial uses. As stated by the Supreme Court:

If, indeed, commerciality carried presumptive force against a finding of fairness, the presumption would swallow nearly all of the illustrative uses listed in the preamble paragraph of §107, including news reporting, comment, criticism, teaching, scholarship, and research, since these activities are generally conducted for profit in this country.[8]

The public benefits from uses providing information (i.e., criticism, comment and news reporting) and uses related to education (i.e., teaching, scholarship and research). These types of uses are therefore more likely to be fair than uses that do not fall within these categories. Additionally, a use that has a productive or transformative purpose is more likely to be fair than a use that merely replaces the original work. If a use changes an original work in some way to create something new, its transformative character may outweigh its commercial purpose.

Example 11.5:

In *Withol v. Crow,*[9] a court held that it was not fair use for a teacher to make a new arrangement (i.e., a derivative work) of a copyrighted musical work and distribute copies to a school choir without the copyright owner's permission.

In certain situations, the character of a use may be incidental. For instance, if a copyrighted work is used incidentally and as background in a different type of work, the use is likely to be fair since does not compete with the copyrighted work.

Example 11.6:

A television broadcast of a parade which included a band playing a copyrighted song was held to be a fair use describing the use as an "incidental and fortuitous reproduction, in a newsreel or broadcast, of a work located in the scene of the event being reported."[10] Similarly, the use of fifteen seconds of a copyrighted song as part of a political campaign advertisement was held to be fair use when the song was in the background of an opposing politician's radio commercial.[11]

Courts have also weighed a defendant's bad faith against a fair use finding and a defendant's good faith in favor of a fair use finding. Although a defendant's good faith is relevant in fair use analysis, the failure to obtain the copyright owner's permission to use a copyrighted work does not constitute bad faith.

Example 11.7:

In *Campbell v. Acuff-Rose Music, Inc.*[12] (discussed in detail below), the court stated that the 2 Live Crew's failure to obtain permission to use the song "Oh, Pretty Woman" in a parody did not evidence bad faith. Instead, the Court believed that 2 Live Crew's license request may have been a good faith effort to avoid litigation, showing that they were willing to pay the customary price for their use.

(2) The Nature of the Copyrighted Work

The second factor to be considered under § 107 is "the nature of the copyrighted work." This factor is concerned with the copyrighted work itself rather than the use made of the copyrighted work. The use of an unpublished work is less likely to be fair than that of a published work since the copyright owner may have decided not to make the work available to the public. Additionally, the use of a factual work is more likely to be fair use than the use of a creative work since facts should be free for everyone to use. Since musical works such as songs and sound recordings are virtually always creative in nature, this factor will normally weigh against fair use. However, the second factor is also usually viewed as the least important of the four factors.

(3) The Amount and Substantiality of the Portion Used

The third factor involves the amount and substantiality of the portion of the copyrighted work used compared to the copyrighted work as a whole. In general, the greater the amount of the copyrighted work used, the less likely that a use will be fair. In evaluating this factor, it is important to consider only copyrightable material that has been copied rather than uncopyrightable ideas that may be contained in the copyrighted work. It is also important to realize that there are no absolute rules as to how much of a copyrighted work may be copied and still be considered fair use.

Example 11.8:

In a 1978 case,[13] a candidate for political office used fifteen seconds of his opponent's copyrighted campaign song in a political ad. The court found that this was a fair use since the song was part of a political message and the portion copied was relatively brief. However, if a more substantial portion of a song was used under similar circumstances, the result could be different. In the 1996 presidential campaign, Bob Dole's campaign staff adapted the song "Soul Man" so that it was performed as "Dole Man." Steve Cropper, the song's author and copyright owner, did not approve of this use (quite likely due to his much more liberal political orientation) and threatened the Dole campaign with a copyright infringement lawsuit. Wisely, Dole's campaign stopped using the song.

In addition to the quantity of material copied, the quality of that material must also be considered. In other words, even if only a small portion of a copyrighted work is used, if the portion used is an essential part of the copyrighted work, it will weigh against fair use. Courts often make numerical comparisons (i.e., of words, musical notes, measures, etc.) between the total length of the plaintiff's work and the amount copied by the defendant. For instance, in *Fisher v. Dees*,[14] a court held that the use of the first six bars of a 38 bar song was a fair use. However, more emphasis is normally placed on the quality of the amount copied. Even if only a very small part of a work is copied, the use will not usually be fair if the part taken is of critical importance to the work as a whole. Especially in the case of musical composition, the use of even a very small amount of a copyrighted work may be considered substantial.

If I were to copy the four-note theme from Beethoven's 5th Symphony, most people would recognize that theme. Even though the copying only involves four notes and would be quantitatively insubstantial, it is qualitatively substantial since those four notes constitute the most recognizable part of the work. In this situation however, there would be no risk of copyright infringement because Beethoven's 5th Symphony is in the public domain.

Tip: Most uses of music, even if only a few bars are used, will not be fair unless they are non-commercial and for purposes of criticism, comment, education or news reporting. In most circumstances, it is advisable to obtain a license rather than rely on fair use.

(4) The Effect of the Use upon the Potential Market for or Value of the Copyrighted Work

Under the fourth factor, an analysis must be made of how the defendant's use will affect the value of the copyrighted work. This factor is generally viewed as the most important of the four. In the broadest sense, every fair use involves some degree of harm to the copyright owner since fair uses are not licensed and do not produce income for the copyright owner. However, some degree of harm to the copyright owner is tolerated in certain circumstances due to the public benefit obtained from the use of the work.

Example 11.10:

If a movie producer uses a copyrighted sound recording as part of the soundtrack for a movie without obtaining a license, this will not be a fair use. Obviously, such a use negatively impacts the market for the copyrighted work since this type of use is normally licensed and is one of the ways the copyright owner of a sound recording earns income.

The analysis of the fourth factor must include consideration not only of any actual harm to the market for the work, but also any harm to potential markets for the work. In other words, you have to not only consider what uses of the work the copyright owner has made, but also any future uses the copyright owner might make. Some courts will only consider the impact of the use on traditional or reasonable markets. If the defendant's use produces a work that competes with the plaintiff's work or reduces the potential market for the work, it is likely that there will be an adverse effect on that work and that the use will not be fair. Using a work no longer available to the public (i.e., out of print) will be likely to be fair since the use will not impair the market for the original work.

When a use is commercial, an adverse impact on the market for the copyrighted work will often be presumed and the copyright owner will only have to prove that if the use were to become widespread, it would harm potential markets for the work. On the other hand, if the use is transformative, an adverse impact on potential markets for the work will not be presumed.

Example 11.11:

A magazine publishes a record review that contains part of the lyrics of a song. This use will probably be fair since the purpose of the use is comment or criticism and it does not adversely affect the market for the original work. Even so, magazine publishers often obtain permission to quote lyrics and music publishers are normally glad to give permission provided that copyright notice and the phrase "used by permission" accompany the use.

(5) Parody as Fair Use

Parody is one type of use that will often qualify as fair use. One court defined parody as "a literary or artistic work that imitates the characteristic style of an author or a work for comic effect or ridicule."[15] In order for a parody to be protected as fair use, the work copied to make the parody must, at least in part, be the object of the parody. In other words, a parody must comment upon or criticize the original work. The legal definition of parody is different from what is commonly known as satire. Parody involves the use of a copyrighted work in order to criticize or make fun of the work. Satire involves the use of a copyrighted work in order to comment on or make fun of something other than the copyrighted work such as society in general. Satire, unlike parody, is not likely to be fair use since it is not necessary to use a copyrighted work to comment upon something other than the copyrighted work.

Although parodies will often be considered to be fair use, there is no rule that all parodies will qualify as fair use. As with any other fair use determination, the specific facts must be analyzed under the four-factor test of § 107.

a. The 2 Live Crew–Pretty Woman Case

In order to illustrate how the four-factor fair use test is applied to parody, it is helpful to examine how the Supreme Court utilized this test in an actual case. In 1994, the Supreme Court decided a case that clarified some of the confusion and inconsistency of prior case law applying the fair use doctrine to parody. In *Campbell v. Acuff-Rose Music, Inc.*,[16] a music publisher, Acuff-Rose, sued Luther Campbell of the rap group 2 Live Crew for infringing its copyrighted song "Oh, Pretty Woman," written by Roy Orbison and William Dees. 2 Live Crew had recorded a song called "Pretty Woman" that copied parts of the music and lyrics from "Oh, Pretty Woman." 2 Live Crew had requested a license to use the song from Acuff-Rose, but Acuff-Rose denied the request and 2 Live Crew released their version of the song anyway.

2 Live Crew asserted that their song was a parody that should be protected under the fair use doctrine. The District Court agreed, holding that 2 Live Crew's "Pretty Woman" was a fair use parody of the Orbison song. Acuff-Rose appealed the decision and the Court of Appeals reversed, holding that the "blatantly commercial purpose" of 2 Live Crew's parody prevented it from being a fair use. 2 Live Crew appealed this decision and the Supreme Court agreed to decide the case.

The Court first addressed whether 2 Live Crew's song constituted a legal parody of the Orbison song. The Orbison song involves a 1960s romance and begins with a man who notices a beautiful woman walking down the street. He pleads with her to spend the night with him, but she rejects his advances and walks on by. However, in the last verse, she walks back to him. 2 Live Crew's song also involves a man who notices a woman walking down the street. However, it's a different time period (i.e., the 1990s) and a different street (i.e., in the hood) where the idealism of the Orbison song no longer exists. According to the Court, 2 Live Crew's version of the song "derisively demonstrates how bland and banal the Orbison song seems to them" stating that:

Although the parody starts out with the same lyrics as the original, it quickly degenerates into a play on words, substituting predictable lyrics with shocking ones … The physical attributes of the subject woman deviate from a pleasing image of femininity to bald-headed, hairy and generally repugnant. To complete the thematic twist, at the end of the parody, the "two-timin" woman turns out to be pregnant.

Under its analysis of the first factor, the Court rejected the idea that the commercial purpose of a use automatically makes the use unfair.[17] Instead, the Court found the transformative nature of the use to be more important. Parody is by definition a transformative use. The value of transformative works is that, rather than merely copying the original work, they also add something new, thereby creating a new work with a different purpose or character. As explained by the Supreme Court:

The central purpose of this investigation is to see whether the new work merely supercedes the objects of the original creation or instead adds something new, with a further purpose or different character, altering the first with new expression, meaning or message; it asks, in other words, whether and to what extent the new work is "transformative." Although a transformative use is not necessary for a finding of fair use, the more transformative the new work, the less will be the significance of other factors, such as commercialism, that may weigh against a finding of fair use.

The Court held that the second factor, the nature of the copyrighted work, weighed against fair use due to the creative nature of the Orbison song. However, the Court didn't place too much weight on this factor since the vast majority of parodies are based upon creative works.

Under the third factor, the amount and substantiality of the portion used in relation to the copyrighted work as a whole, the Supreme Court expanded the degree to which a parodist may copy from an existing work. Earlier cases had held that a parodist is allowed to recall or conjure up the original work. In other words, a parodist could copy enough of a work to make the work recognizable as the object of the parody. Acuff-Rose argued that the 2 Live Crew had taken more of "Oh, Pretty Woman" than was necessary to make it recognizable since 2 Live Crew used almost identical music throughout their parody. The Supreme Court, however, held that parody allows for greater use of a copyrighted work than other types of use since a song is difficult to parody effectively without exact or near-exact copying. Certainly, a song parody would not be as effective if the music of the original song was not used throughout the parody. As to exactly how much a parodist can copy, the Court related the third factor to the first and third factors, stating that:

Once enough has been taken to assure identification, how much more is reasonable will depend, say, on the extent to which the song's overriding purpose and character is to parody the original or, in contrast, the likelihood that the parody may serve as a market substitute for the original.

The Court also stated that in order for a parody to be effective, it must utilize the heart of the original work since:

It is true, of course, that 2 Live Crew copied the characteristic opening bass riff (or musical phrase) of the original, and true that the words of the first line copy the Orbison lyrics. But if quotation of the opening riff and the first line may be said to go to the "heart" of the original, the heart is also what most readily conjures up the song for parody, and it is the heart at which parody takes aim. Copying does not become excessive in relation to parodic purposes merely because the portion taken was the original's heart. If 2 Live Crew had copied a significantly less memorable part of the original, it is difficult to see how its parodic character would have come through.

Finally, the Court also mentioned that the amount copied must be balanced against the amount of original material contributed by the parodist. In this case, the Court found that 2 Live Crew had contributed substantial new material (i.e., new lyrics and certain musical effects). The Court remanded to the trial court the issue of whether 2 Live Crew's use of the famous bass line throughout its song was excessive.

In analyzing the fourth factor, the effect of the use upon the potential market for or value of the copyrighted work, the Court began by stating that a use which has no demonstrable effect upon the potential market for, or the value of, the copyrighted work need not be prohibited in order to protect the author's incentive to create. Parodies will be normally be held to be fair use when the parody is unlike any use the copyright owner could reasonably be expected to make of the work.

In terms of direct competition, the 2 Live Crew song would not seem to have much effect on the market for the Orbison song. In other words, a person desiring the Orbison song is not likely to be satisfied with the 2 Live Crew song. However, harm to the market for potential derivative works must also be considered. Noting that the 2 Live Crew song is not only a parody, but also a rap song, the Court determined that the market for derivative rap version of "Oh, Pretty Woman" should be considered and remanded this issue to the trial court.

The Court also noted that a parody may harm the original work by criticizing it, thereby potentially reducing its demand. However, such critical impact should not be considered under fair use analysis since parody's primary function is to criticize. The Court stated that:

parody may quite legitimately aim at garroting the original, destroying it commercially as well as artistically.

Although the Court remanded two issues in the 2 Live Crew case for determination by the district court, these two issues were never actually resolved. Apparently, both Acuff-Rose and the 2 Live Crew decided they had spent enough time and money fighting over Pretty Woman and settled the dispute in 1996 with Acuff-Rose issuing a mechanical license for the 2 Live Crew song.

Example 11.12:

The lyrics of both "Oh, Pretty Woman" and 2 Live Crew's "Pretty Woman" as well as sound files of both songs are posted at **www.benedict.com/audio/crew/crew.htm**. Does this web site's use of the various copyrighted musical compositions and sound recordings qualify as fair use? It probably does, because the use is non-commercial, for educational purposes, and is not likely to harm the market for any of the copyrighted works.

The Supreme Court's decision in the 2 Live Crew case has been misinterpreted by many people as setting forth a strict rule that all parodies are fair use. In reality, the Supreme Court merely ruled that parodies may qualify as fair use, but are subject to evaluation under the four-factor test of § 107. The Supreme Court did indicate that the two most important factors in analyzing whether a particular parody is a fair use are whether the use is transformative and the effect of the use on the potential market for the original work.

> **Tip:** Since fair use is never guaranteed, it is often advisable to obtain permission to make a parody of a copyrighted work. For example, Weird Al Yankovic obtains licenses for his parody versions of popular songs such as "Eat It" (Michael Jackson's "Beat It"), "Like a Surgeon" (Madonna's "Like a Virgin"), "Pretty Fly For A Rabbi" (The Offspring's "Pretty Fly for A White Guy") and "Smells Like Nirvana" (Nirvana's "Smells Like Teen Spirit").

b. Other Parody Cases

There have been many copyright lawsuits involving parodies, many of which are very interesting and entertaining. The following are several notable parody cases involving musical works:

1. *Fisher v. Dees*[18]—Disc jockey Rick Dees recorded a parody song entitled "When Sonny Sniffs Glue," which used the music from the 1950s hit song "When Sunny Gets Blue" recorded by Johnny Mathis. The parody was determined to be a fair use because it did not unfairly diminish the value of the parodied work (i.e., no one interested in hearing a romantic ballad would be satisfied to hear the parody instead). Although the plaintiff had argued that the parody reflected negatively on the original song and therefore affected its marketability, the court stated that "the economic effect of a parody with which we are concerned is not its potential to destroy or diminish the market for the original—any bad review can have that effect—but whether it fulfills the demand for the original . . . Parodists will seldom get permission from those whose works are parodied. Self-esteem is seldom strong enough to permit the granting of permission even in exchange for a reasonable fee." In other words, a parody's critical impact on the market for the parodied work is not relevant to the fair use analysis.

2. *Berlin v. E.C. Publications*[19]—Mad Magazine published an issue that contained various parody lyrics (i.e., lyrics that were to be sung to the tune of popular songs). One example involved Irving Berlin's "A Pretty Girl Is Like a Melody," which was turned into "Louella Schwartz Describes Her Malady," in which Berlin's tribute to feminine beauty became a parody of a hypochondriac. This was held as fair use because the use had neither the intent nor the effect of fulfilling the demand for the original songs.

3. *Elsmere Music, Inc. v. NBC*[20]—The television show *Saturday Night Live* did a skit making fun of New York City's public relations campaign with actors singing a song called "I Love Sodom" to the tune of "I Love New York." The only parts of the original song copied were the words "I love" and four musical notes, but the court held this to be qualitatively substantial. The court ruled it to be a fair use, primarily relying on the fourth factor ("the defendant's version of the jingle did not compete with or detract from the plaintiff's work").

4. *Walt Disney Productions v. Mature Pictures Corp.*[21]—Mature Pictures produced a movie entitled "The Life and Times of the Happy Hooker" which contained a scene in which three teenagers sing part of the lyrics of the "Mickey Mouse March" after which the "Mickey Mouse March" is played as background music while the three young men have a sexual encounter with the heroine. Held not to be fair use since the use was not legally a parody (it did not comment or criticize the original song). Further, the defendants used the original work without changing or adding anything, so their use was not transformative.

5. *MCA v. Wilson*[22]—A musical play called *Let My People Come*, which was billed as an "erotic nude show," contained a song entitled "Cunnilingus Champion of Company C" sung to the tune of the Andrews Sisters' "Boogie Woogie Bugle Boy of Company B." Held not fair use since it did not comment on the original work. The court stated that "[w]e are not prepared to hold that a commercial composer can plagiarize a competitor's copyrighted song, substitute dirty lyrics of his own, perform it for commercial gain, and then escape liability by calling the end result a parody or satire on the mores of society."

Tip: Although fair use questions are decided on a case-by-case basis and there is no way to guarantee that a use is fair, in order to get an idea of whether a use is likely to be fair, ask yourself the following questions:

1. Are you just copying from someone else's work or adding substantial original material in order to transform it into a new work? The more transformative your work, the more likely it will be a fair use.

2. Will your use compete with the work you are copying from? If your use harms or even potentially harms the market for the original work or any derivatives of the original work, it will not likely be fair.

3. How much copyrighted material have you copied? The more you have copied, the less likely your use will be fair.

4. How important is the part of the work you have copied to the original work? The more important the material copied (even if only a small portion), the less likely your use will be fair.

V. De Mimimis Copying

In some circumstances, a court might decide that, although material from a copyrighted work was copied, the amount copied is insubstantial and inconsequential or de minimis. For example, it is possible that if a recording artist incorporated a sample of a very small, unrecognizable portion of a copyrighted sound recording in a new sound recording, the use might be excused as de minimis. However, it is risky to rely on this defense since there are no clear legal rules on how much can be copied and courts tend to be quite conservative in applying the de minimis defense.

VI. Fraud on the Copyright Office

In rare circumstances, if a copyright owner files a registration with the Copyright Office containing false information that would have caused the Copyright Office to reject the application, a court may declare the registration invalid and deny enforcement of the copyright. This will only happen when the copyright owner has knowingly supplied false information on a registration application or recordation of a transfer of copyright ownership. If an error is only clerical in nature or is made inadvertently, the registration will not be invalidated.

VII. Misuse of Copyright

Another very rarely successful defense involves situations where a copyright owner has engaged in some type of anticompetitive behavior. The rationale for this defense is that the defendant has engaged in wrongful conduct that should prevent it from being able to enforce its copyright.

Example 11.13:

In the recording industry's lawsuit against Napster (see chapter 14 for a detailed discussion of the Napster case), Napster alleged that the major record labels had been using their monopoly power to beyond the scope of their copyrights by controlling the distribution of music over the Internet and restricting the distribution of artists not signed to the major labels. The court ruled that the misuse defense was inapplicable because Napster could not prove that the record labels had engaged in any illegal conduct.

VIII. Innocent Intent

The fact that a person does not realize that his actions constitute copyright infringement is not a defense to a copyright infringement action. A person who infringes a copyrighted work unintentionally, even without reason to believe that he is infringing, is liable for infringement. Innocent infringement can occur when an infringer believes that a copyrighted work is in the public domain. It can also occur when a music publisher, record company or record distributor relies on a songwriter's promise that an infringing song was written by the songwriter when it was actually copied from someone else's copyrighted work. The primary reason for not allowing innocence as a defense is that, as between the copyright owner and the infringer, it is fairer to put the burden on the infringer to guard against infringing.

6. The Court of Appeals had relied on the presumption that a use for any commercial purpose is unfair. This presumption originated in a previous case, *Sony Corp. v. Universal City Studios, Inc.*, 464 U.S. 17, 451 (1984). However, the Supreme Court in *Campbell* held that the Court of Appeals had placed too much emphasis on the commercial purpose and failed to take into account the transformative character of the use.

7. 794 F.2d 431 (9th Cir. 1986).

8. 329 F.2d 541 (2d Cir. 1964).

9. 623 F.2d 252 (2d Cir. 1980).

0. 389 F. Supp. 1397 (S.D.N.Y. 1975).

1. 677 F. Supp. 180 (2d Cir. 1992).

2. 420 F. Supp. 177 (1976).

3. Black's Law Dictionary 415 (6th ed. 1991).

4. *Stewart v. Abend*, 495 U.S. 207 (1990).

5. 9 F. Cas. 342 (C.C.D. Mass. 1841).

6. H.R. Rep. No. 94-1476, 94th Cong., 2d Sess. at 65 (1976).

7. *Harper & Row Publishers, Inc. v. Nation Enterprises*, 471 U.S. 539, 562 (1985).

8. *Luther R. Campbell aka Luke Skyywalker v. Acuff-Rose Music, Inc.*, 510 U.S. 569 (1994).

9. 309 F.2d 777 (1962).

10. *Italian Book Corporation v. American Broadcasting Companies, Inc.*, 485 F. Supp. 65 (1978).

11. *Keep Thompson Governor Committee v. Citizens for Gallen Committee*, 457 F. Supp. 957 (1978).

13. *Luther R. Campbell aka Luke Skyywalker v. Acuff-Rose Music, Inc.*, 510 U.S. 569 (1994).

12. *Keep Thompson Governor Committee v. Citizens for Gallen Committee*, 457 F. Supp. 957 (D.N.H. 1978).

13. 794 F.2d 432 (9th Cir. 1986).

14. *Luther R. Campbell aka Luke Skyywalker v. Acuff-Rose Music, Inc.*, 510 U.S. 569 (1994).

15. *Luther R. Campbell aka Luke Skyywalker v. Acuff-Rose Music, Inc.*, 510 U.S. 569 (1994).

Remedies for Copyright Infringement

▼

"Creative work is to be encouraged and rewarded, but private motivation must ultimately serve the cause of promoting broad public availability of literature, music, and the other arts." Sony v. Universal

If you win a copyright infringement suit, there are several different legal remedies that you may be entitled to. Some of these remedies are coercive in nature and are designed to prevent further infringement, while others are compensatory in nature and are designed to compensate the copyright owners for losses incurred as a result of the infringement. Finally, some copyright infringements are subject to criminal as well as civil prosecution.

I. Coercive Remedies

A. INJUNCTION

Courts deciding copyright infringement actions, have the authority under § 502(a) of the Copyright Act to grant injunctions on terms that the court believes reasonable to prevent or restrain infringement. An injunction is a court order telling someone to stop doing something. In a copyright infringement claim, a court might grant an injunction ordering the defendant to stop its infringing conduct.

Example 12.1:

In one case,[1] rap artist Biz Markie used an unauthorized sample from the Gilbert O'Sullivan song "Alone Again (Naturally)" on a song contained on his album on Warner Brothers Records. The court issued an injunction ordering Warner Brothers to stop selling the album containing the infringing song. Warner Brothers consequently had to discontinue sales of the album and take back unsold copies from retailers and distributors.

An injunction may be temporary (pending resolution of the suit) or final. A temporary restraining order may be granted shortly after a complaint is filed for infringement. A hearing must then be held within ten days to determine whether a preliminary injunction should be ordered. A preliminary injunction is effective until the case is finally decided. A judge will usually order a preliminary injunction when it is likely that the plaintiff will be successful in its infringement suit and the plaintiff would be irreparably harmed if the injunction is not issued. In copyright infringement claims, irreparable harm (harm that can't be cured otherwise) is normally presumed to exist. An exception would be when an infringement involves a defendant's recording of a musical work. In this situation, irreparable harm would not be presumed since the defendant's use would be subject to compulsory mechanical licensing under the Copyright Act and therefore would be fully compensated by a monetary award in the amount of the mechanical license fees that would have been paid if a license had been obtained.

In some cases where a preliminary injunction is issued, the court also orders the plaintiff to post a bond as a form of security. If the plaintiff loses its suit, the defendant will be allowed to collect the damages incurred as a result of the injunction from the bond. If a defendant continues the infringing conduct after an injunction has been issued, it is subject to fines and potential imprisonment.

B. IMPOUNDMENT

In addition to an injunction, a court may also order the impoundment of allegedly infringing articles. Section 503(a) of the Copyright Act provides that a court may:

order the impounding, on such terms as it may deem reasonable, of all copies or phonorecords claimed to have been made or used in violation of the copyright owner's exclusive rights, and of all plates, molds, matrices, masters, tapes, film negatives, or other articles by means of which such copies or phonorecords may be reproduced.

Under an impoundment order, all infringing goods as well as instruments used to make such goods are collected and held until the court makes a final judgment on the infringement claim. After a plaintiff files an affidavit identifying the number, value and location of the alleged infringing copies or devices and a bond, the court can order a federal marshal to seize and hold the materials identified in the affidavit. The defendant has the right to ask the court to order the return of impounded articles by filing an affidavit showing that the articles are not infringing.

Example 12.2:

In a copyright infringement action involving record piracy, a court could order the impoundment of not only the allegedly pirated recordings, but also any recording equipment, blank tapes and discs, labels and packaging materials used to manufacture the pirated recordings.

C. DESTRUCTION

If a court finds a defendant guilty of infringement, it may order the destruction of infringing articles. Section 503(b) of the Copyright Act provides that:

[T]he court may order the destruction or other reasonable disposition of all copies or phonorecords found to have been made or used in violation of the copyright owner's exclusive rights, and of all plates, molds, matrices, masters, tapes, film negatives, or other articles by means of which such copies or phonorecords may be reproduced.

Courts have some flexibility in ordering the disposition of infringing articles since § 503(b) allows, as an alternative to destruction, the other reasonable disposition of infringing articles. A court could therefore order that the infringing articles be sold or delivered to the plaintiff.

II. Compensatory Remedies

Many people who want to sue for copyright infringement have overly optimistic expectations of the amount of money they can recover. On several occasions, I have been approached by songwriters who believe that someone has infringed one of their songs and wants to sue for millions of dollars. In reality, you cannot just pick an amount of money to sue for out of thin air no matter how much you might believe you are entitled to. This is due to the fact that the Copyright Act specifies the monetary damages you can sue for. Unfortunately for songwriters, copyright law does not allow you to recover for emotional distress or mental anguish that may have resulted from an infringement.

The Copyright Act allows a plaintiff who wins a copyright infringement action to recover several different types of monetary remedies. Some of these remedies are designed to compensate the copyright owner for losses incurred due to the infringement and expenses incurred in connection with the infringement action while others are designed to deter copyright infringers.

A. ACTUAL DAMAGES AND PROFITS

Under § 504(b) of the Copyright Act, a successful copyright plaintiff may recover:

the actual damages suffered by him or her as a result of the infringement, and any profits of the infringer that are attributable to the infringement and are not taken into account in computing the actual damages.

Actual damages are intended to compensate the copyright owner for the losses incurred as a result of the infringement. Allowing the plaintiff to recover the defendant's profits, in addition to actual damages, is intended to prevent the defendant from profiting from the infringement and to act as a deterrent to infringement.

Actual damages are the revenues lost by the copyright owner as a result of the infringement. In order to be awarded actual damages, the copyright owner must prove the amount of money it has lost because of the infringement. Generally, actual damages will be equal to the fair market value of the use made by the infringer. For instance, if someone made an unauthorized recording of a copyrighted song, the amount of actual damages would be easy to determine. You would merely multiply the number of records distributed by the statutory mechanical license rate (currently 7.55 cents). However, if the song is released as a single from an album, determining its fair market value is a bit more difficult. Since a single promotes sales of the album, its fair market value may be higher than other songs on the same album that are not singles.

Example 12.3:

In an infringement suit brought by the Isley Brothers against Michael Bolton, the jury decided that the Isleys were entitled to 66 percent of the profits from Bolton's song as well as 28 percent of the royalties from the album it was contained on. This amounted to $5.4 million at that time since Bolton's album had sold over 7 million copies and the song was a huge radio hit. Reportedly, the Isleys had been willing to settle for about $500,000, but Bolton refused. Sony Music, Bolton's record company, came out the worst as a result of this decision, owing $4.2 million, while Bolton was ordered to pay $932,924, his co-writer $220,000, and their publishing companies $75,900.

In other situations, proving the amount of actual damages can be a bit more difficult. For example, if a copyrighted song were used in a national television commercial without authorization, the plaintiff would have to prove the amount of money it lost due to the defendant's use of the song. If the plaintiff could prove that a synchronization license for this type of use would have cost $100,000 (by offering evidence of licenses issued for similar uses or expert testimony), a court would probably award actual damages of $100,000.

In addition to actual damages, a copyright owner is allowed to recover the profits of the infringer that are attributable to the infringement and are not taken into account in computing the actual damages. The copyright owner must prove the amount of the infringer's gross profits resulting from the infringement. The infringer can then offer proof of any expenses that should be deducted from these gross profits. It would do so in the discovery period before trial by requesting financial documents from the defendant or taking the defendant's deposition. Deductible expenses would include any expenses that are directly attributable to the production, distribution, performance or display of the copyrighted work. Additionally, the infringer may offer proof of any elements of profit attributable to factors other than the copyrighted work, which would also be deducted from gross profits.

Example 12.4:

In a case involving the unauthorized use of compositions contained on a record company's release of a five-record album of Scott Joplin compositions,[2] the court awarded the copyright owner one-half of the profits earned from sales, even though the infringed works occupied only one side of the five-record set. The defendant argued that, on a strictly proportional basis, the plaintiff should receive only 10 percent of its profits, but the court held that the inclusion of the infringing compositions allowed the defendant to advertise the album as the only complete set of Joplin's works and that the defendant had failed to produce evidence disputing the contributions of the infringing compositions to the album's marketability.

In addition to profits earned directly from infringing conduct, a copyright owner may also be able to recover profits that the infringer earned indirectly as a result of its infringement. However, since indirect profits are often difficult to quantify, courts will often be hesitant to award them.

Example 12.5:

In one case,[3] the defendant used the plaintiff's musical compositions in a musical revue performed at its hotel without permission. In addition to holding the defendant liable for direct profits, the court also awarded the plaintiff a portion of the indirect profits from the defendant's hotel and casino operations that may have resulted from increased patronage generated by the infringing show. This portion of indirect profits was found to be $699,963.10, while the direct profits were $551,884.54.

B. STATUTORY DAMAGES

In many situations, it is difficult to prove the amount of actual damages and the defendant's profits from an infringement. Further, in many instances, actual damages and profits may be a very small amount of money. For example, if someone makes a recording of a song without a license, the amount of actual damages would be the statutory mechanical royalty rate multiplied by the number of records sold. If only 1000 records were sold, the amount of actual damages would be a whopping $75.50, which would often have to be split among several publishers and songwriters. Even if 100,000 records were sold (a sales figure that only a small percentage of recordings achieve), the actual damages would only be $7550.00, which would be unlikely to cover the plaintiff's costs and attorney's fees incurred in connection with an infringement suit.

In order to make it potentially worthwhile to sue for infringement in situations where actual damages and profits are hard to determine or a relatively small amount, the Copyright Act allows a copyright owner to elect to receive monetary damages within a specified range (known as "statutory damages") instead of actual damages and profits.

Unlike actual damages and profits, a plaintiff who chooses to receive statutory damages does not have to prove the amount of its losses or the defendant's profits from the infringement. A copyright owner may elect to receive statutory damages at any time before the court makes its final judgment of liability in the case. However, in order to be eligible to elect statutory damages, the copyrighted work must have been registered either before the infringement began or within three months after the work's initial publication.

Under § 504(c)(1), the general range of statutory damages is from $750 to $30,000.[4] However, the range is expanded in cases involving willful infringement and reduced in cases involving innocent infringement. In cases where a court finds that the infringement was committed willfully (i.e., the defendant knew, had reason to know, or recklessly disregarded the fact that its conduct constituted infringement), a court can increase the award of statutory damages up to $150,000.[5] Alternatively, in cases where a court finds that the infringement was committed innocently (i.e., the defendant was not aware and had no reason to believe that its acts constituted infringement), the court may reduce the award of statutory damages to $200 and may even decide not to award any statutory damages at all in certain cases where the defendant reasonably believed that its use of a work was a fair use.[6]

Within the statutorily prescribed range, courts have discretion as to the actual amount to be awarded. Most courts will try to approximate actual damages and profits when possible and in cases where a plaintiff suffered little or no actual damages and the defendant made little or no profits, courts will usually award the minimum statutory amount. When actual damages and profits cannot be easily estimated, courts tend to rely on the rationale for statutory damages—sustaining copyright incentives while deterring infringement. Statutory damage awards will normally be at the low end of the range when the infringement was technical rather than substantive. However, awards will usually be toward the high end of the range when the defendant's conduct indicates that a greater deterrent is necessary. For example, courts tend to make statutory damage awards at the high end of the range in the following types of situations:

• A defendant continues the infringing conduct after a copyright owner's objection and request that the defendant obtain a license.

• A defendant continues selling allegedly infringing goods after being served with process in a copyright infringement suit.

• A defendant fails to cooperate with the plaintiff's discovery efforts intended to determine actual damages (e.g., failing to provide documentation of record sales containing the infringing work).

• A defendant is a repeat offender such as a record pirate.

An award of statutory damages covers all infringements that occur with respect to any single work.[7] For instance, an infringer who sells a recording containing one unlicensed song is liable for one statutory damages award regardless of how many records were actually sold although the number of sales might affect the court's determination of the actual amount of the award within the statutory range (e.g., sales of a million records would result in a greater single award than sales of 100 records). However, if the infringing recording contained ten unlicensed songs, the infringer is liable for ten statutory damage awards (one for each work infringed).

C. COSTS AND ATTORNEY'S FEES

Under § 505 of the Copyright Act, a court may award reasonable attorney's fees to the prevailing party as well as the costs or expenses incurred in connection with an infringement lawsuit. The right to recover attorney's fees can be very important since many copyright infringement suits involve long, expensive trials that result in relatively small amounts of money being awarded.

Costs which may be awarded include court filing fees, expert witness fees, photocopying and postage expenses and transcription costs for witness depositions. As a incentive to encourage copyright owners to register their works, the Copyright Act requires that in order to be entitled to attorney's fees, the copyrighted work must have been registered before the infringement began or within three months of the work's publication.

The rationale for allowing a plaintiff to recover its attorney's fees and costs is to deter potential infringers and to encourage copyright owners to bring infringement suits even when actual damages and profits or statutory damages may not sufficiently cover the expenses of litigation. The rationale for allowing an award of attorney's fees and costs to prevailing defendants is to encourage defendants to defend against claims they believe to be invalid (rather than settling solely to avoid litigation expenses) and to discourage copyright owners from bringing frivolous claims.

It is important to note that the authority to award attorney's fees is discretionary and courts are therefore not required to do so. Until a few years ago, there was some disagreement among courts on the factors to be considered in determining whether to award attorney's fees. Further, some courts applied a different standard to prevailing plaintiffs and defendants in deciding whether to award attorney's fees. These courts generally required prevailing defendants to prove that the plaintiff acted in bad faith or that their claim was frivolous. In *Fogerty v. Fantasy*, an appeal of a decision by a court awarding $1,374,519 in attorney's fees to musician John Fogerty, the Supreme Court held that courts must treat prevailing plaintiffs and prevailing defendants alike. The lower court's ruling held that successful copyright defendants had to prove that the suit was frivolous or in bad faith in order to recover attorney's fees. The Supreme Court's ruling is likely to make prospective plaintiffs give more thought to bringing infringement claims and to settling their claims since if they lose, they may have to pay substantial attorney's fees to the defendant.

When deciding whether or not to award attorney's fees to the prevailing party, courts will normally consider the losing party's frivolousness, motivation, good or bad faith, as well as general considerations of compensation and deterrence. Bad faith generally occurs when a defendant willfully infringed the copyrighted work, unnecessarily delayed the litigation or refused a reasonable settlement offer. Similarly, a court may find that a plaintiff has acted in bad faith when its infringement claim clearly lacked merit, when its real motive is to harass the defendant, or when it has rejected a reasonable settlement offer. One court, for instance, held that a plaintiff had acted in bad faith when its claim "rested ultimately on alleged showings of similarities which ranged from the patently erroneous to the ridiculous or involved palpable trivialities."[8] Making a misrepresentation in an application for copyright registration may constitute bad faith justifying an award of attorney's fees against the plaintiff.[9]

Since § 505 provides that a court may award a "reasonable" attorney's fee, the question arises as to what a reasonable fee is. A court may decide to award attorney's fees, but decline to award the full amount of attorney's fees actually incurred. Some factors that courts tend to consider in determining how much to award are the time and labor required for the services performed, the customary fee, the amount involved, the results obtained and the experience and reputation of the attorney. In one case,[10] a court awarded the plaintiff its actual attorney's fees of $22,000 even though the plaintiff had only been awarded $250 in statutory damages. Although the statutory damage award was quite low, the plaintiff also received an injunction preventing any further infringement and the court therefore felt that the amount of attorney's fees was reasonable.

III. Criminal Copyright Infringement

The vast majority of copyright infringements are civil in nature and are not subject to any criminal penalties. Congress has historically been hesitant to impose criminal liability for copyright infringement in fear of deterring technological progress and due to the ease with which any individual can violate a copyright. Consequently, in the past, criminal liability has only applied to situations of large-scale piracy of copyrighted works. More recently however, Congress has increased the scope of criminal copyright liability in response to lobbying by the entertainment and computer software industries. Congress realized that with the widespread availability of copying technology and that technology's ability to make perfect reproductions, anyone can now commit large-scale copyright infringement.

A. THE 1976 COPYRIGHT ACT

The criminal provisions of the 1909 Copyright Act did not apply to sound recordings. Due to estimates that record piracy cost the recording industry over $100 million annually, the 1976 Copyright Act made certain instances of infringement of sound recordings subject to criminal penalties. If an infringement is made willfully and for purposes of commercial advantage or private financial gain, the infringer may be subject to criminal liability. For an infringement to be considered willful, the government must prove that the defendant knew that its acts constituted copyright infringement or, at least, knew that there was a high probability that its acts constituted copyright infringement. In order to prove that the defendant's conduct was for purposes of commercial advantage or private financial gain, the defendant does not have to actually make a profit, but only hope or intend to make a profit.

Under § 506(a) of the Copyright Act, criminal copyright infringement of any of the copyright owner's exclusive rights is a misdemeanor, punishable by imprisonment for up to one year, a fine, or both. However, criminal infringement of the reproduction or distribution rights may also be punishable as a felony if the defendant reproduced or distributed at least 10 copies or phonorecords of one or more copyrighted works with a retail value of more than $2,500 during any 180-day period. Felony copyright infringement is punishable by imprisonment for up to five years (and up to ten years for subsequent offenses), a fine, or both.

In criminal cases, infringing articles as well as any equipment used in the manufacture of infringing articles can be impounded and destroyed. Under § 506(b), impoundment and destruction in criminal cases is mandatory.

Under § 506(c) of the Copyright Act, criminal liability may also be imposed upon anyone who knowingly puts false information on a copyright notice with fraudulent intent. It is also a crime, under § 506(d), to remove or alter a copyright notice on a copy containing a copyrighted work with fraudulent intent (also subject to a fine of up to $2,500). However, since § 506(d) only mentions copies, it is not clear whether this provision would also apply to removing or altering the copyright notice on a phonorecord. Finally, § 506(e) makes it a crime to knowingly make a false representation of a material fact in an application for copyright registration or in any written statement filed in connection with the application. All of these actions are punishable by a fine of up to $2,500.

B. THE NO ELECTRONIC THEFT ACT

On December 16, 1997, the No Electronic Theft ("NET") Act was signed into law.[11] The NET Act expanded the applicability of criminal penalties for copyright infringement to situations where an infringer acts without direct financial motivation. Congress stated the reasoning for passing this legislation as follows:

What we are essentially saying is if you trash somebody else's property, even if you are not doing it for money but you are just doing it because you want to show how smart you are and because you are seriously maladjusted and cannot make an impression on anybody in any other way, it is as criminal as if you stole.[12]

The NET Act's passage was in response to a legal loophole that was brought to light in *United States v. LaMacchia*. In *LaMacchia*, David LaMacchia operated a web site bulletin board that allowed subscribers to upload and download copies of pirated computer software. LaMacchia not only encouraged people to upload and download copyrighted software over his bulletin board, but also warned his subscribers to act cautiously in order to avoid detection. Even though the unauthorized distribution of software facilitated by LaMacchia resulted in more than $1 million in lost revenue to copyright owners, the court found that LaMacchia was not subject to criminal liability due to a loophole in then existing copyright law.

Section 506(a) of the Copyright Act requires that in order to be guilty of criminal copyright infringement, the infringing conduct must be "for purposes of commercial advantage or private financial gain." Since the government did not have any evidence that LaMacchia had received any financial gain from his infringing conduct, he could not be convicted of criminal copyright infringement although he would clearly have been liable for civil copyright infringement if any of the software copyright owners sued him.

Despite its ruling, the LaMacchia court encouraged Congress to reexamine the state of criminal copyright law and suggested that criminal penalties should be applicable to blatantly willful, large-scale infringements, even in the absence of a financial incentive. Congress took the court's advice and passed the NET Act which expanded the Copyright Act's definition of "financial gain" to include the "receipt, or expectation of receipt, of anything of value, including the receipt of other copyrighted works." It provides for criminal penalties for the "reproduction or distribution, including by electronic means, during any 180-day period, of one or more copies or phonorecords of one or more copyrighted works, which have a total retail value of more than $1000." If an offense involves ten or more copies of one or more copyrighted works that have a retail value of $2500, the maximum penalty is three years in prison, a fine of $250,000, or both. Although the NET Act may help to deter online piracy, criminal prosecutions are not likely to be too frequent since copyright infringement is not one of the FBI or U.S. Attorney's main concerns.

Example 12.6:

In 1999, Jeffrey Levy, a 22 year-old college student at the University of Oregon became the first person convicted under the NET Act. Levy pled guilty to criminal infringement of copyright in violation of the NET Act and the Copyright Act. He admitted that in January 1999, he illegally posted thousands of MP3 files of copyrighted musical recordings as well as computer software and digitally recorded movies on his Internet web site, allowing the general public to download and copy these copyrighted products. The University of Oregon brought the matter to the attention of the Oregon State Police after it noted a very large amount of bandwidth traffic being generated from Levy's web site on its server. The Oregon State Police and the FBI investigated and confirmed that thousands of pirated music recordings, software programs and movies were available for download from the site. Levy was fined $2500, the minimum amount under the NET Act, and given two years of probation.

C. THE DIGITAL MILLENNIUM COPYRIGHT ACT

On October 28, 1998, Congress passed another piece of legislation that increased the penalties for criminal copyright infringement—the Digital Millennium Copyright Act (the "DMCA"). The DMCA, discussed further in chapter 14, provides criminal penalties for circumventing copyright protection systems and tampering with copyright management information. If the circumvention is willful and for commercial advantage or private financial gain, an infringer is subject to a fine up to $500,000, imprisoned for five years, or both. Further, the penalty may be increased to a fine of up to $1,000,000, imprisonment for up to ten years, or both for repeat offenders.

1. *Grand Upright Music Limited v. Warner Brothers Records, Inc.,* 780 F. Supp. 182 (1991).

2. *The Lottie Joplin Thomas Trust v. Crown Publishers, Inc.,* 592 F.2d 651 (9th Cir. 1978).

3. *Frank Music Corp. v. Metro-Goldwyn-Mayer, Inc.,* 886 F.2d 1545 (9th Cir. 1989). Interestingly, this suit was instituted in 1975 and was not finally resolved until 1989.

4. The statutory damages minimum and maximum amounts were recently increased by the Digital Theft Deterrence and Copyright Damages Improvement Act which was singed into law by President Clinton on December 9, 1999. Prior to that date, the range was $500 to $20,000.

5. 17 U.S.C. § 504(c)(2).

6. 17 U.S.C. § 504(c)(2).

7. 17 U.S.C. § 504(c)(1).

8. *Burnett v. Lambino,* 206 F. Supp., 517 (S.D.N.Y. 1962).

9. *Whimsicality, Inc. v. Maison Joseph Battat,* Ltee, 27 F. Supp. 2.d 456 (U.S.P.Q. 1998).

10. *Rockford Map Publishers, Inc. v. Directory Service Company of Colorado, Inc.,* 768 F. 2d 145 (1985).

11. Criminal Copyright Improvement Act of 1997, S. 1044, 105th Cong. (1997).

12. Quoting 143 Cong. Rec. H9885 (daily ed. Nov. 4, 1997).

CHAPTER 13

International Copyright Protection

▼

"The recent introduction of copyright into the general trade process, in which new rights can be facilely traded for subsidies to rice and rapeseed oil, promises to complicate both domestic and international copyright." Goldstein on Copyright

It has been estimated that westerners account for a mere 700 million people out of a worldwide population of 9 to 15 billion people.[1] The worldwide economy has consequently become increasingly important to the United States and intellectual property (such as copyrighted works) has correspondingly gained importance, because intellectual property is one of the few positive trade areas in the American economy (i.e., exports exceed imports). In 1998, foreign sales and exports of intellectual property products (music, films, software, etc.) totaled $60.18 billion, more than any other major industry sector.[2]

As the worldwide economy and international trade has grown, it has become crucial that copyrighted property be protected on an international basis. However, protecting anything on an international basis poses substantial problems because each country operates independently with its own laws. There is no such thing as an international copyright law that would provide copyright protection on a worldwide basis. Instead, most countries have their own copyright laws, which are not applicable outside of their borders. The United States Copyright Act, for instance, has no effect outside the borders of the United States. If a work copyrighted under U.S. copy-

right law is infringed in another country, the United States has no jurisdiction over that infringement.

Does this mean that copyrighted works can be infringed at will outside of the United States? Fortunately not. Since it is crucial that copyrighted works are protected on a worldwide basis, a system of treaties has developed under which different countries agree to give protection to other countries' copyrighted works. In fact, the vast majority of the nations in the world are members of one or more copyright treaties that collectively assure a degree of international protection for copyrighted works. In essence, the various treaties between countries are like a network of copyright laws. As international protection and enforcement of copyright has become more important, a trend toward the harmonization of copyright law in different countries has started to emerge and is likely to continue in the future.

I. History of the United States' Attempts at International Protection

The United States has only become a strong advocate for strengthening international copyright protection over the past few decades. Previously, the United States took a much more isolationist position. According to former Register of Copyrights, Barbara Ringer:

Until World War II, the United States had little reason to take pride in its international copyright relations; in fact it had a great deal to be ashamed of. With few exceptions its role in international copyright was marked by short-sightedness, political isolationism, and narrow self-interest."[3]

In fact, the United States did not grant protection to foreign works at all until 1891. Although the United States is currently one of the strongest advocates for international copyright enforcement, the United States itself was the most notorious pirate country slightly over a century ago. At that time, many British works were legally used in the United States without any compensation to their authors. Charles Dickens, for one, was very vocal about how Americans unfairly used his works and even came to the United States in 1842 to lobby for international copyright protection.

A. BILATERAL TREATIES

In 1891, an amendment to the United States Copyright Act, known as the Chace Act, allowed the President to extend copyright protection by proclamation to works originating in foreign countries if they in turn provided protection for American works. As a result, the United States gradually entered into bilateral treaties with other countries concerning copyright. (Bilateral treaties are treaties between two countries.) The United States has many bilateral treaties with individual foreign countries dealing with copyright. Many of these treaties have been superseded by multinational treaties such as the Berne Convention and the UCC. However, some countries, such as Taiwan, Singapore and Angola, are not members of any of the multinational treaties. In order for copyrighted works to be protected in these countries, the United States has bilateral treaties with some of them.

B. MULTINATIONAL TREATIES

By the 1950s, it had become more important that the United States insure the protection of copyrighted works abroad. The growth in foreign markets for American goods and the piracy of copyrighted works abroad were important reasons for doing so. Additionally, some foreign countries believed that the United States was not really committed to international protection. As a result, the United States eventually joined several multinational treaties (agreements between more than two countries). The two most important multinational treaties dealing with copyright are the Berne Convention and the

Universal Copyright Convention. Most of the countries of the world have signed one or both of these treaties.

(1) The Berne Convention

The first international copyright convention was held in Berne, Switzerland in 1886 and resulted in an agreement called the Berne Convention for the Protection of Literary and Artistic Works (commonly known as the Berne Convention). Since its inception in 1886,[4] most of the major countries in the world have become members of the Berne Convention.[5] Since it also provides for the greatest degree of copyright protection of any multinational treaty, it has consequently become the most important international copyright treaty. The Berne Convention is administered by the World Intellectual Property Organization (WIPO), an agency of the United Nations based in Geneva, Switzerland.

The Berne Convention is intended to promote uniform international law to protect copyrights. It applies to "literary and artistic works, which shall include every production in the literary and artistic domain, whatever may be the mode or form of its expression."[6] The Berne Convention does not include sound recordings as protectible works due to the fairly common belief that performers are not equivalent to authors.

a. The National Treatment Principle

The Berne Convention is based on the principal of national treatment. This principal realizes that it would be impossible to implement a uniform international copyright law, applicable to every member country. One goal of Berne was to end the practice of reciprocity under which one country granted copyright protection to the citizens of another country only if the other country granted similar protection to citizens of the first country. Under the national treatment principle, each country agrees to give citizens of foreign countries at least the same degree of copyright protection that it gives to its own citizens. Consequently, when an American copyright owner sues for an infringement occurring in a foreign country that is a member of the Berne Convention, the foreign country's copyright law will be applied.

Since the Berne Convention became effective in the United States on March 1, 1989, any copyrighted works created after that date are entitled to national treatment by all other Berne Convention members. The Berne Convention is not applicable to works published in the United States prior to March 1, 1989 unless the work was simultaneously published in a Berne member country. Before March 1, 1989, some American book publishers published their books simultaneously in the United States and Canada in order to be eligible for protection under the Berne Convention, a practice that became known as "the back door to Berne."

b. Minimal Protection

In addition to national treatment, the Berne Convention also imposes certain minimum standards of protection that all member countries must guarantee. Some of the most important of these minimum standards are:

- The duration of copyright protection must be at least for the life of the author plus 50 years.

- Each member country's laws must provide for some fair use of copyrighted works for purposes such as education and news reporting (such as § 107 of the U.S. Copyright Act).

- Each member country must provide moral rights, which can never be transferred by an author.

c. Formalities

Under Article 5(2) of the Berne Convention, formalities such as copyright registration and notice cannot be required as a condition to copyright protection. However, some countries provide greater copyright protection conditioned upon compliance with such formalities. For example, in countries such as the United States and Japan, registration, although not required, can be an important form of evidence in a copyright infringement action.

d. Term of Protection

The Berne Convention provides for a minimum term of copyright protection lasting for the life of the author plus 50 years.[7] However, many European countries chose to provide a longer term of protection, lasting for the life of the author plus seventy years. In 1998, the United States extended its copyright term by 20 years to the life of the author plus 70 years, thereby bringing the United States into conformity with most European countries. However, prior to this time, American copyrights received a shorter term of protection in such European countries than

those countries provided for their own works under what is known as "the rule of the shorter term." Under the rule of the shorter term, copyright for foreign authors in Berne member countries is limited to the same term as the authors enjoy in their home countries if that term is shorter.

Example 13.1:

An American songwriter writes a song in 1980 and dies in 1990. If the song is infringed upon in France in 2050, under the rule of the shorter term, the author's heirs would not be able to sue for copyright infringement in France since the song's copyright would have expired in 2040 even though under French law, the copyright would last until 2060. However, since the United States added 20 years to its copyright term, France will now accord the extra 20 years to American works.

e. Exclusive Rights

The exclusive rights required to be protected under the Berne Convention are similar to those specified by § 106 of the 1976 Copyright Act. These rights include reproduction,[8] translation,[9] adaptation[10] and public performance.[11] Berne however, does not mention any rights of distribution or public display. Berne also requires the recognition of the moral rights of attribution and integrity, stating that:

the author shall have the right to claim authorship of the work and to object to any distortion, mutilation or other modification of, or other derogatory action in relation to, the said work, which would be prejudicial to his honor or reputation.[12]

The Berne Convention also encourages its members to recognize new authors' rights and expressly authorizes members to provide higher levels of protection in their own copyright laws.[13] Article 10 of the Berne Convention specifies exceptions for fair quotation from copyrighted works and permits exemptions for educational uses of copyrighted works. Article 10 also authorizes limitations on the recording of musical works such as the compulsory license provision of § 115 of the 1976 Copyright Act.

f. Enforcement

Article 33(1) of the Berne Convention provides for the submission of treaty compliance disputes to the jurisdiction of the International Court of Justice. However, the International Court of Justice's jurisdiction is of little practical value since Article 33(2) allows countries to declare that they are not bound by Article 33(1). The United States as well as several other countries have declared that they are not bound by Article 33(1) and the International Court of Justice has never heard a case arising under the Berne Convention. Consequently, countries have a lot of discretion as to the extent to which they interpret the provisions of the Berne Convention.

g. United States' Membership in Berne

The United States finally became a member of the Berne Convention on March 1, 1989, due mostly to its interest in combating piracy on an international basis. In order to join Berne, Congress passed the Berne Convention Implementation Act of 1988, which added certain amendments to the 1976 Copyright Act, including the following:

• Sections 401(a) and 402(a) were amended to make copyright notice optional rather than mandatory for works published after March 1, 1989.

• Section 205(d) was repealed so that copyright transfers no longer have to be recorded in order to file a copyright infringement suit.

In some respects, the Berne Convention Implementation Act is a cautious approach by the United States regarding the provisions of the Berne Convention. For example, the Berne Convention Implementation Act refused to recognize moral rights required by Berne as part of American copyright law. Instead, Congress stated that legal protection under other types of law such as unfair competition, defamation, privacy and contract law were sufficient to protect moral rights. Additionally, § 12 of the Berne Convention Implementation Act states that no retroactive protection is available for works that have entered the public domain in the United States and § 13 provides that the Act does not apply to claims arising before March 1, 1989.

h. Protocols to the Berne Convention

Several issues that remained unresolved under the Berne Convention have been subsequently addressed in supplementary treaties known as protocols to the Berne Convention. Member nations can ratify these protocols without having to revise the Berne Convention as a whole. Two of these protocols, the 1998 WIPO Treaties, deal with copyright and digital technology (discussed below).

i. Protection of Foreign Copyrighted Works

For foreign works that are owned by citizens of Berne member countries and were first created or published after March 1, 1989, full protection is afforded under U.S. copyright law.

Example 13.2:

Wolfgang, a German citizen, composes a symphony in 1998. Since Germany is a member of the Berne Convention, Wolfgang's symphony is protected in the United States to the same extent as works of American citizens. If, however, the symphony had been composed and published before March 1, 1989, it would not be protected in the United States under the Berne Convention.

---

(2) The Universal Copyright Convention

Another important multinational treaty is the Universal Copyright Convention ("UCC"), which the United States joined on September 16, 1955. The main goal of the UCC was to bring the United States into the international copyright community. By 1952, 36 countries had joined the Universal Copyright Convention.

The UCC is similar to the Berne Convention except that it allows member countries to require some formalities as conditions to copyright protection. However, the copyright owner of a work published in one UCC member country can avoid complying with the formalities required by another UCC member country by placing copyright notice on all published copies of the work.

The UCC, like the Berne Convention, requires its members to give foreign copyrights national treatment. It also requires certain minimum levels of protection such as a term of at least the life of the author plus 25 years. The UCC however, does not provide any protection for sound recordings.

Many countries are members of both the UCC and the Berne Convention. In these countries, the Berne Convention takes priority over the UCC. When the United States signed the Berne Convention on March 1, 1989, the UCC's relevance to American works was limited to countries that are UCC members but not Berne members and works published in the United States prior to March 1, 1989 that were not simultaneously published in a Berne member country.

Example 13.3:

If Wolfgang's symphony from the previous example had been composed and published in the United States prior to March 1, 1989, although it would not be protected under the Berne Convention, it would be protected in the United States under the Universal Copyright Convention.

(3) The Geneva and Rome Conventions

Many countries, including the United States, have been hesitant to recognize producers of sound recordings and performers as authors under copyright law. Consequently, ownership rights in sound recordings have historically been protected by several neighboring or related rights treaties that are not technically part of copyright law. The Convention for the Protection of Producers of Phonograms Against Unauthorized Duplication of Their Phonograms (the "Geneva Convention") was passed in 1971 and became effective in the United States on March 10, 1974. The Geneva Convention is designed to provide international protection against record piracy by recognizing the rights of reproduction, distribution and importation of sound recordings. Another treaty, the International Convention for the Protection of Performers, Producers of Phonograms and Broadcasting Organizations (the "Rome Convention") provides a higher level of protection than the Geneva Convention. However, the United States has not joined the Rome Convention.

(4) The Buenos Aires Convention

The Buenos Aires Convention, passed in 1910, was the result of a gathering of all of the North and South American countries. Under this convention, the phrase "all rights reserved" is required at end of copyright notices placed on copies and phonorecords.

(5) The North American Free Trade Agreement

Starting in the 1980s, the United States began a campaign to link intellectual property protection more closely to international trade by incorporating copyright provisions into multinational trade-based agreements. This resulted from the relatively newly developed economic rights philosophy for copyright protection and rests on the assumption that the failure to adequately protect intellectual property on an international basis is an unfair trade practice.

The North American Free Trade Agreement (NAFTA) was entered into in 1992 by the United States, Canada, and Mexico. NAFTA requires copyright protection for computer programs, data compilations and sound recordings, recognition of rental rights for sound recordings, limitations on compulsory licensing and recognition of rights against unauthorized importation of copies of protected works.

NAFTA contains detailed provisions providing for the protection of sound recordings.[14] Producers of sound recordings can authorize or prohibit a recording's direct or indirect reproduction, importation of unauthorized copies, first public distribution, and commercial rental.[15] NAFTA also provides for a minimum copyright term of 50 years for sound recordings.[16]

(6) The General Agreement on Trade and Tariffs

The General Agreement on Trade and Tariffs (GATT) is a multinational treaty designed to encourage free international trade. GATT includes an agreement on intellectual property called the Trade Related Aspects of Intellectual Property Rights (TRIPS). Under TRIPS, member countries must agree to enact copyright laws that give effect to the substantive provisions of the Berne Convention. TRIPS incorporates most of the minimum standards specified by the Berne Convention.[17] However, due primarily to pressure by the United States, TRIPS does not require recognition of moral rights.

TRIPS incorporates the Berne Convention's requirement of a minimum term of copyright protection lasting for the life of the author plus fifty years. If a work's term is not based on the life of a natural person, the term must be at least fifty years from either the year of publication or the year of the creation of the work if the work has not been published within fifty years of its creation.

The implementation of the TRIPS provisions is a gradual process. TRIPS has been adopted by 107 countries, including the United States. Most developed countries implemented the TRIPS provisions between 1994 and 1996. Developing countries and countries in transition from centrally planned to market economies (such as countries that were part of the former Soviet Union) have four additional years to comply with TRIPS. Least developed countries have until 2006 to comply without the risk of sanctions being imposed. Unfortunately, many developing nations have yet to take sufficient measures to ensure that their laws and enforcement systems are compatible with their obligations under TRIPS.

Quite possibly the most important part of TRIPS is that it provides for a practical enforcement system for intellectual property rights which has been a major weakness among all of the other multinational treaties. Under the Berne Convention, the United States could sue another country in the International Court of Justice. However, even if the United States won its case, the International Court of Justice cannot enforce a judgment unless the country the judgment is to be enforced against agrees to it. TRIPS, however, provides for a much more practical enforcement system, which includes provisions for injunctions and damages, seizure and interdiction at the border, and criminal penalties. TRIPS also provides for international panels to hear complaints about copyright violations.

a. Neighboring Rights

In order to implement the obligations imposed by TRIPS, the United States passed the Uruguay Round Agreements Act (URAA) in 1994. The URAA added a new Chapter 11 to the United States Code (which is not technically a part of the Copyright Act) that provides for protection for performers against the unauthorized fixation of performances and reproduction of such fixation.[18] It also provides performers with a right to prevent the unauthorized broadcast or communication to the public of a live performance.[19] TRIPS similarly gives broadcasting organizations the right to prevent unauthorized fixation of broadcasts, the reproduction of such fixations, the rebroadcasting of such broadcasts by wireless means, and the communication to the public of television broadcasts.[20] TRIPS provides for a term of protection for performers and producers of phonograms of fifty years from the date of the performance or fixation and twenty years for broadcasts from the year in which the broadcast took place.[21] Violations of these provisions are subject to criminal penalties and seizure and forfeiture of copies of unauthorized fixations.[22]

b. Restoration of Foreign Copyrights

One of the main features of copyright law is that once the term of a copyright expires, the work enters the public domain. In general, once a work has entered the public domain, it stays there forever and can never be brought back under copyright protection. However, this rule is subject to some exceptions that apply solely to certain foreign works.

Under NAFTA, a new section 104A was added to the 1976 Copyright Act providing for the restoration of copyright in motion pictures produced in Mexico or Canada that had previously entered the public domain in the United States due to publication without copyright notice between January 1, 1978 and March 1, 1989. In order to restore copyright in such works, the copyright owner had to file a statement of intent with the Copyright Office.

The 1994 Uruguay Round Agreements Act entirely rewrote section 104A of the 1976 Copyright Act, providing for automatic restoration (i.e., without the necessity of filing for restoration) of copyright for a much greater amount of works than those restored under NAFTA. In order to qualify for restoration, a work must not be in the public domain in its source country but in the public domain in the United States for one of the following reasons:[23]

- Failure to comply with U.S. copyright formalities.

- Lack of subject matter protection if the work is a sound recording fixed before February 15, 1972.

- Lack of national eligibility if the work's source country had no copyright relations with the United States at the time of publication.

In addition, there must be at least one author or right holder who was a national or domiciliary of a Berne Convention or World Trade Organization (WTO) member nation at the time the work was created.[24] Finally, if the work was published, publication must have initially been in a Berne Convention or WTO country and publication cannot have been in the United States until greater than thirty days after the initial publication.[25]

The restoration provisions are subject to a limitation that applies to parties who previously relied on foreign works that had fallen into the public domain (who are known as "reliance parties"). This limitation provides that any party who committed any infringing act with respect to a public domain work before the work's restoration is immune from infringement claims for one year.[26] If a copyright owner of a restored work intends to enforce the copyright against a reliance party, it must provide a notice of intent to enforce the copyright to the reliance party or must file a notice with the U.S. Copyright Office. Notices filed with the Copyright Office are published in the Federal Register and the reliance party is then deemed to have constructive notice of the intent to enforce the copyright. After receipt of actual or constructive notice, the reliance party has immunity for one year for any use of the copyrighted work other than reproduction.

(7) The WIPO Treaties

The World Intellectual Property Organization ("WIPO") is an agency of the United Nations that works toward increasing international legal protection for copyright and other intellectual property. In 1998, WIPO drafted two treaties designed to balance the interests of creators and owners of copyrighted works with the interests of users and distributors of such works in digital media. The WIPO treaties require member countries to provide protection to certain works from other member countries that must be no less favorable than the protection provided for domestic works. Both WIPO treaties contain provisions requiring the protection of copyright management information against tampering and circumvention of technical safeguards. When ratified by 30 countries, the WIPO treaties will establish binding international rules.[27] The United States ratified these treaties by passing the Digital Millennium Copyright Act in 1998 *(see chapter 14)*.

a. The WIPO Copyright Treaty

The WIPO Copyright Treaty updates the Berne Convention with respect to technological developments. Most importantly, it clarifies that the reproduction right under Article 9 of the Berne Convention applies in the digital environment by providing that the storage of a work in a digital or electronic medium is a reproduction. For example, digitally downloading a recording from a web site would constitute reproduction. It also prevents member nations from taking advantage of Berne Convention provisions that would permit them to allow a lesser term of protection to sound recordings than for other types of copyrighted works.

b. The WIPO Performances and Phonograms Treaty

The WIPO Performances and Phonograms Treaty is the first international law that provides protection for U.S. sound recordings distributed digitally over computer networks. The treaty requires that member countries provide at least fifty years of protection after the first fixation of a recording. It also gives sound recording copyright owners the exclusive right to authorize others to make their recordings available by interactive Internet communications, including by wire or wireless means, in such a way that members of the public can access the recordings from places and at times individually chosen by them.

Under the Performances and Phonograms Treaty, performers receive greater protection than under TRIPS. In addition to economic rights, the treaty also provides for moral rights for performers of live audio performances fixed in phonorecords.

III. Countries Having No Copyright Relations With the United States

There are some countries that do not have any copyright relations with the United States since they are not members of any of the multinational treaties and are not parties to a bilateral treaty with the United States. In these countries, American copyrighted works are not given any protection. These countries include Afghanistan, Bahrain, Bhutan, Estonia, Ethiopia, Iran, Iraq, Latvia, Mongolia, Namibia, Nepal, Oman, Qatar, Saudi Arabia, Tonga, United Arab Emirates, and Yemen.

IV. Use of Economic Pressure to Enforce Copyright

Although the United States currently has copyright relations with virtually all of the major countries in the world, problems can still arise over enforcement of copyright protection. During the last decade of the 20th century, the United States has resorted to threatening, and in some instances, actually using economic pressure against foreign countries to encourage them to strengthen their copyright laws and enforcement efforts. For example, the United States may impose trade sanctions against countries that allow widespread copyright violations.

Under § 301 of the Trade Act of 1974,[28] Congress has authorized the United States Trade Representative to identify and investigate countries that fail to adequately enforce or protect copyrights and to recommend retaliatory trade measures if the offending states refuse to take steps to increase copyright protection. Each year, the U.S. Trade Representative identifies certain foreign countries that it believes lack sufficient intellectual property protection and the United States then puts pressure on these countries to increase their level of protection. For example, United States pressure recently led to a major revision of Thailand's copyright laws.

Example 13.4:

In 1999, the United States Trade Representative identified Israel as the country most seriously lacking in enforcement of intellectual property rights, asserting that it produces and imports pirated intellectual property that dwarfs its legitimate domestic demand while its government sits idly by promising to act in the future.

The best example of the use of economic pressure by the United States involved the People's Republic of China. In 1995, the United States threatened to impose 100 percent import duties on Chinese products. United States ambassador Mickey Kantor stated that the main reason for the threatened sanctions was annual losses of one billion dollars to Chinese intellectual property piracy. Although much of the concern was due to piracy of computer software, piracy of American music and sound recordings was also a major concern. For example, China had allowed 29 manufacturing plants to operate that produced 75 million pirated compact discs a year. After strong pressure from the United States, China promised to enact new laws to protect intellectual property. Although piracy in some Asian nations as well as other countries is still a major problem, economic pressure by the United States has resulted in the enactment and enforcement of intellectual property laws that are helping to substantively reduce international piracy.[29]

V. What to Do if Your Work Is Infringed in a Foreign Country?

If you own a copyrighted work that is infringed in a foreign country, there are several issues that should be considered. First of all, it is necessary to determine what, if any, treaties the foreign country is a member of. If the foreign country is a member of a treaty to which the United States is also a member, you can pursue legal action against the infringer. However, you should also consider whether it is practically worthwhile to take such action since it can be very complicated, costly, and time consuming to do so.

In some circumstances when a copyrighted work is infringed abroad, you can sue the infringer in the United States. However, the U.S. court will apply the copyright law of the foreign country where the infringement occurred. In other circumstances, you would have to sue the infringer in the foreign country. Either way, it is important to understand that the foreign country's copyright laws will govern and that you will be entitled to the same protection that a citizen of the foreign country would receive. Consequently, it is very important to determine what remedies are available if you are successful under the law that will be applied before pursuing legal action.

1. Stephen Budiansky, *World Report: 10 Billion for Dinner, Please*, U.S. NEWS & WORLD REP., Sept. 12, 1994, at 58.

2. *Copyright Industries in the U.S. Economy: The 1998 Report,* prepared for IIPA by Economists, Inc.

3. Ringer, *The Role of the U.S. in International Copyright—Past, Present & Future,* 56 Geo. L.J. 1050, 1051 (1968).

4. The Berne Convention has been revised seven times since it origin in 1886. The most recent revision is the Paris Act of 1971, of which the United States is a member.

5. As of the writing of this book, the Berne Convention had been signed by 136 states.

6. Berne Convention, Art. 2(1).

7. Berne Convention, Art. 7(1).

8. Berne Convention, Art. 9(1).

9. Berne Convention, Art. 8(1).

10. Berne Convention, Art. 12.

11. Berne Convention, Art. 11.

12. Berne Convention, Art. 6.

13. Berne Convention, Art. 19.

14. Article 1706

15. Article 1706(1)(a)-(d).

16. Article 1706(2).

17. Articles 1-21 of the 1971 Act of the Berne Convention with the exception of Art. 6 which deals with moral rights.

18. 17 U.S.C. 1101(a)(1) (1995).

19. TRIPS, Article 14(1).

20. TRIPS, Article 14(3).

21. TRIPS, Article 14(5).

22. 18 U.S.C. 2319A (1995).

23. Pub. L. No. 103-465, 514, 108 Stat. 4809, 4980 (codified at 17 U.S.C. 104A(h)(6)(A)-(C) (1995)).

24. 17 U.S.C. 104A(h)(6)(D), (h)(3) (1995).

25. 17 U.S.C. 104A(h)(6)(D), (h)(3) (1995).

26. 17 U.S.C. 104A(d)(2)(A)-(B) (1995).

27. At the time this book was written, at least twelve countries have ratified the WIPO treaties. These countries are Argentina, Belarus, Burkina Faso, El Salvador, Hungary, Indonesia, Kyrgyzstan, Panama, Republic of Moldova, Slovenia, St. Lucia and the United States.

28. 19 U.S.C. § 2242(a)(1)(A).

29. China became a member of the Berne Convention in 1992 after amending its copyright laws to bring them in line with international standards.

CHAPTER 14

The Future of Copyright

▼

"The perceived value of music must be maintained. Just because you can download someone's work through your home computer in five minutes doesn't mean that time and sweat wasn't invested in that work and doesn't mean the artist and the labels and publishers who still help to expose that artist don't deserve to get paid."
Michael Greene, President, The Recording Academy

"No manufacturer would ship his or her goods on a highway if his trucks were routinely hijacked." Senator Orrin Hatch

I. Introduction

At the beginning of the 21st century, copyright is in a transitional state. Over the past several years, copyright has received much more public attention than ever before due to lawsuits against companies such as Napster and MP3.com. Unfortunately, much of the media coverage has been biased and inaccurate, helping to create a public view of copyright as a tool of the entertainment industries to maintain control of music and other creative works. Although it has sometimes been used as such, it was not intended for that purpose and has more often fulfilled its intended purpose of providing incentives to authors to create new works of art while assuring the public of access to those works.

Adversaries of copyright law tend to oversimplify the issues that copyright law seeks to resolve. Using slogans such as "information wants to be free"

and "the genie is out of the bottle," and relying on misplaced ideas of "free speech," "fair use," and "file sharing," these people avoid the difficult balance that copyright law attempts to strike between providing access to creative works while providing authors with incentives to create such works. Instead, they attempt to convince the courts, the legislature, and the public that they should be allowed to use creative works without permission from or compensation to the owners of these works.

Some people believe that we have reached the end of the copyright era, and that intellectual property should be free to all in the Internet age. According to John Perry Barlow, a former lyricist for the Grateful Dead and current copyright critic:

Intellectual property law cannot be patched, retrofitted, or expanded to contain digitized expression any more than real estate law might be revised to cover the allocation of broadcasting spectrum (which, in fact, rather resembles what is being attempted here). We will need to develop an entirely new set of methods as befits this entirely new set of circumstances.[1]

Barlow's analogy ignores the fact that copyright has always been an evolving body of law. Just because expression can be stored in digitized form does not mean that copyright has outlived its usefulness. If all laws were thrown out when any new set of circumstances challenged their application, society would be in a constant state of chaos. Certainly, there are new circumstances which copyright law must adapt to, but copyright has been adapting for over two centuries and to think that any new technology, no matter how innovative it may be, automatically eliminates its necessity or applicability seems a bit narrow minded.

The Internet is merely a relatively new medium to which existing laws such as copyright must be applied. Music in digital form copied and distributed using computers and the Internet is protected by the same provisions of copyright law that apply to music in more traditional formats such as compact discs. The Copyright Act specifically recognizes that technological advances will alter the mediums in which works are fixed in tangible form and the Copyright Act was specifically intended to include works fixed in digital form in such media as computer files, compact discs, etc.[2] There have also been some amendments to copyright law dealing specifically with digital music. According to the presiding judge in the case involving MP3.com discussed later in this chapter:

Defendant's copyright infringement was clear, and the mere fact that it was clothed in the exotic webbing of the Internet does not disguise its illegality.

Currently, many people and organizations are proposing additional amendments to the United States Copyright Act. Copyright owners are attempting to convince Congress that greater protection is required, while new industries that use copyrighted works are attempting to limit copyright law and obtain exemptions favorable to them. Some copyright scholars are also worried that some of the recent amendments to copyright law have gone too far and unfairly limit the rights of individuals to build upon existing works, thereby stifling rather than promoting creativity. In the author's opinion, passing legislation in response to every technological change is likely to be a self-defeating prophecy. Although some amendments to copyright law will be required, too much legislation (especially as the result of lobbying by affected industries) results in the creation of complicated, impractical laws, many of which will become obsolete as technology continues to evolve.

II. New Technologies

Technological developments have always provided a challenge to copyright law. In fact, copyright law initially developed as a response to the invention of the printing press. Innovations in technology have led to new ways to reproduce and distribute copyrighted works and have consistently expanded the boundaries of copyright.

New technologies provide both threats and opportunities for copyright owners. Initially, the threats must be dealt with, but in the long run, copyright owners have benefited greatly from technological advances. After the invention of the photocopy machine, the print publishing industry worried that its business would be ruined by people photocopying rather than buying print publications. However, many books, newspapers, magazines and other print publications continue to be sold. Similarly, the motion picture industry originally believed that the VCR would destroy the movie business. In fact, people continue to pay to watch movies in theaters while selling videocassettes to rental stores has provided motion picture companies with a substantial additional revenue stream.

The music industry has also been no stranger to technological advances. Since Thomas Edison invented the gramophone in 1877, advances in recording technology have challenged copyright law and forced it to adapt. The gramophone was followed by inventions such as the phonograph, eight-track, analog cassette, compact disc, and digital audiotape. In the early years of radio, many felt that it would destroy the record business and several decades later worried that video would supplant radio. Generally, each new invention has been an improvement over its predecessors and has changed the way people listen to music.

It is important to note that none of the new technologies mentioned above have destroyed their respective industries. In fact, some such as the VCR and the compact disc have actually rejuvenated their industries, bringing in huge new sources of revenues. However, the concern of the various entertainment industries when a major new technology is introduced is not totally misplaced. The mistake is that the concern should be over the use of technology rather than technology itself. No technology is inherently bad. Instead, it is the illegal and unethical use of technology by individuals that poses the real threat to copyrighted works.

The evolution of copyright law has not always been smooth, but it has managed to work quite well overall. Copyright law was designed to be fairly flexible. In fact, some provisions of copyright law may seem to be quite broad. This is often because these provisions were designed to apply not only to existing technologies, but also to technologies that had not yet been invented. Even so, it has been necessary to revise and update certain provisions of the law from time to time in order to accommodate technological advances.

At the dawn of the 21st century, the newest challenge to copyright and the music industry is actually the combination of two technologies, digital technology and the Internet. These technologies are changing the way people listen to music. Through these technologies, copyrighted works are much more easily accessible than in the past. This also means that copyrighted works can be much more easily infringed than in the past.

A. DIGITAL TECHNOLOGY

Digital technology involves converting information such as sounds into mathematical bits that are represented by a series of 0s and 1s. With analog recording, each successive copy results in a decrease in sound quality. The main advantage of digital audio technology is that there is virtually no loss of sound quality regardless of how many generations of copies are made. Additionally, digitization provides an easy and inexpensive way to reproduce and distribute an unlimited number of copies.

B. THE INTERNET

The Internet is made up of a worldwide network of computers connected by telephone and cable lines. The Internet allows computers and their users to communicate with each other. Information is transmitted over the Internet in analog form through the use of modems. A modem converts digital information stored on a computer into analog form so that the information can be transmitted to another computer over phone or cable lines. The receiving computer's modem converts the analog information back into digital form.

III. How Music Is Used on the Internet

In order to understand how copyright law applies to the Internet, it is first necessary to examine how the copyright owner's exclusive rights are commonly exercised in the Internet medium. Additionally, there have been some amendments to the Copyright Act during the past decade addressing specifically the use of copyrighted works in digital forms. Finally, there have been several court decisions that have interpreted copyright law in connection with the Internet.

There are two main ways music is distributed over the Internet, digital downloading and streaming. Both of these technologies allow music to be transmitted over the Internet to individual's computers.

A. STREAMING

Streaming technology allows for the continuous transmission of music over the Internet in real time so that listeners hear the music as it is transmitted to them from a website. Streaming can be thought of as the equivalent of Internet radio. No permanent copy of the music transmitted is made on the listener's computer since the audio is merely "streaming," or passing, through the computer on its way to speakers connected to the computer. Many radio stations transmit their broadcasts over the Internet through websites, a process known as "webcasting." In order to play the webcasted music, you need software that can often be downloaded for free. One disadvantage of streaming is that the listener must be online to hear the music. Additionally, the music is usually of lesser sound quality than downloaded files since it has to be heavily compressed in order to flow through typical modems. Many record companies use streaming technology to allow consumers to preview recordings and videos.

B. DIGITAL DOWNLOADING

Digital downloading allows people to make (or download) copies of digital music files from websites. Downloaded files can be stored on a computer hard drive or other storage device and played on demand. In order to play a downloaded file, you need to have a software program that can read the particular file type, but such programs can be downloaded for free.

Example 14.1:

One popular website offering downloads is **www.MP3.com,** which offers tens of thousands of free downloadable recordings, mostly by unknown recording artists. A pioneer in the digital downloading arena is **www.emusic.com,** where you can download recordings, mainly by artists on independent record labels. Ironically, both MP3.com and emusic, which originally marketed themselves as alternatives to the traditional record industry, are now owned by the largest record label conglomerate in the world, Universal Music Group.

(1) MP3 – The Latest Challenge

Traditionally, when audio files are copied to a computer hard drive, they take up a lot of the computer's memory. Consequently, audio files must be compressed in some manner in order to transmit and store them effectively. Compression involves taking digital data such as a recording and representing it with a smaller number of bits. Compression algorithms delete redundant parts of a digital file as well as parts of the file that are inaudible to the human ear. The result is a smaller or compressed file that reduces the amount of bandwidth and storage space needed. MPEG Layer 3 (MP3) is a compression format that reduces the size of digital audio files by a ratio of 11 to 1 without much loss of sound quality.[3] Whereas a typical four-minute music file in uncompressed format takes up about 40 megabytes of hard drive space, the same recording in MP3 format takes up only 3.5 megabytes. The MP3 compression format is not owned by anyone and has become the most commonly used compression format for music files.

There are two ways you can obtain and store MP3 files. The first involves using a search engine to locate websites where MP3 files are located and then downloading a file to your computer's hard drive. You can then play the MP3 file using software known as an MP3 player. Although some recordings are available for downloading in this manner, many of them have been posted illegally. It has been estimated that in the first six months of 1999, three billion MP3 files were downloaded from the Internet, equaling seventeen million MP3s each day.[4]

You can also create MP3 files from compact discs. To do so, you must use a software program called a "ripper" which extracts music tracks from the compact disc while it is loaded in the computer's CD-ROM drive. The extracted tracks can then be saved on the computer's hard drive and converted to MP3 format.

Once you have a music file stored on your computer hard drive in MP3 format, you can play the music using your computer (equipped with a sound card and speakers) or record it onto compact discs if you have a compact disc recorder (CD-R). You can make an infinite number of copies, which if made from a lawfully acquired file and used solely for your own personal use is perfectly legal. However, you cannot legally give away, sell or upload copies to websites without the copyright owners' permission.

(2) The Legality of MP3

There is nothing inherently illegal about the MP3 compression format. However, it is often used illegally. Uploading and downloading an MP3 file containing a copyrighted work is legal when the copyright owner gives the uploader or downloader permission to do so. However, if you upload or download an MP3 file containing a copyrighted work without the copyright owner's permission, you will generally be infringing upon the copyright owner's exclusive rights.[5]

Example 14.2:

MP3.com users can download recordings from a vast selection of over 50,000 relatively unknown artists. These artists voluntarily make their music available over MP3.com. Assuming that the artists own the copyrights to the songs and sound recordings they are making available, downloading this music is perfectly legal. However, if an artist posted a file containing a copyrighted song owned by someone else, downloading such a file would constitute infringement unless the artist had obtained a license from the copyright owner.

---

(3) The Music Industry's Concern over MP3 and Internet Piracy

The use of MP3 software for the distribution of music has generated considerable fear in the music industry. Many individuals have ripped MP3 files of their entire CD collections and the trading of illegal MP3 files over the Internet has become rampant. Worsening the problem, more and more consumers are buying compact disc recorders and many are using them to burn CDs of illegal MP3 files. Due to the compressed nature of the MP3 format, many more audio tracks can be recorded onto a single CD than the typical 10-12 tracks on commercially released CDs.

IV. How Does Copyright Apply to the Internet?

One of the main problems for businesses attempting to legally offer music over the Internet is the complexity involved in licensing music. This can be a complicated process since most uses will involve two separate copyrighted works (a musical work and a sound recording), which are normally owned by different parties. Additionally, there are different rights and limitations on those rights applicable to musical works and sound recordings.

A. THE REPRODUCTION RIGHT

Copyright owners of musical works and sound recordings have the exclusive right to reproduce or make copies of their works. The reproduction right is exercised continuously by Internet users, often without users even being aware of it. Whenever someone receives an e-mail or visits a website, a copy of the computer file accessed is made on the computer user's hard drive. Reproduction occurs when a work is entered into a computer for more than a temporary period. For instance, a reproduction occurs in each of the following situations:[6]

• A work is copied to a computer file, whether on the computer's hard drive, a floppy disk, CD-ROM or other storage medium. This includes "ripping" an MP3 file from a compact disc.

• A digitized file is uploaded from a computer to a website.

• A digitized file is downloaded from a website.

• One person's computer is used to access a file on another computer. This process is commonly known as file-sharing and is the basis for software programs such as Napster.

• A file is transferred from one computer on a network to another.

If you operate a website which allows digital downloads of files containing copyrighted sound recordings and musical compositions, you need to obtain licenses from the copyright owners or their agents. Licenses to reproduce copyrighted sound recordings are obtained directly from the record company or artist who owns the sound recording. In some instances, independent artists may be willing to license the right to reproduce their sound recordings for free. For instance, MP3.com requires that all artists who make recordings available for download on their website give them the right to allow reproduction of the recordings without any payment to the artist. Record companies on the other hand, are not usually willing to license the right to download their recordings for free since the only way they make money is by selling recordings.

In addition to the license for a sound recording, a license is also required for any copyrighted musical compositions contained on a sound recording. MP3.com also requires artists to give them the right to reproduce any musical compositions contained on recordings without any payment to the songwriter. Artists cannot grant this right unless they also happen to be the songwriter and publisher of the musical compositions. Licenses to reproduce musical compositions can be obtained either from the publisher that owns them or a licensing agent authorized by the publisher (such as The Harry Fox Agency which represents many music publishers in the United States).

The compulsory mechanical license provision of the Copyright Act limits the copyright owner's exclusive right to reproduce musical works. As discussed in more detail in chapter 5, once the copyright owner of a musical work has authorized the first reproduction and distribution of a musical work, anyone can make their own recording of the work as long as they comply with the compulsory license provisions. In 1995, the compulsory license provision was amended to allow the reproduction and distribution of musical works by "digital phonorecord delivery." In other words, when you download a recording from a website, a digital phonorecord delivery has taken place. If the website has a mechanical license to reproduce and distribute the musical work, the transmission will not infringe the copyright owner's rights. The royalty rate for digital phonorecord deliveries is set every two years and is currently the same as the rate for the reproduction of physical phonorecords such as compact discs (i.e., 7.55 cents).[7]

B. THE PUBLIC PERFORMANCE RIGHT

A copyright owner has the exclusive right to publicly perform a copyrighted work, directly or through a means of communication or transmission. The transmission of music over the Internet can constitute a public performance. When you listen to music over the Internet, the music is certainly being performed, but it may not seem that the performance is a "public" one. However, the fact that a performance occurs at different times for different users does not prevent it from being a public performance. Similarly, when you download a music file, the public performance right may be implicated. This is true even if you do not listen to the music immediately after it is downloaded since copyright law only requires that the performance is transmitted.

Licensing of the public performance right for musical compositions is handled predominantly by performing rights organizations (such as ASCAP, BMI and SESAC in the United States). All three of these organizations offer licenses authorizing performances of musical compositions over the Internet. It is also important to realize that under the Digital Performance Right in Sound Recordings Act of 1995 *(see chapter 7),* sound recordings transmitted over the Internet are also subject to a performance right. Licensing of the performance right for sound recordings is handled by a relatively new organization called Sound Exchange.

C. THE REPRODUCTION/PERFORMANCE CONTROVERSY

Before the digital distribution of music over the Internet, the difference between a reproduction and a performance of music was usually clear. Unfortunately, music transmitted over the Internet does not always fit within these distinct categories. Often, both rights are involved when music is transmitted over the Internet.

Resolving this controversy has not been easy, in great part due to the turf war between reproduction right licensing agents and performance right agents, neither of which want to give up a potentially lucrative source of commissionable royalty income. The transmission of music over the Internet makes the act of copying automatic since the digital representation of the music is copied into Random Access Memory (RAM) so that it can be played. Consequently, reproduction rights agents such as the Harry Fox Agency believe that virtually all transmissions of music involve a reproduction. At the same time, the performance rights agents (ASCAP, BMI and SESAC) believe that all transmissions also constitute public performances. The result is that a website wanting to make music available by digital transmission over the Internet is forced to obtain several licenses for the right to transmit musical compositions as well as separate licenses to transmit sound recordings.

Example 14.3:

A website which allows users to download from a choice of many copyrighted musical compositions and sound recordings would have to obtain at least the following licenses: mechanical licenses for the reproduction of musical compositions from the Harry Fox Agency or individual publishers; blanket performance licenses from ASCAP, BMI and SESAC; and licenses for the reproduction and performance of the sound recordings from Sound Exchange or a similar licensing agent.

There seem to be two potential solutions to this problem. One would be to amend the definitions of reproduction and performance in the Copyright Act to classify certain types of transmissions as reproductions and others as performances. Transmissions that result in a permanent copy could be classified as reproductions while transmissions that are listened to while being made and do not result in a permanent copy could be classified as performances. A second solution would be to reach some type of compromise allowing website operators to obtain a single license covering both the reproduction and performance rights for musical compositions. For instance, copyright owners could appoint a licensing agent to grant the rights of reproduction and public performance for a single fee, thereby simplifying the online licensing process. At this point, such a compromise seems unlikely due to the vested interests of existing licensing agents. Ultimately, however, what is important is that copyright owners are adequately compensated for the use of their works rather than how those uses are classified or who collects for them.

The United States Copyright Office has recently weighed in on the webcasting reproduction/performance controversy and has taken the position that it is likely that the reproduction of a temporary or "buffer" copy in the course of streaming is a fair use, which would not require an additional payment to the copyright owner.[8] The Copyright Office's reasoning is based on the fact that buffer copies exist only for a short period of time and consist of only small portions of a work. The Copyright Office stated that:

The sole purpose of making the buffer copies is to permit an activity that is licensed by the copyright owner and for which the copyright owner receives a performance royalty. In essence, copyright owners appear to be seeking to be paid twice for the same activity.[9]

Although the Copyright Office's position has no legal effect, it is possible that Congress may eventually decide to resolve this issue and Congress often gives a great deal of deference to the Copyright Office's recommendations.

D. THE DISTRIBUTION RIGHT

Another complication brought about by the transmission of music over the Internet involves the copyright owner's exclusive right to distribute a copyrighted work. Under the first sale doctrine, once someone has legally acquired a copy or phonorecord containing a copyrighted work (e.g., a compact disc, cassette, etc.), they can sell or otherwise distribute that copy or phonorecord without the copyright owner's consent.[10] The first sale doctrine applies to the material object containing a copyrighted work, and is limited to that material object. For example, someone who has lawfully acquired a compact disc is free to distribute that compact disc to someone else. However, the compact disc owner is not free to make and distribute copies of the copyrighted works contained on that compact disc.

In the online environment, the concept of distribution becomes a bit fuzzy. When a copyrighted work such as a sound recording is transmitted over the Internet, it seems like a distribution has taken place. However, this is not technically true since such a transmission does not involve the transfer of a material object. Instead, the owner of the copy or phonorecord transmitted still possesses that copy or phonorecord and the recipient has received a copy of the original. Instead of a distribution, what has taken place is really a reproduction of the original work that results in a new copy being created. Since a reproduction rather than a distribution has taken place, the first sale doctrine does not apply, because the first sale doctrine is limited solely to the distribution right. The new copy resulting from a digital transmission would therefore be an infringement unless made with the copyright owner's permission.

Some critics have argued that the first sale doctrine should be partially extended to reproduction. They say it should be expanded to allow the digital transmission of a work by the owner of a legally made copy of the work as long as the owner of the copy destroys his or her copy after making the transmission. For example, a proposed piece of legislation called the Music Online Competition Act[11] would expand the first sale doctrine to permit the reproduction that occurs during the course of a digital transmission, provided that the transmitter deletes his or her copy after making the transmission.

The United States Copyright Office, in a recent report to Congress, recommended that Congress refrain from expanding the first sale doctrine as proposed by the Music Online Competition Act, basing its recommendation on the inherent differences between physical copies and digitally transmitted copies. Physical copies of works (especially those in analog formats) degrade over time, making used copies less desirable than new ones. However, digitally transmitted copies do not degrade over time regardless of how much they are used. Additionally, with an Internet connection, digital copies can be transmitted almost instantaneously to an infinite number of people worldwide. The Copyright Office Report states that:

The need to transport physical copies of works, which acts as a natural brake on the effect of resales on the copyright owner's market, no longer exists in the realm of digital transmissions. The ability of such "used" copies to compete for market share with new copies is thus far greater in the digital world.[12]

The Copyright Office also expressed doubt about the practicality of the Music Online Competition Act's requirement that a transmitter delete his or her copy after transmitting it. It would be very difficult for a copyright owner to prove or disprove that users deleted digital files from their hard drives or other storage devices after transmitting a copy to someone else. Further, the Copyright Office believes that this difficulty would likely result in "greatly increased risk of infringement in a medium where piracy risks are already orders of magnitude greater than in the physical world."[13] It does not appear to be realistic to expect people to voluntarily comply with a legal requirement to delete their copies of digital files that they transmit to others and the costs to copyright owners of policing and enforcing such a requirement would be prohibitive.

V. The Digital Millennium Copyright Act

The Digital Millennium Copyright Act (DMCA), signed into law in 1998, is an amendment to the 1976 Copyright Act. The DMCA's enactment was prompted by advances in technology and the exponential growth of the Internet as a communications medium. Before its passage, a considerable amount of lobbying took place and many of its provisions reflect legislative compromises. The end result is a very detailed and complicated piece of legislation. The three most important issues addressed by the DMCA relevant to the music industry are anti-piracy provisions, limitation on liability for online service providers, and rules for webcasters *(discussed in Chapter 7)*.

A. ANTI-PIRACY PROVISIONS

(1) Anti-Circumvention

Due to the threat of widespread infringement of works in digital format over computer networks, copyright owners have begun to use several technological devices to make their works more difficult to infringe. For instance, a digital computer file can be transmitted in encrypted form requiring someone who receives the file to have a software code to be able to read or listen to the file. However, no protection technology is infallible and there are people (commonly referred to as "hackers") who will attempt to deactivate technologies used by copyright owners. The DMCA makes it illegal to manufacture, import, distribute or provide products or services that are primarily designed or produced for the purpose of circumventing technological measures used by copyright owners to protect their works.

Section 1201 of the DMCA specifies the obligation to provide protection against circumvention of technological measures used by copyright owners to protect their works. Circumvention of technological measures means descrambling a scrambled work, decrypting an encrypted work or otherwise bypassing, removing, deactivating, or impairing technological measures without the authority of the copyright owner.

One major criticism of the DMCA is that it makes some conduct that does not constitute copyright infringement illegal. For instance, a person who circumvents copyright protection technology for a lawful purpose such as to make a fair use of the work is still violating the DMCA.

Example 14.4:

A court held that the distribution of software that enables users to defeat copy protection technology encoded into DVD movies violates the anti-circumvention provisions of the DMCA.[14] Movies released in DVD format are protected by encryption software called the Contents Scramble System (CSS), which can only be decrypted and viewed on a DVD player that has a licensed CSS key (DeCSS). Computers using the Windows and Macintosh operating systems that come with DVD players have the DeCSS key built in. But computers using the free Linux operating system do not have the decryption key and cannot view DVD movies. The defendant, who publishes a publication called *2600:*

The Hacker Quarterly, had posted the DeCSS software on his Web site where it could be downloaded by Linux users. The movie studios allege that DeCSS is a piracy tool and that without the anti-circumvention protection afforded by the DMCA, copyright owners would be reluctant to make encrypted works available. The defendant claims that DeCSS is merely a way to help Linux users watch DVD movies they already own, contending that DeCSS has legitimate uses. So far, the court has sided with the plaintiffs, issuing a preliminary order banning the defendant from posting, linking to, or otherwise trafficking in the DeCSS code. At the time of this book's writing, an appeal of this decision was pending.

(2) Protection of Copyright Management Information

In addition to prohibiting circumvention of technological measures, the DMCA also provides for protection of copyright management information. Copyright management information is information embedded into a digital file that identifies the work such as the author, the copyright owner, the performer, and the terms and conditions for the use of the work. Copyright management information can be embedded so that it remains in a file regardless of where the file is transmitted, allowing the copyright owner to detect unauthorized uses and track royalty payments.

Section 1202 of the DMCA prohibits the falsification, alteration or removal of copyright management information, or trafficking in copies of works that are linked with copyright management information that has been falsified, altered or removed, if the offending party knew or should have known that its actions would facilitate infringement.

(3) Remedies

In addition to civil damages, the DMCA provides for criminal penalties for violating the anti-circumvention and copyright management provisions willfully and for purposes of commercial advantage or private financial gain. A person convicted of violating these provisions is subject to a fine of up to a $500,000 or up to five years imprisonment for a first offense. For subsequent offenses, the penalty is up to $1 million or up to ten years imprisonment.

B. ONLINE SERVICE PROVIDER LIABILITY

One of the problems in applying copyright law to the Internet involves determining who is responsible for infringements. Clearly, people who, without permission, upload copyrighted music to the Internet or download it from the Internet are direct infringers. However, copyright owners face several problems in enforcing their copyrights against such individuals. First, it can be difficult to determine the identity of individual infringers in some circumstances. Second, it is often not economically practical to sue individuals for copyright infringement since copyright owners would have to sue thousands or millions of people, often for relatively small amounts of money. Third, copyright owners are often afraid of the negative publicity that will result from suing individual consumers.

Fortunately for copyright owners, in addition to direct infringers, the law also imposes liability on third parties who aid in infringement (contributory infringement) or financially benefit from infringement (vicarious liability). This allows copyright owners to sue websites and online service providers for infringements by individuals who use their services to commit infringements. Prior to the enactment of the DMCA, several courts had indicated that online service providers may be contributorily liable for copyright infringement by website operators.[15] The fear of liability resulted in heavy lobbying by service providers, which led to the enactment of Title II of the DMCA.

The DMCA added a new § 512 to the Copyright Act that creates limitations on the liability of online service providers for copyright infringement. An online service provider is defined as "a provider of online services or network access, or the operator of facilities therefore."[16] The DMCA does not totally immunize online service providers from liability. Instead, it limits the remedies available against online service providers in certain circumstances and provides for a procedure to aid in limiting online infringement.

The DMCA specifies four types of conduct for which an online service provider is not subject to damages or other monetary relief. In order to fit any of the four categories, a service provider must satisfy two general conditions: (1) it must adopt and reasonably implement a policy of terminating the accounts of subscribers who are repeat infringers; and (2) it must accommodate and not interfere with technical measures that copyright owners use to identify or protect copyrighted works such as watermarks and encryption. In addition, there are specific conditions applicable to each of the four categories of conduct.

(1) Transitory Communications

Section 512(a) limits the liability of service providers for copyright infringements of third parties (i.e., their users). In other words, this section limits the liability of service providers which act merely as data conduits, transmitting digital information from one point on a network to another at the request of users. A service provider must satisfy the following conditions to qualify for this limitation:

• The transmission must be initiated by a person other than the service provider.

• The transmission must be carried out by an automatic technical process without selection of material by the service provider.

• The service provider must not determine the recipients of the material.

• Any intermediate copies must not be accessible to anyone other than anticipated recipients, and must not be retained for longer than necessary.

• The material must be transmitted with no modification to its content.

(2) System Caching

Section 512(b) limits the liability of service providers for system caching. System caching refers to the process by which a service provider retains a temporary copy of frequently accessed Internet material for a limited time so that subsequent requests for the material can be fulfilled by transmitting the retained copy instead of retrieving the material again from the original source. This reduces the waiting time on subsequent requests for the same material. This limitation is subject to the following conditions:

• The content of the retained material must not be modified.

• The service provider must comply with rules about updating material and replacing retained copies of material with material from the original location, when specified in accordance with accepted industry standards.

• The service provider must not interfere with technology that returns hit information to the person who posted the material.

• The provider must limit users' access to the material in accordance with conditions on access (e.g., password protection or access fees) imposed by the person who posted the material.

• Any material posted without the copyright owner's authorization must be removed or blocked promptly once the service provider has been notified of its existence.

(3) Hosting at the Direction of Users

Section 512(c) limits the liability of service providers for infringing material on websites hosted on their systems. To be eligible for this limitation, the following conditions must be satisfied:

• The service provider must not have actual knowledge of infringing activity, must not be aware of facts or circumstances from which infringing activity is apparent, or upon gaining knowledge or awareness, must respond expeditiously to take the material down or block access to it.

• If the service provider has the right and ability to control the infringing activity, it must not receive a financial benefit directly attributable to the infringing activity.

• Upon receiving proper notification of any claimed infringement, the service provider must promptly take down or block access to the material. The service provider is responsible for filing a designation of an agent to receive notifications of claimed infringement with the Copyright Office and must make contact information available through their websites in an accessible location.

The DMCA creates a notice and takedown procedure, allowing a copyright owner to submit a notice of claimed infringement to the service provider's designated agent. If the service provider promptly removes or blocks access to the material identified in the notice after receiving it, the service

provider will be exempt from monetary liability. The service provider will also be protected against liability to any person due to its having taken down the material, provided that it notifies the subscriber that it has removed or disabled access to the material. The subscriber can then file a counter notice including a statement that the material was removed or disabled through mistake or misidentification. It is then up to the copyright owner to file an action seeking a court order against the subscriber. If the copyright owner neglects to do so, the service provider must put the material back up within 10-14 business days after receiving the counter notice.

(4) Information Location Tools

Section 512(d) limits the liability of service providers which link users to websites (through hyperlinks, directories, search engines, etc.) containing infringing material. The conditions for this exemption are the same as those required for the § 512(c) exemption specified above.

VI. Enforcing Copyright in Cyberspace

A. LEGAL ENFORCEMENT

Any legal right is worthless on a practical basis if it is not enforced. Especially in an area of law such as copyright, which many people are unaware of or do not understand, it is crucial for copyright owners to assert and protect their rights. Consequently, one of the ways that the music industry enforces its rights is by taking legal action against copyright infringers.

In addition to copyright infringement lawsuits filed by individual copyright owners, several music industry organizations bring lawsuits on behalf of their members. For instance, the Recording Industry Association of America (RIAA) often brings lawsuits on behalf of its member record companies. Similarly, the performing rights organizations (ASCAP, BMI and SESAC) often bring lawsuits on behalf of their publisher and songwriter members against infringers of the public performance right.

In connection with infringements involving the use of music over the Internet, the RIAA has taken the most active role in enforcing its members' copyrights. In 1997, the RIAA began to actively monitor the use of music on the Internet. It does so by using an automated webcrawler and a group of specialists to search the Internet for infringing uses of sound recordings. When the RIAA locates a website engaging in infringing conduct, it sends the person or company operating the website a cease and desist letter informing them that they are infringing and demanding that they stop doing so. Under the DMCA, copyright owners can obtain subpoenas from federal courts, which order service providers to disclose the identity of users who are allegedly committing copyright infringements. This helps to allow copyright owners to deal with direct infringers, who might otherwise be difficult to identify. It has also encouraged service providers to cooperate in disconnecting infringing sites after they are notified of them by the RIAA since service providers can avoid liability by doing so. Many websites voluntarily cease their infringing conduct or attempt to secure licenses after receiving cease and desist letters from the RIAA. However, some websites choose to ignore the RIAA's warning and continue operating, either believing that they are not really infringing or not caring whether they are infringing or not. Consequently, the RIAA may eventually file a copyright infringement suit against them, usually after several more warnings and attempts to get them to stop infringing.

Example 14.5:

In 1997, the RIAA sent several hundred letters to website operators notifying them that they were violating copyright law and requesting that they stop the infringing conduct. Over 250 websites were shut down after receiving these letters. The RIAA filed copyright infringement suits against three sites that failed to stop infringing.[17] All three cases resulted in judgments in the RIAA's favor requiring the site operators to agree to refrain from further infringements, to destroy any unauthorized sound recordings in their possession, and to pay $100,000 in damages for each infringed sound recording (totaling more than $1 million against each defendant). The RIAA, however, agreed not to enforce the judgments as long as there were no future infringements.

(1) Frank Music Corp. v. CompuServe, Inc.[18]

The first lawsuit involving digital music was brought in 1993, when a group of 140 publishing companies represented by the Harry Fox Agency filed a class action copyright infringement lawsuit against CompuServe. The suit involved a forum on Compuserve from

which copyrighted music files could be downloaded. Neither Compuserve nor the operator of the forum had obtained licenses from any of the copyright owners for uploading and downloading the copyrighted compositions. Although Compuserve was not involved in direct infringement, which was committed by individual Compuserve subscribers downloading copyrighted songs, the publishers claimed that it was guilty of contributory infringement and was vicariously liable for the infringing conduct of its subscribers.

Prior to trial, the suit was settled with Compuserve agreeing to pay the Harry Fox Agency $568,000 to be divided among the publishers involved in the suit. The settlement also provided for a licensing system between CompuServe and the Harry Fox Agency.

(2) A&M Records, Inc. v. Napster, Inc.[19]

The dispute between the recording industry and Napster has received more media and public attention than any other copyright infringement lawsuit in history. However, the media coverage has often been inaccurate and very biased in favor of Napster. The media like to portray Napster as a modern David taking on the recording industry Goliath rather than examining the actual merits of the case, which involves several complicated areas of copyright law.

a. Background

On December 7, 1999, the RIAA, on behalf of eighteen of its member record companies, sued Napster claiming that Napster is guilty of copyright infringement by allowing Napster users to trade copyrighted sound recordings without permission. On January 7, 2000, a group of music publishers represented by the Harry Fox Agency joined the lawsuit on the same grounds for infringement of their musical compositions. Two prominent recording artists, Metallica and Dr. Dre, also sued Napster, claiming that Napster was allowing its users to commit massive infringements of their music. Metallica and Dr. Dre subsequently settled their lawsuits for undisclosed amounts.

Napster is a company that developed software that allows its users to trade MP3 music files using their computers. People who downloaded the Napster software could log onto Napster and share MP3 files with other Napster users. Napster users store MP3 music files on their hard drives and the Napster software sends a list of songs on each user's hard drive to the Napster servers, resulting in a searchable database of all of the MP3 files on each user's hard drive. Files are transferred over the Internet from one user to another rather than through Napster's servers.

At the time the lawsuit was initiated, it was estimated that approximately 10,000 music files were being traded per second using Napster. However, most of the files traded using Napster contain copyrighted songs and sound recordings and neither Napster or its users obtain permission to reproduce and distribute these copyrighted works or pay any royalties for doing so.

At the time of this book's writing, the case against Napster has not gone to trial. However, after filing suit, the plaintiffs asked the District Court to issue an injunction preventing Napster from continuing to assist in the infringement of copyrighted songs and sound recordings. The injunction issue has been decided and in the process of doing so, both the District Court and the Appeals Court have examined the evidence and concluded that it is likely that Napster is guilty of contributory and vicarious copyright infringement.

b. The Ruling

The District Court began its written ruling by stating that:

The matter before the court concerns the boundary between sharing and theft, personal use and the unauthorized worldwide distribution of copyrighted music and sound recordings.

The District Court issued a preliminary injunction ordering Napster to stop

engaging in or facilitating others in copying, downloading, uploading, transmitting, or distributing plaintiffs' copyrighted musical compositions and sound recordings ... without express permission of the rights owner.

The injunction did not, as was commonly reported, order Napster to shut down. Rather, it required Napster to find some way to monitor its service in order to prevent the massive copyright infringements that had been occurring. Napster immediately appealed the injunction order and the injunction was postponed until the appellate court heard the appeal. The Appeals Court eventually ruled that Napster could be held liable for copyright

infringement and that an injunction was not only warranted but required.

c. Napster's Arguments

Napster put forth several legal arguments asserting why it should not be held liable for infringement. All of these arguments were rejected by both the District Court and the Court of Appeals.

1. We Didn't Do It

Napster argued that it had not committed any infringements since the files traded, instead of being stored on Napster's servers, are stored on individual users' computers. Napster claimed that, even if its users were trading copyrighted files, it had no way of knowing they were doing so and could not do anything to prevent it. However, the plaintiffs claimed that Napster should be held liable for copyright infringements committed by its users.

In order for Napster to be contributorily or vicariously liable for copyright infringement, the court first determined that Napster users were directly infringing. Napster users commonly infringe upon two exclusive rights, reproduction and distribution. The reproduction right is infringed when users download copyrighted music files to their hard drives. The distribution right is infringed when users upload copyrighted music files to Napster's search index.

In order to be liable for contributory infringement, a defendant must: (1) have actual knowledge of the infringing activity; and (2) cause or materially contribute to the infringing conduct of another. The District Court believed that there was sufficient evidence that Napster had actual knowledge that its service was being used to commit infringements. In fact, Napster admitted that it knew this on several occasions. For instance, several documents written by one of Napster's co-founders made incriminating statements such as "Napster was created to facilitate unlawful copying," "we are not just making pirated music available but also pushing demand," and that it was important for Napster to remain ignorant of its users' real names and Internet addresses "since they are exchanging pirated music." The court found that these statements proved that facilitating copyright infringement was an important part of Napster's business strategy. There was also evidence that Napster executives had downloaded copyrighted music themselves and promoted the Napster service with web pages listing infringing files.

The court also concluded that Napster materially contributes to the infringing conduct because it provided the software, search engine, and servers used to infringe and enabled users to access each other's computer hard drives. Without these contributions by Napster, its users would not have been able to infringe.

A defendant can also be vicariously liable for the infringing conduct of others if the defendant has the right and ability to supervise infringing activity and has a direct financial interest in the infringing activity. Napster argued that it was not technologically possible for it to distinguish between infringing and non-infringing activity. However, at the time of the preliminary injunction hearing, Napster admitted that it was doing so since it had begun blocking the access of some infringing users. The court also found Napster's assertion that it does not have a direct financial interest in the infringing conduct of its users to be disingenuous. Although Napster had not yet made any money or even decided on a business model, it has always been a for-profit company that intended to develop a business model (whether based on subscriptions, advertising, etc.) by taking advantage of its large user base. The court found that Napster's value is primarily based on the number of Napster users and that the ability to download many popular music files without payment is the main factor that attracts users.

2. Fair Use

Napster claimed that even if its users were trading copyrighted music, they were protected by the fair use defense. The District Court applied the fair use test specified by § 107 of the Copyright Act and concluded that all four factors weighed against a fair use finding.

Under the first factor, the purpose and character of the use, the District Court concluded that downloading MP3 files does not transform the copyrighted work. Transformative uses tend to be fair use while strictly reproductive uses do not. The District Court also determined that Napster users engage in commercial use of copyrighted works because "Napster users get for free something they would ordinarily have to buy." The Appeals Court recognized that a commercial use does not have to result in direct financial benefit. Instead, commercial use is demonstrated by the fact that repeated unauthorized copies of copyrighted works were made to save the expense of purchasing authorized copies.

The Court held that the second factor, the nature of the use, weighs against a finding of fair use since the copyrighted musical compositions and sound recordings at issue are creative in nature. Creative works are less subject to fair use than factual works.

Under the third factor, the amount and substantiality of the portion used, copying an entire work generally weighs heavily against a fair use finding. The District Court determined that Napster users engage in "wholesale copying" of copyrighted works because file transfer necessarily "involves copying the entirety of the copyrighted work."

Finally, the court looked at the fourth fair use factor, the effect of the use on the market for the copyrighted work. If a use of a copyrighted work harms the market for the copyrighted work, the use will not likely be fair. Further, even if harm is not actually taking place, if a use could harm potential markets for the copyrighted work, it is unlikely to be fair. Napster was found to harm the market for copyrighted music in at least two ways. First, a survey introduced into evidence by the plaintiffs indicated that Napster use reduces CD sales among college students. Second, Napster adversely affects the ability of the plaintiffs to enter the market for digital downloading of music. The District Court found that the major record companies had expended considerable funds and effort to begin offering digital downloads. However, having digital downloads available for free using Napster necessarily harms the copyright holders' efforts to charge for the same downloads.

Napster offered expert testimony to indicate that Napster use increased rather than harmed record sales. Both courts however, concluded that Napster's expert did not have any legitimate evidence to support his opinion that Napster use stimulated record sales. Additionally, Napster asserted that since record sales have increased since Napster was introduced, it must be good for the music industry. This assertion seems illogical since there are many factors that could lead to increased or decreased record sales. The mere fact that record sales have increased does not mean that Napster was the cause of that increase. It is also possible that record sales would have increased more if it weren't for Napster.

Napster's fair use defense relied heavily on a Supreme Court decision holding that a technology that has substantial non-infringing uses is protected under the fair use doctrine even if that technology is also used for infringing purposes. In *Sony Corporation of America v. Universal Studios*,[20] two major movie companies (Universal City Studios and Walt Disney Productions) sued claiming that Sony was committing contributory copyright infringement by manufacturing Betamax home video tape recorders. Consumers used the recorders to record television programs for later viewing. The Supreme Court ruled that home video taping for private viewing was fair use since it was primarily nonprofit and non-commercial.

Napster analogized itself to the Sony Betamax, arguing that its software has substantial non-infringing uses. However, anyone who has used Napster probably realizes that it is predominantly used to trade copyrighted music. Although the substantial non-infringing use defense had at least some potential merit, both courts recognized that Napster's situation is different from the Sony situation in several important respects. Further, while Napster claimed to have significant non-infringing uses, it also claimed that the preliminary injunction would put it out of business, thereby indicating that uses other than infringement were not very substantial. Napster claimed to have the following three substantial non-infringing uses:

- We're Just Sampling

Napster argued that people used its service merely to sample recordings. In other words, people were using Napster just to listen to music in order to determine whether they wished to purchase it. Although copyright owners often allow people to listen to their works in the hope that people will ultimately pay for them (e.g., by allowing their works to be played on radio and television), there is no automatic right to sample copyrighted works under copyright law. Additionally, anyone who has used Napster should realize the fallacy of Napster's sampling argument. Sampling generally involves a limited, non-permanent use such as listening to a recording rather than downloading it and allowing millions of other Napster users to download it as well. Although some people might use Napster to sample music, it is up to the copyright owners to decide whether they want to make their works available for sampling in that manner.

- Space-Shifting

Space-shifting involves the process in which consumers convert CDs they own into MP3 format and use Napster to listen to the music using a different computer at a different location. The District Court found that very few Napster users were likely to use Napster for space-shifting purposes since it would be very inconvenient to do so. More importantly, while space-shifting and time-shifting had been recognized as fair use in other situations, those situations did not involve distribution of copyrighted works to the general public as Napster does. For instance, in the Diamond Rio case *(discussed in Chapter 5)*, copyrighted music was transferred from the user's computer hard drive to the user's portable MP3 player. Similarly in the Sony case, VCRs were used to watch taped television broadcasts at home rather than to distribute the taped broadcasts. With Napster, however, in order to access a music file from another location, the file becomes available to millions of other individuals.

- We're Promoting New Artists

Napster also pointed to the fact that it was used to promote new artists. However, the court realized that Napster's "New Artist Program" was only started after Napster was sued and that earlier versions of the Napster website advertised the ease with which users could find their favorite music without "wading through page after page of unknown artists." Additionally, the New Artist Program represented a very small portion of Napster use.

3. The DMCA Safe Harbors

Napster claimed that it was exempt from liability for copyright infringement under 512(a) of the DMCA since it is an online service provider acting as a mere conduit for material to pass through. However, infringements using Napster occur over individual user's networks rather than Napster's networks so Napster does not really operate as an online service provider.

Napster also claimed that it is exempt under § 512(d) of the DMCA, which immunizes service providers that offer information location tools such as a directory or index. In order to qualify for this exemption, a service provider must show that it: (1) has adopted and informs account holders of a policy that provides for the termination of users who are repeat infringers; and (2) accommodates and does not interfere with standard technical measures used to identify or protect copyrighted works. Napster claims that it complies with these requirements since it posts its DMCA policy on its website, has terminated every user for whom it has received notice under the DMCA (over 700,000), and blocks terminated users by placing a code on the user's computer to prevent further use of that computer to access Napster.

Additionally, § 512(d) requires that service providers: (1) do not have actual knowledge of infringement; (2) are not aware of circumstances from which infringing activity is apparent; and (3) upon obtaining such knowledge or awareness, act expeditiously to remove, or disable access to infringing material. Napster argued that it has no duty to monitor its users' activity until it receives notices of infringement, and when it receives such notices, it blocks users' accounts. The District Court concluded that Napster has actual knowledge of infringing activity because the vast majority of music available on Napster is copyrighted and it is common knowledge that virtually all Napster users download copyrighted files.

4. The Audio Home Recording Act

Napster asserted that its users' activity is not infringing since §1008 of the Audio Home Recording Act (AHRA) says that private, non-commercial copying is fair use. However, the AHRA is inapplicable to Napster for two reasons. First, the AHRA only protects digital audio recording devices that incorporate technology to prevent serial copying. Napster users generally download music files onto their computer hard drives, which are specifically exempted from the definition of "digital audio recording devices" in the AHRA. Second, the AHRA only allows private home copying by consumers. Napster users upload and download music files from other Napster users all over the world, which hardly qualifies as "private" copying.

5. Free Speech

Napster argued that the injunction issued by the District Court would restrain free speech and violate the First Amendment of the Constitution. For instance, if the injunction forced Napster to stop operating, artists who allowed their music to be traded using Napster would be prevented from doing so. The Appeals Court stated that although an overly broad injunction might violate the First Amendment, the District Court's injunction did not do so since it

ordered Napster to bar access only to copyrighted music owned by the plaintiffs.

d. What Now?

Although the Appeals Court upheld the District Court's ruling, it sent the case back to the District Court to narrow its preliminary injunction. Originally, the district court had placed the entire burden of ensuring that no "copying, downloading, uploading, transmitting or distributing" of copyrighted works takes place. The Appeals Court placed the burden on record labels to give notice to Napster of copyrighted works and files containing those works available using Napster before Napster has a duty to remove access to those works. However, Napster has a duty to monitor its system to the extent it is reasonable to do so.

Ten days after the Appeals Court's decision, Napster offered $1 billion to the recording industry if it agreed to drop its lawsuit. This proposed settlement was to be paid as licensing fees to all record companies and publishers over a period of five years. Although $1 billion is certainly a lot of money, when split up among the thousands of record companies and publishers not only to compensate for the millions of infringements that have occurred, but also to license all distributions over the next five years, it is really quite a small amount. Consequently, the plaintiffs rejected the offer.

Napster has also begun implementing a filtering system designed to block access to infringing files identified by the plaintiffs. Napster plans on changing its system to a subscription-based model where users pay a monthly fee. However, the subscription model depends on Napster's ability to reach settlements and licensing agreements with copyright owners. One of the major record label parent companies, Bertelsmann, has agreed to withdraw from the lawsuit and make its music available over Napster if Napster can implement a subscription-based service which compensates artists, labels and publishers each time a music file is downloaded. As part of its agreement, Bertelsmann also acquired partial ownership of Napster. One possible settlement scenario is that Napster will be pressured into selling its remaining ownership to one or more of the other major record labels in return for their agreement to settle. Napster could risk going to trial, but it is extremely likely that it would lose and be subject to an astronomical damage award, which would certainly put it out of business.

It appears that Napster's chances for survival depend upon whether it can reach settlement agreements with the record companies and music publishers whose copyrights were infringed. Napster took a step toward doing so on September 24th, 2001, announcing that it has reached a proposed settlement with the Harry Fox Agency under which Napster will pay $26 million for past unauthorized use of music and a $10 million down payment on future royalties. The settlement also provides terms for licenses for Napster's subscription service. The settlement must be approved by the court and Napster must still negotiate settlements with the record companies and the performing rights organizations.

(3) UMG Recordings, Inc. v. MP3.com, Inc.[21]

The RIAA filed suit against MP3.com on January 21, 2000 alleging copyright infringement by MP3.com's service known as My.MP3.com. My.MP3.com is actually comprised of two separate services. First, the Instant Listening service allowed consumers access to music contained on CDs purchased through MP3.com-affiliated online retailers. Consumers who purchased CDs online by credit card could use their My.MP3.com account to listen to the recordings before the compact disc was actually delivered. Second, MP3.com's Beam-It service allowed users to insert a compact disc into their computer's CD-ROM drive which was read by MP3.com's software, allowing the users to listen to the music contained on the CD. Although Beam-It was promoted as only allowing people who had legally obtained compact discs to use the service, the service had no way of assuring this since the Beam-It software could only determine that a user possessed a CD, not that the user owned the CD. Although MP3.com's service agreement required users to promise that they are using CDs that they own, users could use a stolen CD, a copied CD or a borrowed CD without detection.

Both the Instant Listening and Beam-It services provided users with access to MP3 files of recordings from anywhere they have an Internet connection without having to transport CDs. However, both services suffered from a technical flaw since users did not actually upload their CDs onto My.MP3.com, which would have been legal. Instead, MP3.com purchased over 80,000 CDs, which it converted to MP3 file format, stored, and transferred into user's accounts. The RIAA claimed that My.MP3.com was committing copyright infringement since MP3.com

did not own or obtain licenses for any of the recordings in its database. The RIAA alleged that MP3.com was therefore violating the right to reproduce the copyrighted sound recordings under § 106(1) of the Copyright Act.

MP3.com first claimed that since consumers have the right to make copies of recordings for personal use under § 1008 of the Audio Home Recording Act (AHRA), MP3.com should be allowed to make copies for consumers. However, the AHRA exemption is specifically limited to individual consumers and does not allow someone else to make copies for consumers as MP3.com was doing.

MP3.com also claimed that its actions constituted fair use. The court examined MP3.com's actions and found that they did not qualify as fair use. Under the fair use test of § 107, the court determined that: (1) MP3.com's services were commercial since it was able to profit from its expanding client base; (2) the copyrighted works copied by MP3.com were clearly creative in nature; (3) a substantial amount of the copyrighted works were copied (the entire CDs were being copied); and (4) MP3.com's services adversely affected the market for the copyrighted works because other online companies were attempting to obtain licenses from the record companies for services similar to MP3.com's.

The court concluded that MP3.com willingly and consciously infringed the plaintiffs' copyrights. In determining the amount of damages MP3.com was liable for, the court stated that it was important to send a message to similar Internet companies engaged in providing copyrighted materials, commenting that:

Some of the evidence in this case strongly suggests that some companies operating in the area of the Internet may have the misconception that, because their technology is somewhat novel, they are somehow immune from the ordinary applications of laws of the United States including copyright law. They need to understand that the law's domain knows no such limits.

The court awarded damages of $25,000 per CD on approximately 4,700 CDs even though it could have awarded up to $150,000 per CD. However, after the court's decision, MP3.com reached settlements with four of the five major record companies, agreeing to pay each around $20 million. A settlement was also eventually reached with the largest record company,

Universal Music Group, for $53.4 million. MP3.com also reached a settlement deal with the Harry Fox Agency to license musical compositions contained on the sound recordings used in its MyMP3.com service. This deal requires MP3.com to pay publishers 10 cents for each song offered as well as another quarter-cent each time a customer listens to a song.

In a separate lawsuit filed against MP3.com in August, 2002 by Nashville company Copyright.net, a group of independent publishers and songwriters contend that MP3.com is liable for all infringements of their copyrighted songs and recordings which occurred as a result of the songs and recordings being made available through the My.MP3.com online database. Under the plaintiffs' theory of "viral infringement," MP3.com created a large online database of illegal recordings which were subsequently copied and traded using services such as Napster and MP3.com should therefore be held liable for any infringements which occurred after the initial downloads from My.MP3.com. Although it is possible that MP3.com could be held contributorily liable for these infringements, it is not a clear-cut situation, because MP3.com's conduct is a bit farther removed from the direct infringements by its users than in the Napster case.

(4) Publishers v. Universal[22]

Three weeks after MP3.com settled with Universal Music Group, the Harry Fox Agency, on behalf of a group of music publishers, sued Universal for allegedly doing the same thing that MP3.com had been doing. The publishers claim that Universal made unauthorized server copies of their compositions for use on Universal's Farmclub.com website. However, Universal contends that it made the copies legally, under the § 115 compulsory license provision of the Copyright Act. Universal claims that its previously obtained mechanical licenses cover any delivery method including digital downloads.

The difference between Universal and MP3.com is that MP3.com did not attempt to obtain mechanical licenses at all. Universal had existing mechanical licenses for the reproduction of musical compositions on CDs and expected to pay mechanical royalties for digital downloads. The issue in this case is whether Universal's mechanical licenses also apply to reproductions made by digital transmissions. The court ruled that the mechanical licenses issued by The Harry Fox Agency for the use of musical compositions in recordings are limited to the configuration (i.e., CD, Cassette, Digital Phonorecord Delivery) specified in each individual license. Consequently, since the licenses do not specifically mention some form of digital transmission, Universal is guilty of infringing the publishers' copyrights.[23]

(5) RIAA v. Aimster[24]

On May 24, 2001, the RIAA filed a copyright infringement lawsuit against Aimster, a file-sharing program, seeking an injunction similar to the one ordered against Napster to prevent Aimster users from trading copyrighted recordings. The record labels allege that Aimster is facilitating copyright infringement since most of the music files being traded by its users are unauthorized copies.

Prior to the RIAA's suit, Aimster had filed a lawsuit asking for a court ruling that its service does not violate copyright law. Aimster's suit was in response to a letter from the RIAA asking it to block trades of copyrighted music through its service. Aimster claims that it is a service for private communications and that it should not be forced to monitor its users' messages to determine whether they contain copyrighted music.

Aimster's service seems to have been intentionally created to make it difficult to monitor the trading of copyrighted music and to take advantage of some of the provisions of the DMCA. Aimster claims that, since files traded using its system are encrypted, any monitoring system that circumvents the encryption would violate the anti-circumvention provisions of the DMCA.

Aimster also claims that it is exempt from liability for any infringements by its users under the online service provider liability limitations of the DMCA. However, it is unlikely that Aimster qualifies for this exemption because it requires that a service provider not have actual knowledge of infringing activity or be aware of facts or circumstances from which infringing activity is apparent. The court might very well rule that Aimster is at least aware of facts or circumstances indicating infringement since its service appears to have been designed specifically for that purpose. At the time of this book's completion, this case had not been decided.

B. TECHNOLOGICAL ENFORCEMENT

In addition to using the law to enforce their copyrights, the music industry is also using technology to do so. There are several technologies that are currently being used to protect copyrighted works. Many copyright owners are using combinations of these technologies to protect their works, to monitor their use, and to detect infringements.

Although no protection mechanism is perfect, perfection is not really required. There are certainly some people who will find ways to circumvent the various technologies used by copyright owners to protect their works. However, the anti-circumvention provisions of the DMCA discussed above make it clear that it is illegal to do so. Additionally, the vast majority of people are not hackers and are not going to attempt to circumvent technologies used to protect copyrighted works. Consequently, technology can be used to make it more difficult to infringe and to make it easier for most people to buy a copyrighted work rather than steal it.

(1) Encryption

Encryption involves the use of a mathematical algorithm to scramble bits of data into forms that can't be easily deciphered without the use of a key created to decrypt the data. In other words, a file is encoded before being transferred and anyone who receives the file must have the key to be able to decipher it. Encryption can be used to encode recordings so that they will only be playable on a single music player or computer. If an authorized user attempts to copy the file or send it to someone else, the file will be indecipherable.

Various technology companies have developed encryption programs that can be used to protect music files and the programs are becoming more and more sophisticated. For instance, one program developed by three mathematicians at Brown University can be used to encode every second of a music file with a different encryption key. A three-minute song could therefore be scrambled into 180 different codes and a person who broke one code would only gain access to one second of the file's music.

Several of the major record labels have begun experimenting with CD encryption systems, such as Macrovision's SafeAudio, which supposedly prevent copying. Basically, these technologies add small errors to CDs that, although unnoticeable when played on CD players (which are designed to ignore minor errors), are noticeable when played on computer CD drives. Many critics believe that using such technology to prevent copying for personal use violates consumers' fair use rights. However, whether or not consumers have such broad fair use rights has never been legally decided.

(2) Watermarking

Watermarking involves encoding files containing copyrighted works with digital information that can be used to identify the work and specify usage terms. A watermark is basically a series of codes randomly distributed and hidden in the work, making it almost impossible to remove. Further, the removal of a watermark will usually result in a noticeable loss of sound quality. Watermarking does not prevent copying, but it does notify users that a work is copyrighted and enables copyright owners to keep track of the use of their works.

One example of watermarking is the International Standard Recording Code (ISRC) used by record companies to identify sound recordings. The ISRC is a unique twelve-character code that is embedded into recordings. The first two characters identify the country of residence of the record company. The next three characters identify the record company. The following two characters identify the year of the recording's release. Finally, the last five characters identify the specific recording.

(3) Webcrawlers

Webcrawlers or bots can be used to search the Internet for unauthorized music files. A webcrawler is a software program that scans the Internet in search of audio files. Copyright owners or their licensing agents use webcrawlers to search the Internet for unauthorized files of their copyrighted songs and sound recordings. In a way, the Internet has made copyright enforcement easier since it is much cheaper to use a webcrawler to track infringements over the Internet than it is to monitor infringements occurring in private homes and businesses. The

RIAA, the performing rights organizations and several private Internet tracking companies use webcrawlers on a continuous basis to help identify online infringements.

(4) The Secure Digital Music Initiative

In 1998, a group of companies and organizations from the record industry, consumer electronics industry, online music companies and security technology companies formed an organization called the Secure Digital Music Initiative (SDMI). The goal of the SDMI was not to choose a specific format for digital audio files such as MP3, but instead is to develop an open architecture and universal specification for protecting online music.

In July of 1999, the SDMI adopted a specification for portable digital music devices such as the Rio. The specification requires that SDMI-compliant music incorporate a watermark which can be read by SDMI-compliant players. This watermark allows copyright owners to specify how the work can be used. For instance, a copyright owner could encode an SDMI complaint file so as to allow users to make unlimited copies or could alternatively restrict the number of authorized copies.

The SDMI has been slow in achieving its goals and has been harshly criticized for being an effort by major companies to maintain control over the distribution of music. The biggest problem faced by the SDMI has been getting the many member companies, each of which have their own interests and agendas, to cooperate. Whether the SDMI can devise a secured system for online distribution that most, if not all major companies agree to use, remains to be seen.

C. COPYRIGHT EDUCATION

In addition to technological protection and legal enforcement, it is crucial that the music industry educate the public about the importance of copyright. If people have at least a basic understanding of how copyright benefits society, they will be much more likely to respect it. For instance, many people do not perceive downloading an unauthorized copy of a recording for free in the same way as they view shoplifting a CD from a record store. They may believe that since they have not deprived anyone of any physical piece of property such as a CD, they are not hurting anyone. However, if they realized that copyright law makes it possible for creators such as songwriters and recording artists as well as the companies that spend enormous amounts of money making and promoting recordings possible, they may be a bit less likely to download illegal files.

Any educational effort should be centered more on the ethical considerations behind copyright law than on the legal intricacies of the law. Unfortunately, the greatest challenge to educating people about copyright law is that it is not simple. In order for people to comply with the law, they must be able to understand it, at least to the extent that it applies to their individual behavior. Copyright education should stress the reasons for copyright, the basic rights copyright owners have, and the ways in which those rights are commonly violated.

In recent years, the music industry has made some attempts at implementing educational programs. The RIAA's SoundByting Campaign (**www.soundbyting.com**) is intended to inform college students and university administrators about the importance of respecting copyrighted material on the Internet. The SoundByting website provides a basic overview of copyright law and provides some information on how to license music. University administrators can also order SoundByting kits, which contain materials that can be used to conduct seminars about the use of music on the Internet.

Many universities have strengthened their computer-use policies regarding copyright infringement over the Internet. A large part of the reason for this is that under the Digital Millennium Copyright Act, universities are liable for copyright infringements committed by their students as soon as they know or have reason to know of the infringing activities.

Example 14.7:

After receiving a letter from the RIAA alerting them of infringements occurring over their computer network (which the RIAA discovered through the use of its automated webcrawler), Carnegie Mellon University conducted a random search of 250 students and found that 71 were violating copyright law by posting copyrighted MP3 files to the university's computer network. The students had their in-room computer connections canceled, but if they agreed to attend a ninety-minute seminar on copyright law, they could have their computer access reinstated after one month.

In addition to copyright education efforts at the college level, there has been talk of instituting programs beginning at the grade school level. Children are growing up using computers and the Internet so it is important that they start to develop an understanding of and sense of responsibility for their actions at an early age.

D. CONCLUSION

Copyright law is becoming increasingly important to individuals and to society at large. Technological innovations have brought about new ways in which copyrighted works can be distributed and used. The beginning of the 21st century has been a great challenge for copyright, but despite copyright owners' fears of piracy and the anti-copyright establishment's cries of a revolution to free music, copyright will continue to survive.

Copyright has survived numerous technological advances over the past two centuries. Often, these new technologies have posed challenges to copyright law's applicability. Although copyright has not always adapted immediately and smoothly, it has not prevented any of these technologies from thriving. Similarly, copyright will survive the challenges posed by the Internet and the digital distribution of music. However, its application will certainly change as new legislation is passed, court precedents are established, and protective technologies are incorporated into copyrighted works.

As always, copyright law must balance the competing interests of copyright owners and the public. Just as the public needs to become educated about copyright law, the music industry needs to educate itself about new ways that music can be used. Although the music industry should not be blamed for protecting its property, it does deserve some blame for failing to be open to new possibilities to legally make music available in ways that consumers desire. If the music industry becomes a bit more flexible and open to new technologies and business models, neither the Internet nor any other technology is likely to destroy it. Instead, technology can be used to enhance the creativity of artists and increase the dissemination of music to the public, which is exactly what copyright is supposed to accomplish.

Example 14.8:

In an effort to finally begin meeting consumer demand for online music, the major record labels have announced plans to make their music available to online subscription services by late 2001. Two subscription services, MusicNet and Pressplay, will offer major label content and will license their content to other services as well. However, music fans used to obtaining whatever music they want from Napster may be less than thrilled with these services. First of all, each service will charge a monthly subscription fee and neither will provide access to recordings of all record labels. Additionally, while allowing subscribers to download music files to their computers, MusicNet and Pressplay will prevent copying the files from their computers to other devices such as portable players. Some critics are worried that the major labels will use MusicNet and Pressplay to dominate online music distribution and to prevent other companies from competing. In August, 2001, a bill called the Music Online Competition Act was introduced which, among other things, would allow consumers to make backup copies of recordings they have legally acquired in order to protect against computer crashes, viruses and accidental erasure. Additionally, the Music Online Competition Act would require record labels which license recordings to MusicNet and Pressplay to offer the same recordings to other online subscription services under similar terms and conditions. The Music Online Competition Act will likely be strongly resisted by the record industry and it is unlikely that Congress will even seriously consider it until the 2002 Congressional session.

Note: For updates on the status of some of the pending copyright lawsuits discussed in this chapter as well as new lawsuits and pending legislation, please visit the author's website at **www.musiccopyright.net.**

1. "The Economy of Ideas," *Wired,* Mar. 1994, at 84, 85.
2. See H.R. Rep. No. 1476, 94th Cong., 2d Sess. 47 at 52 (1976).
3. Some audiophiles would disagree as to the loss of sound quality when music is compressed in MP3 format. However, to most casual listeners, the reduction is sound quality is minor and possibly unnoticeable.

4. See Vito Peraino, "The Law of Increasing Returns," *Wired,* Aug. 1999, at 144.

5. I use the word "generally" since, in limited circumstances, uploading or downloading a copyrighted work without the copyright owner's consent may not constitute copyright infringement if the defense of fair use is applicable. See chapter 12 for a discussion of fair use.

6. See *final report of the national commission on new technological uses of copyrighted works* (1978) at 40.

7. See 17 U.S.C. § 115(c)(3)(B)-(F). The digital phonorecord delivery royalty rate setting procedure allows for negotiation of rates by the industries involved. If negotiations do not result in an agreement, the Copyright Office can hold an arbitration proceeding to set the rate.

8. Digital Millennium Copyright Act of 1998, Section 104 Report, August 2001, pp. 132–148, available online at **http://www.loc.gov/copyright/reports/studies/dmca/ dmca_study.html.**

9. Id.

10. 17 U.S.C. §109.

11. Music Online Competition Act of 2001, H.R. 2724, August 2, 2001, available online at **http://thomas.loc.gov/cgi-bin/query/z?c107:H.R.2724.IH:**

12. Digital Millennium Copyright Act of 1998, Section 104 Report, August 2001, pp. 82-83.

13. Digital Millennium Copyright Act of 1998, Section 104 Report, August 2001, pp. 83-84.

14. *Universal City Studios Inc. v. Reimerdes,* 82 F. Supp. 2d 211 (S.D.N.Y. 2000).

15. *See Religious Technology Center v. NetCom Online Communications Services, Inc.,* 907 F.Supp. 1361 (N.D. Cal. 1995); *Marobie-FL, Inc. v. Nat. Assn. Of Fire Equipment Distributors,* 983 F. Supp. 1167 (N.D. Ill. 1997).

16. 17 U.S.C. § 512(k)(l)(B).

17. The three cases are *A&M Records, Inc. v. Internet Site Known as Fresh Kutz,* No. 97-CV-1099 H (S.D. Cal. filed June 10, 1997), *Sony Music Entertainment, Inc. v. Internet Site Known as ftp://208.197.0.28,* No. 97 Civ. 4245 (S.D.N.Y. filed June 9, 1997), and *MCA Records, Inc. v. Internet Site Known as ftp://Parasoft.com/ MP3s/,* No. 97-CV-1360-T (N.D. Tex. filed June 9, 1997).

18. *Frank Music Corp. v. CompuServe, Inc.,* No. 93 Civ. 8153 (S.D.N.Y. filed Nov. 29, 1993).

19. *A & M Records, Inc., et al v. Napster, Inc.,* 114 F. Supp. 2d 896 (2000).

20. 116. 464 U.S. 417 (1984).

21. *UMG Recordings, Inc. v. MP3.com, Inc.,* 92 F. Supp.2d 349, 350 (S.D.N.Y. 2000).

22. *The Rodgers & Hammerstein Organization, et al. v. UMG Recordings, Inc.* (S.D.N.Y. 2000).

23. At the time of this book's completion, Universal has indicated that it will appeal this decision.

24. *Zomba Recording Corp. v. John Deep,* Complaint No. 01CV4452 (S.D.N.Y. 2001).

Index

file sharing, 155

first sale doctrine, 72-73, 161

Fisher v. Dees, 131

fixation, 18-19, 21-22, 26, 30, 32-33, 95, 151-152

Folsom v. Marsh, 16, 129

Fonovisa, Inc. v. Cherry Auction, Inc., 124-125

Form CA, 108-110

Form PA, 104-107

Form SR, 104

formalities, 14-15, 17, 100, 111, 148-149, 151

Frank Music Corp. v. CompuServe, Inc., 165, 175

Frank Music Corp. v. Metro-Goldwyn-Mayer, Inc., 145

Fred Fisher, Inc. v. Dillingham, 34

Fred Fisher Music Co. v. M. Witmark & Sons, 48, 93

Gaste v. Kaiserman, 118

General Agreement on Trade and Tariffs (GATT), 98, 150

Geneva Convention, 150

Gershwin Publishing Corp. v. Columbia Artists Management, 123

Goldstein v. California, 27, 53

Grand Upright Music Ltd. v. Warner Bros. Records, 62

Harper & Row Publishers, Inc. v. Nation Enterprises, 137

Harry Fox Agency, 57-58, 99, 107, 159-160, 165, 170-171

Harry Fox Agency, Inc. v. Mills Music, Inc., 99

home taping, 59-62, 64, 87, 90

importation, 71, 73, 103, 150

improper appropriation, 114, 119

incentives, 5-7, 9, 11, 13, 141, 155

independent contractor, 42-44

independent creation, 20, 121, 123, 128

infringement, 3, 12, 15-18, 23-26, 28, 30-31, 33, 44-45, 54, 56, 60-64, 70-71, 79-80, 82-83, 89, 96, 99, 101, 103, 108, 110-112, 114-129, 131-132, 136-144, 146-149, 152-153, 156, 158, 161-166, 168-171, 173, 175

injunction, 61, 63, 138-139, 143, 166-169, 171

innocent infringement, 112, 136, 141

International Federation of the Phonographic Industry, 71

International Standard Recording Code (ISRC), 71, 172

Internet, 8, 36, 53, 58-59, 70-71, 75, 80, 85-88, 90, 102, 123, 125, 136, 144, 152, 155-161, 163-164, 166, 170, 172

Italian Book Corporation v. American Broadcasting Companies, Inc., 137

Jerry Vogel Music Co. v. Miller Music, Inc., 40

Jeweler's Circular Publishing Co. v. Keystone Publishing Co., 34

joint authorship, 38-39, 41, 94

joint ownership, 37, 39-40

joint work, 37-39, 41, 92

jukebox, 15, 17, 64, 74, 84

Keep Thompson Governor Committee v. Citizens for Gallen Committee, 137

Kuddle Toy, Inc. v. Pussycat-Toy Co., 34

L. Batlin & Sons, Inc. v. Snyder, 34

La Cienega Music Co. v. ZZ Top, 18

Library of Congress, 17, 48, 98, 100, 102, 104, 107-108, 111

license, 3, 11, 14-17, 22, 26, 28-30, 40, 45-46, 49-51, 54-59, 63-64, 69, 74, 76-79, 82-89, 102-103, 112, 114-116, 123-124, 127, 129, 131-134, 138, 140-141, 148, 158-160, 169, 171, 173-174

Licensing Act, 11, 16, 18, 83

Life Music, Inc. v. Wonderland Music Company, 35

literary work, 23, 28, 55

Lottie Joplin Thomas Trust v. Crown Publishers, Inc., 145

Lulirama Ltd. v. Axcess Broad. Servs., Inc., 53

M. Witmark & Sons v. L. Bamberger & Co., 90

Marks v. Leo Feist, Inc., 25

Marobie-FL, Inc. v. Nat. Assn. Of Fire Equipment Distributors, 175

MCA Records, Inc. v. Internet Site Known as ftp:// Parasoft.com/MP3s, 175

McIntyre v. Double-A-Music Corp., 68

mechanical license, 14-15, 28, 54-55, 57-59, 69, 85, 103, 116, 134, 138, 140, 159

    compulsory mechanical license, 14-15, 28, 55, 57-58, 69, 85, 103, 159

    negotiated mechanical license, 57

Merchant v. Lymon, 126

Mickey Mouse, 7, 97, 135

Millar v. Taylor, 13, 16

Miller Music Corp. v. Charles N. Daniels, Inc., 48

motion pictures, 17, 19, 23, 29, 80, 104, 151

MP3.com, 74, 155-159, 170-171, 175

multinational treaties, 147, 151-152

MusicNet, 174

Music Online Competition Act, 161, 174-175

musical work, 22-23, 26, 29, 54-55, 58-59, 112, 130, 138, 158-159

Napster, 62, 70, 136, 155, 159, 165-171, 174

national treatment, 147-149

natural rights, 12-13

Negativland, 64

neighboring rights, 151

No Electronic Theft Act, 18, 70, 143

nonexclusive license, 45

About the Author

David J. Moser is a professor in the Curb School of Music Business at Belmont University where he teaches courses such as Intellectual Property Law, Music Publishing, Legal Issues in the Recording Industry, and Record Company Operations. Moser is also an entertainment attorney who represents record companies, music publishers, songwriters, recording artists, producers, and managers. He is a frequent guest speaker and panelist at music industry and legal education seminars and can be reached at **www.musiccopyright.net.**